Advance Praise for
Franz Jägerstätter: Letters and Writings from Prison

"Franz Jägerstätter is one of the most important saints and martyrs of Christian history, one of those rare people who takes Jesus at his word, loves everyone, refuses to kill, and pays the price. These extraordinary letters and writings call us to do the same — to take the Gospel personally, live the Sermon on the Mount, love universally, resist the culture of war, and surrender our lives to the God of peace. This collection is a book to return to over and over again, to measure our own work for peace against the Gospel standard set by Franz. I hope we can take Franz's message to heart and pursue the nonviolent Jesus with the same fearless dedication. If we do, we will not only help the church reject war and embrace Gospel nonviolence; we will help give birth to a new world without war, injustice, or nuclear weapons."

— **Rev. John Dear,** author of *A Persistent Peace*

"With these letters, notebooks, and meditative essays, we have a comprehensive record of one of the twentieth century's greatest martyrs for faith and conscience. Everything is here: his mundane worries about paying bills and harvesting the crops; his personal love of his wife and daughters; his persistent refusal to acquiesce in the evils of the Nazi regime; his unswerving devotion to Christ and the Church. We owe a debt of gratitude to Orbis for publishing these documents; to Robert Krieg for translating and commenting on them; to Jim Forest for writing an insightful introduction; to Erna Putz for editing them; to Franziska Jägerstätter for writing the letters that accompanied her husband through his arrest and trial; and most of all to Franz, Blessed Franz, for living, amid this world's most daunting darkness, in the light of Eternity. May this book encourage readers to do the same."

— **Michael Baxter,** Professor of Theology, University of Notre Dame, and National Secretary of the Catholic Peace Fellowship

"These letters of Franz and Franziska Jägerstätter to each other and Blessed Franz's journal entries illustrate the depths of love and fidelity of this holy couple for each other and for their God. This collection makes clear that Blessed Franz's disobedient NO to further Nazi military duty was possible only because of his faithfully obedient YES to the will of God as he understood it."

— **Michael W. Hovey,** Director, Office for
Catholic Social Teaching, Archdiocese of Detroit

"For those who hold that love and responsibility to wife and children is reason not to risk conscience and the Gospel in times of occupation and unjust war ... read these letters and writings from the World War II prison cell of Franz Jägerstätter. Never has a husband and father loved his family more. Never has he sacrificed more — the giving of his life for their sakes, for all our sakes."

— **Mary Lou Kownacki,** author, *A Monk in the Inner City*

FRANZ
JÄGERSTÄTTER

Franz Jägerstätter in his late twenties or early thirties.

FRANZ JÄGERSTÄTTER

Letters and Writings from Prison

Edited by Erna Putz

Translated with Commentary
by Robert A. Krieg

ORBIS BOOKS
Maryknoll, New York 10545

Founded in 1970, Orbis Books endeavors to publish works that enlighten the mind, nourish the spirit, and challenge the conscience. The publishing arm of the Maryknoll Fathers and Brothers, Orbis seeks to explore the global dimensions of the Christian faith and mission, to invite dialogue with diverse cultures and religious traditions, and to serve the cause of reconciliation and peace. The books published reflect the views of their authors and do not represent the official position of the Maryknoll Society. To learn more about Maryknoll and Orbis Books, please visit our website at www.maryknollsociety.org.

The translation of this book was funded by grants from Lyn and Harry Isbell, as well as the Allaire Family Fund of the Winona Community Foundation.

English translation published 2009 by Orbis Books, Maryknoll, NY 10545-0308.

Library of Congress Cataloging-in-Publication Data

Jagerstatter, Franz, 1907-1943.
    [Selections. English. 2009]
    Letters and writings from prison / Franz Jägerstätter ; edited by Erna Putz ; translated with commentary by Robert A. Krieg.
        p. cm.
    ISBN 978-1-57075-826-3 (pbk.)
    1. Theology. 2. Jägerstätter, Franz, 1907-1943 – Correspondence. 3. World War, 1939-1945 – Conscientious objectors – Austria – Correspondence. 4. World War, 1939-1945 – Prisoners and prisons, German. 5. Christian martyrs – Germany – Correspondence. 6. Jägerstätter, Franziska, 1913- – Correspondence. 7. Catholics – Austria – Correspondence. I. Putz, Erna. II. Krieg, Robert Anthony. 1946- III. Title.
    BX4705.J265A25 2009
    282.092 – dc22
                                                                                    2008051698

Contents

Introduction

Jim Forest

Human beings have at least one trait in common with fish: we tend to move in schools. When the drums of war are beating and the latest slogan of mass destruction is announced ("for God and country," "the war to end all wars," "the war to make the world safe for democracy," "the war to defeat the axis of evil," "the war on terror"), few and far between are those who, having been summoned, refuse to take up weapons.

On every side there are those who go willingly, convinced of the war's rightness or at least confident their government knows what it is doing and would not spend human lives for anything less than the survival of the nation. There are still others who have their doubts but avoid knowing better — they rightly sense that it's dangerous to look beyond the slogans. There are also those who know that the war at issue is deeply flawed or even unjustified, but who go along anyway, knowing there is always a price to pay for saying no and not wishing to pay that price.

For many the idea of disobedience simply doesn't occur. There is the joy — at least the sense of security — of being in step with others and acting in unity, even if it turns out that such unity is being put to tragic or murderous uses. We're human beings, after all, and so — for worse as well as better — profoundly social. We like to bond with those around us — to cheer for the same teams, to see things in a similar way, to be "good citizens," to do "what is expected of us." Those of us who are Christians may well find ourselves being urged "to do our part" even by our bishops, pastors, and theologians.

Franz Jägerstätter was one of the least likely persons to question the justifications for war being announced daily by those in charge or to say no to the demands of his government. What did he know? And, for that matter, who would care about his perceptions? He was only a farmer. He had never been to a university or theological school. His formal education had occurred entirely in a one-room schoolhouse. Though active in his parish, which he served as sexton, he was not a person whose name would ring a bell for his bishop. No priest or bishop or theologian, no matter how critical of Nazi doctrine, was announcing it was a sin to obey the commands of the Hitler regime when it came to war. So far as he knew none of his fellow Catholics in Austria, even those who openly disagreed with Nazi ideology, had failed to report for military duty when the notice came.

How could so unimportant a person dare to have such important convictions? How could a humble Catholic farmer imagine he had a clearer conscience than those who led the church in his homeland? And in any event, didn't his responsibility to his wife and children have priority over his views about war and government?

Indeed Franz Jägerstätter did his best, insofar as his conscience allowed, to survive the war and the Hitler years. Submitting to military training, he was in uniform for nearly a year but never took part in the actual war. For an extended period, he was allowed to return to his farm and family, but when summoned to active service, he saw no option but to refuse further compliance. He was immediately arrested and imprisoned. After just over five months in prison, on August 9, 1943, he was taken to a place of execution near Berlin and was beheaded by guillotine.

Franz Jägerstätter was just one more on the long list of the dead. There were so many others who perished in those years that one more fatality was not worth noticing. There were no press reports, no interviews with his grieving wife. But a significant entry was made in the register of his parish in the village of St. Radegund: "Franz Jägerstätter died on August 9, 1943 in Brandenburg [an der Havel, a town near Berlin] the death of a martyr."

Years after the war was over, the name "Franz Jägerstätter" gradually came to light almost by chance. Gordon Zahn, an American sociologist, had written a book, *German Catholics and Hitler's Wars*. In the course of his research, he had found a reference to an Austrian peasant who had paid with his life for refusing any part in Hitler's wars. With the one book finished, he started researching what became *In Solitary Witness: The Life and Death of Franz Jägerstätter.*

Zahn's book generated a great deal of discussion, especially in the Catholic Church. How was it possible that "a man of no importance" could have possessed a moral clarity absent from those who were supposed to provide spiritual leadership to Austrian and German Catholics? Had any bishop expressed the view that Hitler's wars were unjust? Answer: not one.

At the Second Vatican Council, Archbishop Thomas Roberts, a Jesuit who had formerly been archbishop of Bombay, recounted Jägerstätter's life, pointing out that the heroic stand taken by this remarkable Austrian could not be credited to pastoral guidance from those leading the church in Austria or Germany or from the text of any existing Catholic catechism. In fact rulers could count on their Catholic subjects to obey them no less unquestioningly than they obeyed their church.

Should not the church, asked Archbishop Roberts, speak more clearly about the responsibility for its members to say no when they were required by their rulers to commit sins or be part of a system based on lies and injustice? Should the church not make clear that conscientious objectors to war have the support and admiration of their church for bearing witness to the Gospel? Should the church not rejoice that Franz Jägerstätter had given such a witness against an unjust war—a witness Roberts compared to that of another beheaded hero of the church, St. Thomas More? Should not the church express itself in such a way that it would be more likely that Catholics in the future would be better equipped by their church to take a similar stand, even if, like Jägerstätter, it cost them their lives? Was not a martyr's death far preferable to complicity in evil?

Archbishop Roberts's intervention was not without effect. While it was simply a bishop's reflection on the life of an as-yet uncanonized saint and the implications of that saint's witness, it turned out to be a factor in the direction taken by the bishops in the final document issued by the Second Vatican Council, known as *Gaudium et Spes* (its first three Latin words), or the Pastoral Constitution on the Church in the Modern World, as it was called in its more lengthy English title.

The Council declared, "Every act of war directed to the indiscriminate destruction of whole cities or vast areas with their inhabitants is a crime against God and humanity, which merits firm and unequivocal condemnation." The Council also condemned other crimes against life: abortion, euthanasia, slavery, and torture among them.

Emphasizing the role of conscience, the Council called on states to make legal provision for those "who, for reasons of conscience, refuse to bear arms, provided that they agree to serve the human community in some other way." Those who renounce violence altogether, seeking a more just and compassionate society by nonviolent means, were honored: "We cannot fail to praise those who renounce the use of violence in vindication of their rights and who resort to methods of defense which are otherwise available to weaker parties too, provided this can be done without injury to the rights and duties of others or to the community itself." Those who, in the name of obedience, obey commands that condemn the innocent and defenseless were described as "criminal," while those who disobey such corrupt commands merit "supreme commendation."

It was a text that would have made Franz Jägerstätter rejoice. So too all the other Christian martyrs down through the centuries who have obeyed God rather than man.

For nearly every bishop who came to Rome to attend the Council, the name of Franz Jägerstätter was unknown before Archbishop Roberts made his intervention. Today there are few if any bishops in the Catholic Church who are unaware of Jägerstätter's name and story. On October 26, 2007, Franz Jägerstätter was officially beatified. His wife and descendants were among those taking part in the event. Franz Jägerstätter is now known throughout his church as Blessed Franz. Perhaps before too many years it will be Saint Franz.

◆ ◆ ◆

Though Franz Jägerstätter's life has come to be a matter of significance in the history of the twentieth century, and his beatification a vivid indication that the Catholic hierarchy today is taking to heart what the bishops who took part in the Second Vatican Council had to say about war, peace, and individual conscience, few people on the calendar of saints had a more unpromising beginning in life.

Franz Jägerstätter was born on May 20, 1907, in the Austrian village of St. Radegund. His mother was an unmarried farm servant, Rosalia Huber. His father, Franz Bachmeier, was the unmarried son of a farmer from Tarsdorf in the Austrian province of Salzburg; he died in the First World War. After Franz's birth, Rosalia's mother, Elisabeth Huber, a shoemaker's widow, took charge of Franz's care.

It was not uncommon for those with little money or property to conceive children outside marriage, but marriage often followed. It wasn't so in this case, perhaps due to parental objections regarding one or the other potential partner. When Rosalia Huber at last married years later it was in 1917, a decade after Franz's birth, and not to Franz's father but to Heinrich Jägerstätter. He was a man of property — the owner of the Leherbauernhof farm in St. Radegund. In addition to marrying Rosalia, Heinrich Jägerstätter adopted her son, thus giving him the family name we know him by. They were to have no children of their own.

Franz's formal education was slight and brief. From 1913 to 1921 he attended the one-room school in St. Radegund, where a single teacher taught seven grades. At a given time, there were about fifty to sixty children in all.

But one sees from his writing that he was a quick learner with a well-organized and independent mind.

Franz's birthplace was as inauspicious as his education. The village of St. Radegund, on the River Salzach, is on the northwestern edge of Austria. The village, with a population of about five hundred, appears only on the most detailed maps of Austria. Mozart's Salzburg is to the south, Linz to the east, Vienna much further east. The closest major German city is Munich. Hitler's birthplace, the Austrian town of Braunau, isn't far from St. Radegund. St. Radegund's major claim to fame for many years was the four-hour passion plays it organized from time to time, the last one occurring in 1933. Like nearly everyone in the community, Franz had a part to play: he was one of the Roman soldiers involved in the crucifixion of Christ.

Franz grew up mainly among farmers. The Jägerstätter farm was one among many in the area. It was a region in which Catholicism was deeply embedded. The idea of not being Catholic was, for nearly everyone Franz knew, as unthinkable as moving to another planet, though he did have a cousin who became a Jehovah's Witness.

One reads in the accounts of saints' lives how amazingly pious some of them were from the cradle to the grave. The stories local people tell of Franz as a young man go in the opposite direction. In his teens he wasn't hesitant to get involved in fistfights. He enjoyed all the pastimes that his friends enjoyed. Along with all his neighbors, he went to church when everyone else did, but no one would have remarked on his being a saint in the making.

In 1930, at age twenty-three, Franz worked for a time in the Austrian mining town of Eisenerz. This was his first encounter with a secularized factory culture. Here he met people who didn't bother with church or have any good words to say about Christianity. Under their influence, in that period Franz slept in on Sunday mornings, skipping Mass.

Returning to St. Radegund, Franz surprised his family and neighbors by arriving on a motorcycle he had purchased with money he earned in the city. No one else in the area had a motorcycle.

Far more important, though the most attentive neighbor would have realized it in the early stages, was the fact that after his return to St. Radegund Franz's religious life not only revived but gradually came into sharper focus. Unfortunately, letters that might give a clue about this period of his life either do not survive or were never written. It may be that Franz's brief encounter with a more secular culture in his time away ultimately had the effect of bringing him closer to a faith he had previously taken for granted.

Not that anyone would have regarded Franz as notably pious or altogether converted from his former rowdy ways. In August 1933, a local farm maidservant, Theresia Auer, gave birth to a daughter, Hildegard. Franz was the child's father. The fact that there had been no marriage before the birth, nor would there be afterward, was attributed locally to the determined opposition of Franz's mother, who seemed to doubt that Franz was in fact Hildegard's father. What is striking is that for the rest of his life, Franz not only provided material support for Hildegard, but remained very close to her, visiting her often. Just before his marriage to Franziska Schwaninger, Franz and his wife-to-be offered to adopt Hildegard, but Hildegard's mother and grandmother (who was raising the child) declined.

According to local consensus, the most important single factor attributed to bringing about a change in Franz was his marriage to Franziska Schwaninger. Nearly everyone who lived in the area saw this as the main border-crossing event of his adult life. Franz was, neighbors said, "a different man" afterward, a fact most of all reflected in the intensity of his religious life.

But in fact the transition was not quite as abrupt as it seemed to neighbors. Prior to marriage, Franz had thought seriously of entering a monastery. One of Franziska's initial concerns regarding Franz, once they met, was to make sure he had a more than superficial commitment to his faith. She was relieved not only that he attended Mass regularly, but also that he was a committed and thoughtful Catholic.

Franziska Schwaninger, six years younger than Franz, had grown up on a farm in the village of Hochburg, about five miles away from St. Radegund. She came from a deeply religious family; her father and grandmother were both members of the Marian Congregation. Her grandmother also belonged to the Third Order of St. Francis. Before Franziska's marriage, she had considered becoming a nun.

After a short engagement, the two were married on April 9, 1936. Franz was almost twenty-nine, Franziska twenty-three. The honeymoon that followed startled everyone in or near St. Radegund. The couple went to none of the usual places visited by the newly married, but opted instead to go as pilgrims to Rome, at the same time ignoring deeply embedded local tradition by declining to have a wedding feast. Married at six in the morning, before noon they were on their way to Rome, a city crowded with churches built over the tombs of martyrs of the early church or the locations of their execution. To be in so many martyr-linked places of worship must have helped prepare the newly married couple for what would happen in the years to come.

The Roman pilgrimage had been Franz's idea, but Franziska had eagerly agreed. Returning home, Franz proposed to Franziska that they go on a similar pilgrimage every ten years. It wasn't to be. (After fewer than seven years of marriage, Franz's ashes were buried by the church wall in St. Radegund. Nonetheless Franziska was able to go on pilgrimages to Rome that marked her fiftieth and sixtieth wedding anniversaries.)

While Franz was already a committed Catholic Christian, in the early months of their marriage it was Franziska whose spiritual life was the most developed. Franziska went to Mass on many weekdays, often received communion, and kept the Friday devotions associated with the Sacred Heart of Jesus. But Franz was quickly influenced by her example. Neighbors were surprised and in many cases critical. The general view was that it was all right for women to do these things, if they had the time, but a man must give priority to his farm and keep the church and its services in their place. Franz, while remaining a productive and efficient farmer, increasingly put the church first.

It was a happy marriage. Franz once told his wife, "I could never have imagined that being married could be so wonderful." In one of his letters to Franziska during his period of army training in 1940, he mentions how "fortunate and harmonious" have been their years of marriage. "This good fortune is unforgettable, and will accompany me through time and eternity. You also know how the children bring me joy. For this reason, a feeling of good fortune often comes over me here so that tears of joy flow from my eyes when I think about our reunion."

Years after her father's death, the Jägerstätters' eldest daughter, wondering aloud whether she would ever marry, recalls her mother warning her that married couples often fight. Her daughter responded, "But you and daddy didn't fight."

Looking back on the days when her husband was still alive, Franziska observed, "We helped one another go forward in faith." Indeed, Franziska was not only an equal partner in their marriage, someone whose example brought Franz closer to a fearless Christian faith, but also a partner in her husband's martyrdom, even while hoping against hope that Franz's refusal to be a soldier would not lead to his execution.

The Jägerstätters had three children, all daughters: Rosalia (Rosi) in 1937, Maria in 1938, and Aloisia (Loisi) in 1940.

Theirs was not a marriage out of touch with the world beyond their farm. Franz and Franziska were attentive to what was going on just across the river from St. Radegund in Germany, where Hitler had been German chancellor since 1933. They were aware of Hitler's pagan ideology, the brutality of his followers, and they also knew of the intensive effort underway to build up Germany's military. They also were aware of the anti-Nazi writings of the bishop of Linz, Johannes Maria Gföllner, who in 1933 had stated in a pastoral letter read aloud in every parish of the Linz diocese: "Nazism is spiritually sick with materialistic racial delusions, un-Christian nationalism, a nationalistic view of religion, with what is quite simply sham Christianity." The racial purity so dear to the Nazis was condemned by Bishop Gföllner as "a backsliding into an abhorrent heathenism.... The Nazi standpoint on race is completely incompatible with Christianity and must therefore be resolutely rejected." In 1937, four years later, he declared, "It is impossible to be both a good Catholic and a true Nazi." (By 1941, Linz had a new bishop, who was to speak much more cautiously.)

Meanwhile, Nazism's dark shadow was spreading in Austria as well. There was more and more talk of Austria fully incorporating itself into Germany, though in St. Radegund, as in many places throughout Austria, the Nazis had little support.

One important factor in helping people keep their distance from Nazism was the widespread awareness that the Nazi movement was only a degree less hostile to Christianity than the Bolsheviks in Soviet Russia. Nazis regarded the values of the New Testament with contempt and saw those who attended church as stupid and weak. In Germany, they knew, Christians found themselves living in a steadily tightening noose of restrictions. The Nazis had made clear that one of their most urgent priorities was to separate children and young people from the church and in its place make them into Hitler Youth members.

The Nazis didn't hide their hostility to the teachings of Christ and the churches that spread his teaching. In the words of one prominent Nazi, Roland Freisler, state secretary of the Reich Ministry of Justice: "Christianity and we are alike in only one respect: we lay claim to the whole individual.... 'From which do you take your orders? From the hereafter or from Adolf Hitler? To whom do you pledge your loyalty and your faith?'"

On March 12, 1938, the Eighth Army of the German Wehrmacht crossed the German-Austrian border. Assisted by the local Nazi movement and supported by the vast majority of the Austrian population, German troops quickly took control of Austria then organized a national plebiscite on April 10 to confirm the union with Germany. With few daring to vote against what had already been imposed by military methods, the annexation (*Anschluss*) of Austria by Germany was even ratified by popular ballot. Austria, now an integral part of the Third Reich, ceased to exist as an independent state. What had been Austria was renamed Ostmark.

Well before the *Anschluss,* Franz had been an anti-Nazi, but the event that brought his aversion to a much deeper level was a remarkable dream he had in January 1938. Perhaps it was triggered by a newspaper article he had read a few days earlier reporting that 150,000 more young people had been accepted into the Hitler Youth movement.

In the dream he saw "a wonderful train" coming around a mountain. The gleaming engine and carriages seemed especially attractive to children, who "flowed to this train, and were not held back." Then a voice said to him, "This train is going to hell." He woke Franziska to tell her of his dream and continued to think about it long afterward. The train, he realized, symbolized the glittering Nazi regime with all its spectacles and its associated organizations, Hitler Youth being one of the most important and spiritually corrupting.

The dream seemed to Franz a clarifying message from heaven. The Nazi movement — with its racism, its cult of violence, its elimination of those members of society regarded as unfit, its efforts to suppress Christianity — was satanic. It was nothing less than a gateway to hell.

In St. Radegund it was widely known that Franz, ignoring the advice of his neighbors, had voted against the *Anschluss,* but, in the reporting of the results to the new regime in Vienna, Franz's solitary vote was left unrecorded. It was seen as endangering the village to put on record that even one person had dared raise a discordant voice. After all, as Franz was painfully aware, even Austria's Catholic hierarchy had advocated a yes vote. Afterward Cardinal Innitzer, principal hierarch of the Catholic Church in Austria, signed a declaration endorsing the *Anschluss.* The words *Heil Hitler!* were above his signature. Innitzer was among the first to meet Hitler following the Führer's triumphant entry into what was now the Ostmark region of Germany. That same year, in honor of Hitler's birthday, he ordered that all Austrian churches fly the swastika flag, ring their bells, and pray for Hitler. Presumably the cardinal hoped such an action on his part would be repaid by the Nazi regime with a more tolerant attitude toward the church. In fact, following the *Anschluss,* the situation for Austrian Catholics proved to be even worse than it was for their counterparts in Germany. Many priests were jailed or sent to concentration camps, youth education by the church was all but eliminated, church newspapers were closed, church processions were banned, and, in many parish churches, Mass on important feast days, even Christmas, was prohibited unless the feast fell on a Sunday.

If someone greeted Franz with the Nazi salute and the words *Heil Hitler,* Franz would respond, minus the salute, with the words *Pfui Hitler.* As Franz saw it, the *Anschluss* was similar to what had happened in Jerusalem during Passion Week: the crowd had chosen the criminal Barabbas rather than their savior, Christ.

The *Anschluss* was only the beginning of a rapid campaign of German territorial expansion. Following the annexation of Austria, Germany occupied the Sudetenland, a region of Czechoslovakia. In March 1939, the rest of Czechoslovakia was taken over. In September 1939, Hitler began the invasion of Poland, at which point Britain and France responded with declarations of war and World War II began. In May 1940, France and the Low Countries were invaded. In June 1941, Germany launched its war on the "eastern front" with the Soviet Union, at the same creating for itself an urgent need for a much larger army.

Having become citizens of Germany, every able Austrian was subject to conscription. Franz was called up in June 1940, taking his military vow in Braunau, Hitler's birthplace, but a few days later he was allowed to return to his farm, as farmers were needed no less than soldiers. In October he was called back for training as an army driver, but in April 1941, six months later, he was again allowed to return to his farm.

While in the army, Franz made a significant commitment: he joined the Third Order of St. Francis in December 1940. He may not have known that the Order's original rule, as written by Francis, obliged those who joined not to possess or use deadly weapons, but without doubt he knew that Francis was a man who, following his conversion, never threatened or harmed anyone.

Franz's brief period in the army, coupled with his recognition that to assist the Nazi movement in any way was to oppose Christ and his church, made him realize that a return to the army was not possible for him. If he were summoned again, even at the cost of his life, he would have to say no.

Returning home from the army, Franz was ready for a deeper engagement in his parish. He agreed to become sexton, a responsibility that involved keeping the church and its grounds in good repair, assisting at daily Mass, and helping arrange baptisms, weddings, and funerals. His priest was surprised at how quickly Franz learned all the Latin responses.

It was not possible for Franziska to offer her wholehearted endorsement — how could she sanction a course of action that would result in the death of her beloved husband? — but she was equally determined not to seek to change Franz's mind. She knew her husband was simply following Christ in the same way as the martyrs at whose tombs in Rome they had prayed in the days following their wedding.

Franz readily talked about his views with anyone who would listen. Most often he was told that his main responsibility was to his family and that it would be better to risk death in the army on their behalf than to take steps that would almost certainly guarantee his death. While he would certainly do what he could to preserve his life for the sake of his family, Franz noted that self-preservation did not make it permissible to go and murder other people's families. He pointed out that to accept military service also meant leaving his family without any assurance he would return alive. If he had to risk his life, was it not better to do so for Christ rather than Hitler? As for his family, surely God would not forget them. How good a husband and father would he be if he chose social conformity over obedience to Christ's teaching? Did not Christ say, "He who loves father or mother more than me is not worthy of me; and he who loves son or daughter more than me is not worthy of me"?

Most of all Franz sought advice from the church's pastors. At the time Fr. Ferdinand Fürthauer was the priest in St. Radegund, filling in for Fr. Josef Karobath, who in 1940 had been jailed for delivering an anti-Nazi sermon and then banished from the district. Far from encouraging Franz, Fr. Fürthauer—a young man who felt unprepared for such a situation—wondered if refusing military service, given that execution was the almost certain penalty, was not the same as committing the mortal sin of suicide. In later years Fr. Fürthauer wrote to Franziska, "I wanted to save his life, but he did not want any pretense and rejected all falsehood. I often pray that Franz Jägerstätter may forgive me."

Franz turned for guidance to his former pastor, Fr. Karobath. "We met in the Bavarian town of Tittmoning," Karobath recalls. "I wanted to talk him out of it [Franz's decision to refuse further military service], but he defeated me again and again with words from the scriptures."

Franz even managed to meet with the bishop of Linz, Joseph Fliesser, successor to Bishop Gföllner. A list of questions Franz had written down in preparation for the encounter has survived. Franz asked if it was not sinful to support an ideology (Nazism) whose goals included eradicating Christianity; if "the predatory raids" that Germany was making in various countries could be regarded as acts of "a righteous and holy war"; how is it possible for the church, in burying the remains of German soldiers killed in the war, to permit its priests to describe the fallen as heroes and even saints; would it not be truer to regard as heroes those who defended their homelands rather than those who invade other countries; could the church regard as righteous and good whatever the crowd happens to be shouting; and, finally, can one be both a soldier of Christ and a soldier of Nazism, thus both fighting for the victory of Christ and his church while at the same time fighting for the victory of Nazism?

While Franz met with Bishop Fliesser, Franziska was in the adjacent waiting room, no doubt praying. When Franz came out of the bishop's consulting room, Franziska recalls that he "was very sad and said to me: 'They don't dare commit themselves or it will be their turn next.'" Franz had the impression that the bishop didn't discuss his questions because it was possible that his visitor might be a Gestapo spy.

In later years, Bishop Fliesser said, "In vain, I explained to him the basic principles of morality concerning the degree of responsibility that a private person and citizen bears for the actions of those in authority, and reminded him of his far higher responsibility for those within his private circle, particularly his family."

It was, in fact, an answer any Catholic might have heard from any bishop in any country at the time: if not a doctrine found in any catechism, it was widely believed that any sins you commit under obedience to your government are not your personal sins but are regarded by God as the sins of those who lead the state. God would judge the leader, not those who had obeyed his orders. But for Franz it seemed obvious that, if God gives each of us free will and a conscience, each of us is responsible for what we do and fail to do, all the more so if we are consciously aware we have allowed ourselves to become servants of evil masters.

Franz later made the compassionate observation that "the bishop has not experienced the grace that has been granted to me."

In a notebook entry Franz made early in 1942, he remarks, "They [the bishops and priests] are human beings of flesh and blood as we are, and they can be weak. Perhaps they are even more tempted by the evil foe than we are. Perhaps, too, they were too little prepared to take on this struggle and decide for themselves whether to live or to die."

Having gone through his training, nearly two years went by without Franz's receiving a summons to return to the army. Throughout that period, each time mail was delivered to the Jägerstätter farm, both husband and wife were in dread. Finally on February 23, 1943, the fateful letter arrived. "Now I've signed my death sentence," Franz remarked while putting his signature on the postal receipt. He was ordered to report to a military base in Enns, near Linz, two days later.

The same day he wrote to Fr. Karobath, whom he still regarded as his pastor even though the priest had been sent to another parish, "I must tell you that soon you may be losing one of your parishioners.... Today I received my conscription orders.... As no one can give me a dispensation for the danger to the salvation of my soul that joining this movement [the Nazis] would bring, I just can't alter my resolve, as you know.... It's always said that one shouldn't do what I am doing because of the risk to one's life, but I take the view that those others who are joining in the fighting aren't exactly out of life-threatening danger themselves. Among those fighting in Stalingrad, so I've heard, are also four or five people from St. Radegund.... My family won't forsake God and the Blessed Virgin Mary.... It will be difficult for my loved ones. This parting will surely be a hard one."

It was indeed a hard parting. At the station in Tittmoning, Franz and Franziska could not let go of each other until the train's movement forced them to separate. The conductor was furious.

Even as he boarded the train, Franz was already two days late for his appointment at Enns. But, after all, there was no need to arrive on time — once he reached Enns, he and Franziska had every reason to think, it might be only days or weeks before his execution. His late arrival could not make the punishment any worse.

Arriving at Enns the next morning, March 1, even then Franz took his time, attending Mass in the local church before reporting to the barracks. He also took time to send a letter to Franziska. It ended, "Should it be God's will that I do not see you again in this world, then we hope that we shall see each other soon in heaven." So far as Franz knew, this was his last letter.

The following day, having announced his refusal to serve, Franz was placed under arrest and transported to the military remand prison in nearby Linz. Franz's stay in Linz lasted three months. Though many others were tried and sentenced at Linz (a Catholic priest who visited prisoners there recalled having accompanied thirty-eight men to their executions), Franz was not one among those tried.

Among prisoners at the Linz military prison from that period who survived, there were those who vividly recalled Franz — how often they saw him praying the rosary and his readiness to share with others his meager food rations. Giving away a piece of bread on one occasion, he claimed that a cup of coffee was enough for him.

No one knew better than Franziska how carefully thought out was the position Franz was taking and what a determined man he was in matters of faith. Even so, it was impossible for her not to encourage him occasionally to search for some alternate path that might not violate his conscience but perhaps would save his life. She wrote to him while he was in Linz, "One does God's will even when not understanding it." Even so, she confessed that she nurtured "the small hope that you would change your decision...because you have compassion for me, and I cannot help [being] me. I shall pray to the loving Mother of God that she will bring you back to us at home if it is God's will."

"I want to save my life but not through lies," wrote Franz to his wife. "In [the army base at] Enns people wanted to trap me by means of trick questions and so to make me once again into a soldier. It was not easy to keep my conviction. It may become even more difficult. But I trust in God to let me know if it would be better for me to do something different."

In a letter dated March 11, he told Franziska that he was willing to serve in the army medical corps "for here a person can actually do good and exercise Christian love of neighbor in concrete ways," but apparently such a noncombatant alternative was never opened to him by those responsible for his case.

Despite the heavy workload at the farm (in Franz's absence, for the first time Franziska had to till the fields), on the feast of Corpus Christi she sought spiritual strength by making a pilgrimage on foot to the Bavarian town of Altötting, home of the Chapel of the Miraculous Image, one of Germany's most visited shrines since medieval times — a place long associated with miracles.

Franz's last Easter before execution was spent in the Linz prison. He wrote that day to Franziska: "'Christ has risen, alleluia,' so the church rejoices today. When we have to endure hard times, we must and can rejoice with the church. What is more joyful than that Christ has again risen and gone forth as the victor over death and hell. What can give us Christians more comfort than that we no longer have to fear death."

Without warning, on May 4 Franz was taken by train to the prison at Tegel, a suburb of Berlin. It had been decided that Franz's was "a more serious case" requiring a Reich Court Martial in the capital rather than a provincial trial. Here Franz would spend the last three months of his life in solitary confinement. (Among Franz's fellow prisoners at Tegel was Dietrich Bonhoeffer, the Protestant theologian who was arrested in April 1943 after money was traced to him that had been used to help Jews escape to Switzerland. After eighteen months as a prisoner, Bonhoeffer was executed in 1945.)

Franz says almost nothing in his letters about the conditions of life at Tegel, but a priest, Fr. Franz Reinisch, who had been in the same prison a year before Franz, described it as "a foretaste of purgatory and hell: the thoughts and experiences: never a friendly face, never to feel any love, always only hard words — if this were to go on forever! And then the screaming of some prisoners who can't bear the loneliness and the wrongful loss of their freedom, the constantly keeping silent, the small cell, etc. and also, in the case of certain men, the spiritual distress that weighs heavily on their hearts, the enchainment of those condemned to death."

On July 6 a brief trial occurred. Franz was convicted of "undermining military morale" by "inciting the refusal to perform the required service in the German army." This was a capital offense. Franz was sentenced to death. From this point on, he was kept in handcuffs. In a letter to Franziska, Franz notes that he is writing with his "hands in chains" (echoing the words of St. Paul when he was a prisoner in Rome).

On July 8, Franz wrote home, "It is a joy to be able to suffer for Jesus and our faith. We have the joyful hope that the few days in this life when we have been separated will be replaced by thousands of days in eternity, where we shall rejoice with God and our heavenly Mother in untroubled joy and good fortune. If we can only remain in the love of God when difficult tests of our faith come to us." Perhaps to spare his family pain, or because the court sentence had not been confirmed, he said nothing in his letter about the trial that had just occurred.

In a final effort to save Franz's life, his court-assigned lawyer, Friedrich Leo Feldmann, arranged a visit by Franziska and the priest of St. Radegund, Fr. Fürthauer, in the hope they could convince his client to change his mind. Were he to do so, Feldmann was confident the court would withdraw its sentence.

Their twenty-minute meeting was Franz and Franziska's last. It happened on July 9 in the presence of armed guards. Not to their surprise, the visitors found that Franz saw no honorable alternative but to continue with his refusal of military service. Fr. Fürthauer later recalled his attempt to persuade Franz to accept army service for his family's sake. "He [Franz] said to me: 'Can you promise me that if I join that movement [the Nazi regime] that I shall not fall into mortal sin?' 'That I cannot do,' I answered. 'Then I won't enlist,' was his reply." (In 2006, Fr. Fürthauer was asked if he would still say the same to Franz were he able to go back in time. "Today," he responded, "I would not try to persuade him to change his resolve, but would just give him my blessing.")

Back in St. Radegund, Franziska wrote to Fr. Karobath to report on the meeting with Franz in Berlin, commenting with bitterness, "They [the military officials] could easily have assigned him to the medical corps, but they were naturally too proud for that, for it might have looked like a compromise on their part."

On July 14, Franz's death sentence was confirmed by the Reich's War Court. On August 9, Franz was taken to Brandenburg/Havel where, at about 4:00 p.m., he was killed by guillotine.

The priest who accompanied Franz to his execution, Fr. Albert Jochmann, standing in that day for the chaplain at Brandenberg, later told a community of Austrian nuns about Franz's final hours. In the early 1960s, one of them, Sister Georgia, having learned that Gordon Zahn was at work on a biography of Franz Jägerstätter, wrote to Zahn to relate what the chaplain had said. Visiting Franz shortly after midnight on August 9, he noticed on a small table in Franz's cell a document that, should Franz sign it, would allow him to leave prison and return to the army. When Fr. Jochmann pointed it out, Franz pushed it aside, saying, "I cannot and may not take an oath in favor of a government that is fighting an unjust war."

Sister Georgia continued: "Later he was to witness the calm and composed manner in which he [Franz Jägerstätter] walked to the scaffold." He told the sisters, themselves Austrian, "I can only congratulate you on this countryman of yours who lived as a saint and has now died a hero. I can say with certainty that this simple man is the only saint that I have ever met in my lifetime."

During his time in Berlin, Franz was permitted to write only one letter to Franziska each month, plus a fourth that was written on the day of his execution. The four letters bear witness to his extraordinary calm, conviction, and even happiness.

Part of the happiness he experienced was thanks to the support he found in the Catholic chaplain Fr. Heinrich Kreutzberg. It was a great consolation for Franz to hear from him that a priest, Fr. Franz Reinisch, had, just a year earlier, been in the same prison and died a similar death for similar reasons. After Franz's death, Fr. Kreutzberg wrote a long letter to Franziska in which he noted, "I have seen no more fortunate man in prison than your husband after my few words about Franz Reinisch."

Franz's final letter home was written the morning of his execution. In it he appeals for the forgiveness of anyone he may have pained or hurt. He adds: "Dearest wife and mother, it was not possible for me to free both of you from the sorrows that you have suffered for me. How hard it must have been for our dear Lord that he had given his dear mother such great sorrow through his suffering and death! And she suffered everything out of love for us sinners. I thank our Savior that I could suffer for him, and may die for him. I trust in his infinite compassion. I trust that God forgives me everything, and will not abandon me in the last hour....And now all my loved ones, be well. And do not forget me in your prayers. Keep the commandments, and we shall see each other again soon in heaven!"

◆ ◆ ◆

FRANZ JÄGERSTÄTTER was a solitary witness. He died with no expectation that his sacrifice would make any difference to anyone. He knew that, for his neighbors, the refusal of army service was incomprehensible — an act of folly, a sin against his family, his community, and even his church, which had called on no one to refuse military service. Franz knew that, beyond his family and community, his death would go entirely unnoticed and have no impact on the Nazi movement or hasten the end of the war. He would be soon forgotten. Who would remember or care about the anti-Nazi gesture of an uneducated farmer? He would be just one more filed-away name among many thousands who were tried and executed with bureaucratic indifference during the Nazi era.

In refusing to change his no to yes, the only thing that Franz could be sure of was that to betray his conscience would put his immortal soul at risk.

While the bishops of Austria had done nothing to sanction conscientious objection, and indeed done a great deal to discourage it, one must note that Franz did not simply invent the stand he took, nor did he feel abandoned by the church. He drew strength from the sacraments and from the awareness that he was walking the same path many saints, some in the recent past, had followed — men and women who had obeyed God rather than man and paid with their lives for doing so. Before his death Franz had the profound consolation of learning that a Catholic priest, Fr. Franz Reinisch, had been held in the very same prison and executed for similar reasons.

Like all the witnesses who had gone before him, Franz was equipped with an acute sensitivity to forgotten or neglected notes of the Gospel. He had read the New Testament countless times and had thought long and hard about its stories and teachings. Given the war-related questions he was facing, no doubt it had impressed him that Jesus neither killed anyone nor called upon anyone to do so.

Aware of such basic Gospel themes and responding to them with uncompromising courage and faith, Franz in turn has made it possible for others to hear them too.

In the Franz Jägerstätter narrative, there are two conversion stories.

The first was his own. Franz had been converted from being the sort of assembly-line Catholic who does what is expected of him within his native Catholic community into a rarer sort of Catholic who actually makes a conscious effort to understand the Gospel and to follow Christ wholeheartedly despite antagonistic social structures prepared to punish severely anyone who fails to stay in line.

The other conversion occurred within his church.

Far from being lost in the past, Franz's witness proved to be a seed cast in the wind, carried along until a time, nearly two decades later, when it would it at last take root and find fitting soil. As a consequence, Franz Jägerstätter helped the Catholic Church change direction. How providential it was that the story of Franz's life began to circulate during the Second Vatican Council and played a part in giving shape to what the Catholic Church today teaches about war, peace, conscience, and individual responsibility — guidance in stark contrast to what was taught in Franz's day: trust your rulers and do as you're told; it is no sin to obey.

Nor did Franz's influence end with a reform of church teaching about war and individual responsibility. Half a century after Franz's death, the church that he loved so much, but that had deeply disappointed him, beatified him. The church had moved from interest in Franz's challenging life to recognizing it as a model of sanctity, a life that rendered nothing less than a modern translation of the Gospel. "Franz Jägerstätter," said Cardinal Christoph Schönborn on the day of Franz's beatification, "is a living page of the Gospel. The Gospel is not only an authoritative report of that which was taking place at that time in Galilee and in Jerusalem. It is a living book.... Franz Jägerstätter was and is for me the most concrete and illustrative commentary on the Beatitudes that I have ever heard."

No one would have been more astonished than Franz to hear himself, or any conscientious objector, described by the cardinal of Vienna in such terms.

Within the cathedral there was resounding applause for Franziska Jägerstätter, who had lived to hear a solemn declaration read aloud recognizing as a model of sanctity a man who had once been dismissed as a model of insanity. Then there was the sight of so many bishops rising to their feet as a thirty-foot banner with Franz's photo was unfurled. But perhaps the high point for all present was to witness Franziska, tears streaming from her eyes, kiss a bronze urn containing some of Franz's ashes before presenting the reliquary to Cardinal Schönborn. One of the persons missing in the Linz cathedral was Gordon

Zahn, absent due to infirmity (Alzheimer's disease) and close to death. It was thanks to Zahn that the name of Franz Jägerstätter had been lifted from obscurity. For someone's life to be formally recognized as saintly by the church, there must first be at least one person who takes special note of that life, recognizes its importance, gathers the available details, and makes it his or her business to bring that life to the attention of others. In the case of Franz Jägerstätter, Gordon Zahn was that person. Had he not written *In Solitary Witness,* it is far from certain that the name of Franz Jägerstätter would be remembered today.

Side by side with Gordon Zahn, we are in debt to an Austrian, Erna Putz. Building on Zahn's research, beginning in 1979 she devoted herself to making Franz better known, obtaining important documents, writing a full-scale biography of Franz Jägerstätter, and collecting all his letters and other writings, now gathered together in the book you hold in your hands.

The impact of Franz's life was not only on the Second Vatican Council and its final document, the Pastoral Constitution on the Church in the Modern World. The year *In Solitary Witness* was published, 1964, happened to coincide with the early stages of U.S. military involvement in the war in Vietnam. *In Solitary Witness* was widely read by the young men, potential or actual soldiers, who were struggling with the question of how to respond to that war. Having been a draft counselor during that period, I can recall how many of the young people I talked with had read Zahn's book and found themselves deeply challenged by Franz Jägerstätter's life. It was one of the reasons that the Catholic Church in the United States produced so many thousands of conscientious objectors during the Vietnam War. While none of them faced the guillotine, many faced prison, exile, or other hardships. How important it was for them to discover that they were not alone; that someone like Franz Jägerstätter, under far more difficult circumstances, had read the Gospel as they did and faced the consequences, despite the incomprehension of their contemporaries.

Franz Jägerstätter remains a challenge, and not only because of his costly refusal to surrender his conscience to the Nazis.

One aspect of that challenge is Franz's deeply traditional faith, an example far from fashionable today even among Catholics. While certainly not unaware of the church's human shortcomings and the ways so many bishops compromise the Gospel in order to be on good terms with political leaders, Franz Jägerstätter was a grateful Catholic committed to the church and its sacramental and devotional life. It is no minor detail of his life that he and Franziska began their marriage by going as pilgrims to Rome, a journey that they could barely afford. No two people were so often seen at Mass in St. Radegund. Both husband and wife were devoted to the rosary; in prison Franz prayed the rosary much of the time. The Jägerstätter household kept all the church-appointed fasts. Both Franz and Franziska made frequent use of the sacrament of confession. It was remembered in St. Radegund that Franz sometimes paused while at work in the fields in order to pray. He not only served his parish as sexton, a voluntary and time-consuming responsibility, but refused to accept any financial rewards offered to him by parishioners for his role in arranging baptisms, weddings, and funerals. Both Franz and Franziska had a special devotion to the Sacred Heart of Jesus, with its stress on Christ's self-giving love for each person. Franz was a member of the Third Order of St. Francis.

Without doubt the hardest part of saying no to further army service was Franz's love of his wife and their children. Franz knew his execution would make many aspects of life harder for his family, especially for Franziska, as indeed it did.

While the widows of soldiers won the widespread sympathy of Austrians, Franziska was shunned. Not only had she lost her husband, but many of her neighbors tuned their back on her. Some blamed Franz's death on her overzealous religious influence.

When Gordon Zahn interviewed Franziska in 1961, she described with composure her last meeting with Franz in Berlin three weeks before his execution, but she broke down in tears while describing the subsequent behavior of her neighbors. Few offered her the help she so badly needed after Franz's death.

In the Nazi period, subsidies and privileges were distributed to compliant farmers; poor and hard-pressed though she was, none of these came to her. An application for cement was once rejected as soon as it was noticed that her family name was Jägerstätter.

Even after the war officials penalized many of those who had opposed Hitler. In the entire period of rationing, Franziska received no coupons for clothing or shoes for herself or her children. She knitted clothes from the wool of angora rabbits.

In post-war Austria, for years she was denied the pension allocated to war widows. The authorities argued that the legislation compensating victims only applied to those who had *fought* for a free and democratic Austria. This did not include Franz, they argued. Franziska only won her right to a pension in 1950, after enlisting the help of a lawyer, Franz's cousin, Franz Huber.

Yet she bore her difficulties bravely and with unwavering respect for her husband's stand.

Throughout her life, Franziska Jägerstätter has been a person who never drew attention to herself. It is only in reading the letters the couple exchanged that the outsider begins to realize how deep the bond was between them.

Franz and Franziska loved each other passionately. It was an extraordinary love, with an all-or-nothing dimension of faithfulness that had as its foundation their shared love of God. What became clear to Franz, once he married Franziska, was that he could truly be a Christian husband and father only to the extent that following Christ stood at the center of his life. What better love could a man give to his family than, by his own example, to follow Christ without fear even to the Cross?

While her neighbors may have overestimated Franziska's influence, she did much to encourage the faith that finally led Franz to martyrdom, though the stand he took was not something she ever advocated. "In the beginning," she once explained, "I really begged him not to put his life at stake, but then, when everyone was quarreling with him and scolding him, I didn't do it any more. . . . If I had not stood by him, he would have had no one."

"I have lost a dear husband and a good father to my children," Franziska wrote soon after Franz's death, "but I can also assure you that our marriage was one of the happiest in our parish — many people envied us. But the good Lord intended otherwise, and has loosed that loving bond. I already look forward to meeting again in heaven, where no war can ever divide us again."

After the war Franz's ashes were brought to St. Radegund and buried beneath a crucifix by the church wall. Little by little, his grave became a place of pilgrimage.

Franziska, still a pilgrim herself, celebrated both the fiftieth and sixtieth anniversaries of her wedding by returning to Rome, the city where she and Franz spent the first days of their marriage.

Perhaps what would have astonished Franz more than anything would have been to see, among the five thousand people packed into the Linz cathedral on the day of his beatification, that not only was Franziska (then ninety-four) present, but their children, grandchildren, and great-grandchildren — sixty family members in all.

Overview

A Prophet, Martyr, and Saint

Robert A. Krieg

Franz Jägerstätter: Letters and Writings from Prison is a collection of texts that this Austrian farmer wrote during the last four years of his life. This book consists of two parts. Part One contains the letters between Franz and Franziska from June 18, 1940, to April 8, 1941, and also from March 1 to August 9, 1943. There are a total of 128 letters. Of these, 74 were written by Franz, and 54 by Franziska. (Some of Franziska's letters to Franz were lost, most likely because of Franz's living conditions in the military and then in prison.) This correspondence between the spouses comprises this book's chapters 1 through 5.

The book's second part consists of Franz Jägerstätter's essays or commentaries on the Christian life and the moral dilemma of Catholics in the Third Reich. It begins with chapter 6, containing three early writings by Franz. Chapters 7 though 10 hold what Franz wrote in three notebooks and on loose sheets of paper from May 1941 until March 1943. In these essays, he laid out the ideas that undergirded his opposition to National Socialism, the Third Reich, and the war. During his imprisonment in Berlin, Franz clandestinely wrote down his thoughts on Christian discipleship and the Third Reich, and arranged to have these writings somehow secretly delivered to Franziska after his execution. Chapter 11 is the notebook that Franz kept in prison from May to August 1943, and chapter 12 contains five separate essays that he put on odd pieces of paper between his trial on July 6 and his execution on August 9.

Franz Jägerstätter's writings remain in the possession of Franziska Jägerstätter, who chose to contribute two texts to memorials for her husband. Frau Jägerstätter donated Franz's handwritten poem "Traumes" ("In a Dream") for the celebration of her husband's beatification at the Cathedral of Linz. Further, she permitted Cardinal Christoph Schönborn, the archbishop of Vienna, to take to Rome on November 4, 2005, Franz's final essay from late July or August 1943. This reflection (text no. 88, page 243 below) opens with the sentences:

"Now I'll write down a few words as they come to me from my heart. Although I am writing them with my hands in chains, this is still much better than if my will were in chains." This text is now on loan to the memorial for the modern martyrs in Rome's San Bartolomeo Church.

The letters between Franz and Franziska Jägerstätter and Franz's essays have appeared in print because of Frau Jägerstätter's initiative. They were first published in 1987 in *Gefängnisbriefe und Aufzeichnungen* (Prison Letters and Notes), edited by Erna Putz. However, this book went out of print many years ago. The letters and essays recently reappeared in *Franz Jägerstätter: Der gesamte Briefwechsel mit Franziska, Aufzeichnungen 1941–1943* (Franz Jägerstätter: The Entire Correspondence with Franziska, [and] Notes 1941–1943), edited by Erna Putz (Vienna: Styria Verlag, 2007), which is translated in this volume.

In her editing of these texts, Dr. Putz retained, as much as possible, the colloquial expressions of Franz and Franziska Jägerstätter. She has also updated the spelling and punctuation in the texts. Since in some cases Franz Jägerstätter wrote two or three versions of the same essay, Dr. Putz chose for publication the manuscript that seemed to be the text's final version. Moreover, she provided commentary on some aspects of the letters and essays in her book's introduction and annotations.

This volume makes available in English for the first time all of the letters between Franz and Franziska and all of Franz's essays. Until now, some of these writings were accessible for English speakers primarily in Gordon C. Zahn's classic *In Solitary Witness: The Life and Death of Franz Jägerstätter* (New York: Holt, Rinehart and Winston, 1964).[1]

This translation is meant to convey the meaning of the texts while manifesting the verbal styles and customs of Franz and Franziska Jägerstätter. However, for the sake of clarity, the translator has recast the long sentences and long paragraphs in German into shorter sentences and paragraphs in English. At the same time, he has retained the German nicknames and ecclesiastical titles. Following German-speaking customs, Franz and Franziska often added "i," "j," or "l" to a person's name. For example, *Franz* became *Franzl,* and *Franziska* became *Fani* or *Fanj.* In German, diminutives such as these are expressions of endearment. Further, Franz and Franziska used the titles "Pastor" (*Pfarrer*) or

---

1. Gordon C. Zahn (b. 1918) died in December 2007. Unfortunately, because of illness, he was not aware of the beatification of Franz Jägerstätter two months earlier. The second edition of his book is *In Solitary Witness* (Springfield, Ill.: Templegate Publishers, 1986). It is to the first edition that citations of Franz Jägerstätter's writings are made here. However, the English translations in this volume were done independently from the translations in Zahn's *In Solitary Witness.* Hereafter, "FJ" in the notes means "Franz Jägerstätter." [RK]

"Chaplain" (*Kaplan*) when they were referring to diocesan priests, and they employed the title "Father" (*Pater*) in reference to a priest in a religious order.

In their writings, Franz and Franziska Jägerstätter were cautious in their comments about Adolf Hitler's political party, ideology, and policies. They spoke about the "National Socialist Party," "the party," and "National Socialism." They did not use "Nazism," which was a derisive abbreviation of "Nationalsozialistische Deutsche Arbeitspartei" (NSDAP), that is, "National Socialist German Workers' Party." Their usage of terms is reflected in this translation, and "N.S." frequently occurs here in place of "National Socialist."

Franz Jägerstätter drew heavily on the Bible as he reflected on the Christian faith and his response to National Socialism. He may have received instruction on the Bible from the priests with whom he was a friend and also from the renewal of biblical studies that flourished in German-speaking Catholicism between the world wars. In any case, Franz frequently quotes, paraphrases, or alludes to the Bible, especially in his essays. When he gives an explicit biblical reference, it appears here in parentheses. When he does not specify the biblical text to which he is referring, the translator has inserted the citation in brackets. Further, when Franz Jägerstätter quotes a biblical text, the translator has used the translation of the New Oxford Annotated Bible, 3rd ed., ed. Michael D. Coogan (Oxford: Oxford University Press, 2001).

Some of the prefaces to the texts and some of the annotations in this volume were written by the German editor, and others were added by the American translator. Those contributed by Erna Putz are unsigned, and those given by Robert Krieg conclude with "RK."

Finally, a word about Franz Jägerstätter's thought. This book discloses that Franz Jägerstätter was not only a martyr and a saint but also a prophet, in the biblical sense. That is, he exhibited many of the personal traits of the Old Testament prophets such as Elijah, Amos, and Jeremiah. For example, Franz Jägerstätter felt an exceptional intimacy with God, as when he meditated time and again on the joy of eternal life. Second, he sensed a divine call, for example, in his dream of January 1938. Third, he attained an insightful analysis of the cultural, political, religious, and social dynamics of his day—an analysis that generated his predictions about life after the war. Fourth, Franz Jägerstätter was acutely aware of human sinfulness and divine compassion. Fifth, he was ready to suffer and die for the sake of his personal integrity and his vocation. Indeed, he even saw his suffering and death as a martyrdom that was part and parcel of his calling. These five qualities of Franz Jägerstätter were evident in the lives of Elijah, Amos, and Jeremiah—and also in the life of Jesus Christ.

Franz Jägerstätter was not, however, a robed figure out of biblical times but a Catholic farmer of the early twentieth century who thrived within a network of familial and social relationships, was impacted by current events, and drank deeply from the Catholicism of his day. Therefore, information concerning the people and events in Franz's life is contained in this book's appendix. The first section of the appendix provides bibliographic information on Jägerstätter's family, neighbors, and friends, and the second gives the dates and short descriptions of key events in Jägerstätter's life in relation to a chronology of the Third Reich and the Second World War.

Participating in the Roman Catholicism of his era, Franz Jägerstätter held assumptions that had emerged out of the Baroque period (1550–1750) and the church's neo-Scholasticism (1830–1965).[2] Four of these convictions run through Franz's letters and essays.

1. The church's sacraments and religious devotions are the primary loci through which we can receive God's grace, which is understood to be a divine energy or power. Prior to his imprisonment, Franz rejoiced when he could attend two Masses on a Sunday and when he could attend his parish's religious devotions, e.g., to the Sacred Heart of Jesus and to the Blessed Mother.

2. The church's primary responsibility is to make the sacraments and religious devotions available to its members. Franz was uplifted when priests brought him Holy Communion in prison, and he and Franziska were troubled when the Third Reich began to stop the celebration of the church's holy days as national holidays.

3. When we suffer, we can gain "merit" with God so that, after death, we can shorten our time in purgatory or other people's time there. Franz believed that he was making up for his sins and others' sins by means of his hardships, such as separation from his family, imprisonment, and execution.

4. The ideal nation is the one that forms a symbiosis of a predominantly Roman Catholic society, Roman Catholic ecclesiastical governance, and a Roman Catholic civil government. Influenced by church teachings, Franz did not support liberal democracy with its separation of church and state. In particular, he was uncomfortable with the idea that if the Reich lost the war, Great Britain or the United States might govern Austria. (See below page 180.)

While holding these four assumptions, Franz Jägerstätter also hammered out for himself personal values that were ahead of his time, indeed prophetic.

---

2. See "Baroque, The" and "Neo-Scholasticism" in the *New Catholic Encyclopedia,* 2nd ed., ed. Berard L Marthaler (Detroit: Gale Publishers, 2003).

He anticipated the Second Vatican Council's *Gaudium et Spes* (1965) as he held the following convictions.

5. Every human being should obey God's voice as known in his or her informed conscience in light of the Bible, the Christian tradition and church teachings. Franz judged that his first responsibility was to obey what he judged to be God's word in his conscience and appealed to Jesus' teaching that discipleship included "hating" one's "wife and children" (Luke 14:26).

6. Every human being should preserve his or her moral integrity. Franz refused to take the Wehrmacht's oath of unconditional allegiance to the Führer because he judged that to do so would be for him to lie. Moreover, he voiced concern about the destruction of the ethical fiber of the Reich's soldiers because they were being required to rob and kill noncombatants.

7. Church officials should publicly confront civil authorities when they adopt policies and engage in actions that violate the Ten Commandments. Franz Jägerstätter held that Austria's bishops erred by remaining silent as the Reich and the N.S. Party violated human rights, including religious freedom.

8. A just war is one in which a nation pursues a just cause (e.g., national self-defense) and respects the dignity and rights of all human beings. Although many people in the Reich maintained that they were not in a position to judge whether Hitler's war was just, Franz insisted that the war's injustice was obvious in its aims — i.e., the acquisition of oil, ore, and in land as well as the forced labor of conquered peoples — and brutal methods.

9. "Active love of neighbor out of love of God is the best means of salvation ... and the surest sign of being a child of God." Franz wrote down this conviction during the final weeks of his life (see below no. 183 on page 232). While becoming increasingly involved in worship and religious devotions since the mid-1930s, he had simultaneously become increasingly generous, giving food and clothing to the poor, even when his family had very little. In Linz's prison, he often gave his ration of bread to his cellmates.

Franz Jägerstätter was a prophetic figure. Similar to the biblical books of Amos and Jeremiah, Franz's letters and essays communicate a great deal about their writer, God, and ourselves. They reveal that Jägerstätter obeyed his dream of January 1938. He did not get on the "train to hell," and tried to warn others about it as he lived in Christian freedom. Refusing to accept Hitler as his idol, he remained faithful to the true God as he followed his conscience, remained in close communication with his wife, Franziska, reflected on the Bible, and participated in the church's worship and prayer.

Franz Jägerstätter's writings also shed light on the God of Christian belief. It was this God who — according to Jägerstätter himself — gave this ordinary Austrian the wisdom and courage to speak the truth, endure imprisonment, and face his execution with "inner peace."[3] This God wills that human beings live not in slavery — as imposed by the Pharaoh (Exod. 3:7–8) or by the Führer — but in the grace-filled freedom that we can taste in this life and can fully enjoy in the next.

Finally, Franz Jägerstätter's letters and essays can show us ourselves. They can function as a mirror in which we can see our souls. These writings may challenge us to examine our consciences — as Jägerstätter urged his family to do — so that we become more faithful to God who speaks in our consciences. In particular, these letters and essays can prompt us to ask, What are today's "trains to hell"? And how well are we walking the way of Jesus Christ in light of the witness of Franz Jägerstätter?

---

3. See Zahn, *In Solitary Witness,* 96. [RK]

Part One

The Correspondence between Franz and Franziska Jägerstätter

Chapter 1

Military Training Letters

June 18–October 30, 1940

Franz Jägerstätter was required by the Third Reich to report for military induction at Braunau am Inn on June 17, 1940. Six weeks earlier, Franz and Franziska had welcomed into the world their daughter Aloisia ("Loisi") and introduced her to her sisters Rosalia ("Rosi") and Maria ("Maridl"). With Franz's departure, it fell to Franziska to care for the three little children and also to manage the family's farm.

After her marriage to Franz on April 9, 1936, Franziska had moved from her family's home and farm in Hochburg to the Jägerstätter home and farm, called Leherbauer, in St. Radegund. There she resided with her husband, Franz, and his mother, Rosalia. While giving birth to three daughters over four years, Franziska also learned about managing Leherbauer and established ties with the families on the surrounding farms.

Of the eighteen letters in this chapter, twelve were written by Franz and six by Franziska. Although these letters were not being censored by military officials — as were the letters that Franz and Franziska exchanged in 1943 — Franz and Franziska were guarded in what they put on paper, lest a letter end up in the wrong hands.

Five days after Franz Jägerstätter entered the army, the Third Reich imposed its armistice on a defeated France. For the remainder of 1940 and into 1941, it consolidated its control of Western Europe. Given this relative calm, Franz and his father-in-law, Lorenz Schwaninger, conjecture in their letters that the war might soon end. [RK]

From Franz to Franziska

Braunau, June 18, 1940

Dear wife!

We arrived safely yesterday. Today we were enlisted and immediately put into uniforms. Very few men were found to be unfit. So far, no one has been found to be superfluous. Otherwise, all goes well for me.

Warm greetings to you.

Yours, Franz

Greetings to Mother and the three little ones and the neighbors.[1]

From Franziska to Franz

St. Radegund, June 20, 1940

Dear husband!

With longing we waited daily — or more frequently — for your letter. Mother is still ill and bedridden.[2] She is in the care of the doctor from Ostermiething. She was not able to travel to a different one. The children are still not behaving any better. They are always demanding my attention.

What I feared has occurred. I have found no one to assist with the work, except for Mari, who has done the work in the barn. Then I sent her to Spreiter to speak with my mother, and afterward my father came here.[3] I would have been truly happy if you could have stayed home at least two weeks. Strohhofer helped us cut down the hay in the lower meadow. Toni helped us in the Tiefenhaler meadow, which we reaped today. Also, Pleikner helped. It is not good when one must rely so much on the neighbors, always asking for help and thanking them.

Today I went to the village office in order to make the inquiry. Herr Huber simply said that they know no one.[4] I'd like to ask you, have you already paid the fire insurance? What is the amount which we must pay?

Also, the pig was picked up. But things got terribly difficult. It almost did not fit into the car. Only a boy came for it. It weighed 326 pounds.

There was a wedding today in St. Radegund. Fred Ofenmacher and his bride were married by [Pastor] Johann Pleikner.

---

1. The "three little ones" are the daughters: Rosalia, Maria, and Aloisia. Concerning them and other key people mentioned in this chapter and subsequent chapters, see the biographical information in the appendix. [RK]

2. "Mother" refers to Franz's mother, Rosalia Jägerstätter.

3. "Spreiter" is the name of Franziska's family home in Hochburg.

4. Ferdinand Huber was St. Radegund's civil registrar.

I received your card today and have made myself immediately write you tonight. It is now 11:00 p.m. The others are already sleeping, and I must end my letter since my eyes are closing.

Warm greetings from your Fani, who is always thinking about you, and also from your parents-in-law.

From Franz to Franziska

Braunau am Inn, June 22, 1940

Dearest wife!

I am finally getting to writing you again. I am still in good health. Hopefully, all of you are as well. How are the three little ones? They will have already forgotten their father. I am hoping that we'll have a reunion on Sunday, June 30.

This morning we had no training exercises. Things are a bit boring on this Sunday.[5] Today's rest is good though. In the early afternoon we made a march of about ten miles, which was not much for me. Would this have been a workout for your father? I hope that he has again visited you this week. Hans Lang and I are in the same barracks but not in the same room. Nor are we in the same platoon for the exercises. There are about 170 newly enlisted men, among whom are many fathers of families.

One of the men told me that his wife gave birth to their first baby two weeks ago. Now things are going poorly for both of them because she got up too soon. The man went to a physician in order to get medicine for his wife, and the physician said that he would not give him a prescription even if his wife were dying. Perhaps you can refer the new mother to a midwife if she contacts you.

Hopefully, you have found a worker to replace me. After eight weeks we shall hopefully be done with this training. At that time will they be done with the war? At the very least, I want to be with my loved ones for some time. Now I can only be with you in my thoughts.

However, the most difficult things can be overcome in God's name.

Warm greetings to you and mother and the three little ones.

Yours, Franz

I look forward to our reunion.

Do not send me anything to eat. I am surely not suffering from hunger. The meals are good. Greetings to father and the neighbors.

---

5. FJ likely wrote this letter on Saturday, June 22, and wrote the next one on Sunday, June 23. In German, Saturday is often called *Sonnabend,* "Sunday evening." [RK]

From Franz to Franziska

Braunau, June 23, 1940

Dearest wife!

I received your letter today, which I had awaited with great longing. I opened it with a joyful heart, and read it to the end with a heavy heart. It is hard to see someone suffer, especially when one cannot help. And most especially when it is one's dearest wife. I ask, dear Fanj, if it is possible, write me often. Spiritual hardships are frequently harder than physical ones, and if one can speak or write a little about everything, then things can become easier for one's heart. We have shared many joys, and so we want also to do the same with suffering.

Dear Fanj, I understand your pain, for I know what is it to feel abandoned by everyone. Therefore, pour out your heart to me for no one — other than God and our heavenly Mother — can better understand your suffering than your beloved husband.

I apologize that I must now write with a pencil. The ink has run out.

Dear Fanj, do not get discouraged even if it often seems that the Lord God has also forgotten us. It is not so. God wants only to test whether we constantly confess our belief even in suffering. It is indeed true that a person's character shows itself in suffering.[6] God did not spare his beloved Son from this experience of abandonment. How much less will it be spared us! We must go courageously on the way of suffering whether we begin sooner or later. They may build many beautiful streets today, but they cannot change the way to heaven. This way will always remain rugged and rocky.

Dear Fanj, do not be angry with me because I did not postpone these two weeks, which I could have arranged. Up until now, I have not regretted that I stuck with my decision. We do not want to condescend to the games of the political leaders. I believe that we must often rely on a strong will.

You must forgive me for being sloppy by once again forgetting to pay the premium for the fire insurance. If you will not miss the money, then be so good as to pay it. It is 18 marks.

Now I must end my writing. This Sunday is slowly coming to a close. We did not go out for exercises today. It was a bit boring. I always have the consolation that there is only one more week, and then there is our joyful reunion.

---

6. FJ included an essay on this theme in his first notebook (see below page 159). [RK]

I shall write you once during the coming week, for there is very little free time. We must get up every day at 5:00 a.m.

Once again, have courage, dear Fanj. And do not immerse yourself too much in the work and the worldly concerns. Leave undone what does not go easily. Your first concern must be our children, and you cannot carry out with thoroughness both the care of the children and the care of the business. So care for the children and mother.[7] You and I must value them more than the business.

I send warm greetings and kisses to you and the children, and I remain concerned about you.

Your husband, Franz.

Many warm greetings to Mother. I wish her all the good that the loving God considers good. Greetings to my parents-in-law and the neighbors.

Be well. See you again on Sunday.

Let me hear something from you soon!

From Franz to Franziska

Franz received a military leave from the end of June until the start of October in order to work on the family farm. When he returned to military duty, he wrote the note below on a postcard.

Enns, October 5, 1940

I arrived safely today and am sending all of you warm greetings.

Yours, Franz.

Franz Jägerstätter, Transportation Specialist Second Class E
Fourth Battalion, Room no. 106, Alpine Rangers Barracks, 17 Enns

From Franz to Franziska

Enns, October 6, 1940

Dearest wife and mother!

Receive my warm greetings. Today I have enough time to write you a few sentences. We have a day of rest today. On Friday we were able to travel to Ried. We were given accommodations in the Gasthof of the Golden Star. But it was not especially golden. One large room was filled with a little straw, already used, that had been there for many days. We had to try to sleep on this straw. Also, there were some vulgar young men who did not remain quiet all night long. Approximately eighty men were billeted in this room.

---

7. FJ's mother was in the hospital recovering from surgery for cancer.

The next day we went to the military installation that was the meeting point. There the older men were separated from the younger ones. The younger ones, including Toni Staiger, went to Linz for the infantry, and we older ones to Enns, where we must now apparently endure things for a few weeks. It may even be a month! It is good that none of us knows how long it will continue and what fate still awaits us. Most of us have the hope that we can return home to our loved ones after our time of training. The military installation would be wonderful if one could be here only for a holiday.

It would have been more satisfactory in Braunau. Here there are large rooms in which approximately seventy to eighty men sleep. In my room there are seventy-six men, almost all of them the fathers of families. The older men are together, most born in 1904 and 1905. There are not many born in 1907. Today we were given uniforms, and tomorrow the dance will begin. The older ones tell us that the longer time is here, and that the meals here are good. Today they were not bad. Hopefully, things will not get worse. If they do not, I'll surely be a fortunate man.

Dearest Fanj, how are things going now for you? Hopefully better than the other time in the summer. What are the three little ones up to? Write me soon and often. Now I must end my writing. It is already dark, and a sad Sunday comes to an end.

Pray for all of us and for peace very soon. I send greetings and kisses to you and to the little ones and mother.

Yours, Franz.

See you again.

Good night.

From Franziska Jägerstätter and Lorenz Schwaninger to Franz

St. Radegund, October 9, 1940

Dear husband!

Today, Wednesday, I received your card and letter. I am very grateful for these, and have made myself write you right now, at 8:00 p.m., since you would like to learn about some things from home.

On Sunday morning, I learned from Josef Strohhofer that on Saturday many men returned to Hochburg. They were not needed. So I hoped to see you on Sunday evening. I thought that you had perhaps stopped to see Pastor Karobath, as you had spoken about at one time. But, sadly, my husband did not arrive home.

I have Strohhofer's daughter working with me.[8] I asked the Strohhofers for help because Maria had to work with the carpenter, and I knew no one else.[9] Perhaps you can send thank-you notes to those people who have assisted me with the work. After Lichtmess she will go to the ironworker. She works very diligently. I think that at home they have insisted that she should hurry.

I am finished with the tilling of the oats. At the start, the planting of the potatoes with the plow was terribly frustrating for me to the point of tears. Then I went to Lang who put everything in order. Today I have received a dispensation from the plowing; father has arrived. I no longer need to shout at the cows [as they pull the plow] but only at our little ones and at the girl whose hearing is terribly bad.

Father said that Hias Erber is at home again because his village applied for his military deferral for community service. Others who have received these leaves were able to return home. As I heard this, I became heavy of heart. If you could have received this deferral, then perhaps you'd be at home again. However, with God's help, you will hopefully not remain away for long.

Things are not going badly for me. I am only very sad about you. Rosi is always asking about you. When we're going to bed, she says, "Papa is locked out." At meals, "Save something for Papa." If I get up at night, "Is Papa home?" Often she begins to weep because "father has not yet come home." Then Maridi says, "He'll bring sausage." They are constantly with Lang at the calves' shed. I'll end my letter. . . .

The letter continues on a note card:

. . . for it is already 10:00 p.m. I did not begin sooner because the Auers picked up the apples tonight. I am attaching the receipt. You can see how we gathered many [apples]. The numbers were not exact. We lumped together the Semoni Spitz apples and Rosmarin apples after we laid out all of them.

Mother continues to think that I should apply for your deferral. What do you think? Warm greetings from your loving wife, as well as from the children and mother.

There follows a note from Franziska's father:

Dear son-in-law!

I came to your family again on Wednesday, October 9. I hoped to see you. Hias Erber is free again because he has received a deferral for community

---

8. Lidwina Eckinger (1924–2006). Her married name was Schett.
9. She is referring to Maria Eckinger.

service as have many others such as Ledige. Perhaps things are going some-what well for you, as I read in your letter. There are surely beautiful churches in Enns, which is your residence at the moment. It had been mine, too. Even my brother wrote: "It is for me most beautiful there in the churches." As God wills, there will soon be an end of this war. I am with you as in heaven, but your angel sings too loudly sometimes! Have patience, dear Franz! I hope to see you soon.

Your father-in-law,

Lorenz Schwaninger.

From Franz to Franziska

Enns, October 13, 1940

Dearest wife and all my loved ones!

I received your letter yesterday. I am grateful for it. I must immediately write a few sentences to you. Today is already the second Sunday that I cannot be with my family for whom I long each day.

Dear Fanj, it saddened me not to tell you the last time that, after the assembling of the men in Ried, most of them were able to travel home because they had received a deferral. Many were not needed. It would have been wonderful if I could have traveled with them. However, one had to provide a guarantee that at the very least one would enlist again in a few months.

Dear Fanj, make no application for my deferral until I am done with my training. We must do infantry training next, and subsequently we must do transport training. All of this should take about two to three months. Then, assuming that there is still the war, a deferral is of course appropriate so that I can again be at home. If you were to have a little luck now with a deferral, then I would have to begin again with the training. If I were to seek a deferral now, I would not be able to go out alone for two or three more Sundays. Everything is already somewhat severe. We still have no good view of things for next Sunday; presumably we may go out in the afternoon.

I had great luck today. I was able to attend two Masses, at which there was preaching. Of course, I did not ask permission. I simply climbed over the wall, which is somewhat high, and went my way. Within two hours, I returned the same way, and everything turned out well. Once again, I am a child of good fortune.

If many hours are severe here, I am still not unfortunate. The training is not hard for me, for I can count on my good health. Things are difficult for me when I think about you at home and consider that I cannot be with you.

It is important that I quickly dismiss these thoughts, otherwise others would notice where my thoughts are. In fact, the Lord God sometimes must send us something hard so that we do not tie ourselves too much to this world.

Dear Fanj, do not take all of this too hard. We have a great, happy anticipation of a joyous reunion. I am astounded that you brought together so many apples. I can now be unconcerned about things because I know that you have attained permanent skills for this work. Your father must exercise much patience with our little ones and also with the cows.[10]

I must now end my writing with many warm greetings and kisses for you and for the three little ones.

Many greetings to Mother and Father-in-Law.

Let me hear something soon.

See you again. Good night.

From Franziska to Franz

Monday, October 14, 1940

Much beloved husband!

I want to write you a few sentences today. I've received no letter from you. I do not know why. Do you not have the time, or are you making the letters too long? We were again in the meadow today. There are already some horses there, belonging to Lenzwastl and Spirner and Hohenauer, along with a couple of horses from Mann. Bäcker and W. also have a couple of horses there. W. will bring me some fodder from there. He ordinarily wants 4 marks. But I'll give him the oats because W. does not want us to pay. You already know this.

One of Moossimmerl's daughters was anointed today. She has diphtheria. Moreover, father learned today that a sergeant in Burghausen was very unfortunate. He was terribly drunk and wanted to lie down on a bed. Instead, he leaned on a windowsill and fell out the window. He was seriously injured. They brought him to the hospital.

I could use your help now in washing the cows. They are always very pleasant in the morning because they are eating the leaves of the sugar beets. I must wash them myself because the young woman washes their udders only when the milking is finished. Mathilde does the same.[11]

I do not know anything more today. Tomorrow I'm going to church. It will be the feast of the Guardian Angels, whom one should especially honor. I'll

---

10. Lorenz Schwaninger was accustomed to having horses, not cows, pull the plow.

11. Mathilde Wagenhammer, now Häusler (b. 1924), primarily cared for the children. Franziska judged that she did not clean the cows satisfactorily before milking them.

surely pray for you and also for the children who are becoming worse. They are sometimes especially funny at meals. The young woman laughs the whole time. Today Rosi went with Lang to the mill. Lang got out the bicycle for me. Yesterday Rosi said, "Father will not come because Maria does not behave and is always very annoying."

Greetings from your Fani.

Tell me what I should send you to eat.

From Franz to Franziska

This letter was dated incorrectly. In it, Franz is responding to Franziska's letter of October 27:

Enns, October 17, 1940

Dearest wife!

I received two of your letters yesterday and another two today. I am deeply grateful for these. I want to apologize to you that I am not getting to write you often. First of all, one should not and cannot speak about everything that plays itself out each day among us. Secondly, much would not interest you because you do not know anyone here.

Dear Fanj, it truly delights me when I receive a letter from you, for everything interests me that I hear from home. As soon as one comes in from training, he immediately looks to see if there is mail. One feels close to home when one often receives mail from home. The time passes also much more quickly than when one seldom receives something. I am enjoying the photograph from you. Loisi will feel ashamed of herself because she is still so small. When I come home, I'll be surprised at how big she already is.

I was surprised as I read about what Frau Huber is going through. It is almost not believable, although such cases often occur, especially in today's world. Have you considered using a horse? With one's help, you could more easily remove the straw. In general, your team of cows would be offended if you put them into retirement.[12] I would gladly help you work with the straw rather than do this training.

Dear Fanj, you have asked whether you should send me food or money. I have enough of both. It would truly be superfluous for you to send me something to eat. I notice nothing bad here, and I need nothing here that will make me fat.

---

12. Two cows were yoked together so that they could pull a wagon.

Forgive my bad handwriting. I am writing in my bed because all the places at the table are already taken. With seventy-five men in the room, there are always too few chairs.

Now I'll end my letter with many warm greetings.

Your husband, Franz

Many greetings to Mother and Father-in-Law.

Write me often.

From Franz to Franziska

Enns, October 19, 1940

Dearly beloved wife!

I received your letter yesterday with delight. I am very grateful for it. In Ried I feared that something would happen just as you spoke of in your letter. Do the people really have so much compassion for me? I am not so sure. Or have things gone badly since I've been away? I know that with so much work you must expend more energy than if I were at home.

Dearest Fanj, I readily believe you when you say that your heart is often heavy, especially when Rosal always asks whether her father has come home yet. Tell her that when she is good about saying her prayers, then her father will return home. Indeed, it would be beautiful and right if I could be at home and remain there.

Yet I do not regret that I did not act differently. I reproach myself for only one thing, that everything here is actually going well. I did not know at the outset where I would end up and that the room and board here would be so excellent. In general, we do not even know whether it will be good for us when things go according to our wishes. Christ said that whoever wants to be my disciple must take up his cross and follow me (see Mark 8:34). I think about whether it would be much better if I had sought a deferral, and then I could have come home from Ried. But if I had, I would perhaps have to leave you now. Anxious rabbits want these deferrals. I do not begrudge those who are able to remain at home. But we need not believe that those at home are so fortunate for they will be anxious every day. In the end, our current situation could be your lucky star.

Dear Fanj, consider this. If my entire life were to go well in all aspects of its physical well-being, I would notice nothing today about my life. I would not see that we have lived fortunate and harmonious years in our marriage. This good fortune is unforgettable and will accompany me through time and eternity. You also know how the children bring me joy. For this reason, a feeling of good fortune often comes over me here so that tears of joy flow from my eyes when I think about our reunion.

Dear Fanj, perhaps you have the desire to visit me here. I would be delighted. Of course, you would need to tell me early enough so that I could request a Sunday leave.

I hope that all of you are well, as I always am. We were already inoculated twice. It did not affect me very much.

Warm greetings to you from your faithful husband, Franz.

Many warm greetings to Mother and Father-in-Law.

See you again.

From Franziska to Franz

Sunday, October 20, 1940

Much beloved husband!

I received your letter yesterday. I am truly grateful for it. I always have great joy when I receive a letter from you.

There are again a few men home on military leave. Hans Speikman has three weeks. Poidl Grüngassler has two weeks. Sterz's stepdaughter said that when Sterz is done with his work, he always goes into the Braunau forest and weeps. (He is working in Ranshofen.) Every two weeks he travels home and then always must leave with great difficulty. How difficult it will be in the future when he may have no children at home. Toni Strohhofer is always very hungry. His family can never send him enough. I think that you do not tell us about this and suffer a great deal. This is my guess. Should I send you a ration card for meat? One cannot always buy things with marks.

Yesterday I received the money for the cream. Sixty marks would have been too little, I judge. When I churn 3 liters [of milk] into butter, I get at least two pounds. This brings 3.15 marks. Over an entire month, I could produce a great amount. I do not have time to rest. Things always take long here. Yesterday I gathered a wagonload of straw with my team of cows. It is small. Perhaps tomorrow I can lay everything out [to dry], then I can get four wagonloads. P. has laid out a lot.

I must now scold the children. They are arguing so terribly with each other that I cannot write you. They are always demanding my attention. Maridl always hits Rosl who says, "You are bad." Then Maridl says, "I am good." Rosl says, "I am good, and you are bad." So they fight all of the time. Helping them is no defense. Sometimes there is a critical moment between the two of them. Recently Maridl pulled the leg off of Rosl's doll and said, "Now I'll pull off the other, too." Rosl said she wanted to go to the doctor who would put the leg back on.

I must end my letter now. I have nothing intelligent to say, for the two are demanding my attention. I am including a pamphlet from the bishop.[13] It cost 3 pfennigs. It was handed out at church. You now owe me 3 pfennigs, dear Franzl. Do not forget them! Tomorrow you will hopefully receive an intelligent letter from me. I'll write it in my little room upstairs. It is not possible down here.

Warm greetings from your Fani.

From Franz to Franziska

This note was written on a postcard:

St. Florian, October 20, 1940

Many warm greetings from St. Florian. Sent to you by your father, Franz.

From Franz to Franziska

Enns, October 24, 1940

Most beloved wife!

Warm greetings to you, as I write from my bed. Yesterday I received the letter from mother and you. Many thanks for it. I am astounded that you are done with the straw. You have energetically slaved at the reaping. We would not be done so soon with it if I were still at home. I have already thanked the Pleikners. I can readily see that what W. did has upset you. You must push it out of your mind. It is good that it is not more public. If you wish to say nothing to Lang about using the straw machine, you could in the future say something to Pleikner. He and Dreschen have offered it if we want to use it. It would be better to speak with Lang about bringing it home.

On Sunday I went alone on a beautiful little trip to St. Florian. By foot, of course. In total I covered approximately ten miles there and back. It was very lovely and interesting there. You are already thinking, "What a dumb guy. Why didn't he rest on a Sunday?" Well, on Sunday we were allowed to go out for the first time. And when the weather is lovely, one must enjoy it. Further, it is good that I not become fat. I also have a good appetite, and I usually eat too much rather than too little. Of course, most people would not believe me, but

---

13. This pamphlet commemorated the twenty-fifth ordination anniversary of Johannes Maria Gföllner, the bishop of Linz (1915–19), who in his pastoral letter of January 1, 1933, urged Catholics to reject National Socialism.

it is the truth. Although they twist us around each day, they cannot make me have a sour view of life. I have not felt ill for one hour since I've been here. Despite the good food, some men want to be pitied here.

Mother thinks that it would be better if I had done the basic training twice so that I would not be needed so soon on the front. I do not hold this view, and few of those who are here hold it. One does not know what will happen after this. But we human beings are such that we always hope that what comes next will be better.

One of the men in our room said that it was written to him that those who had already been called up would be allowed to go home. We shall hardly be able to come again to Enns, and elsewhere the food is not so good. At this time, send me nothing, not a ration card for meat, nor clothing, nor food. I'll likely send you my suitcase this week.

Warm greetings to you from your loving husband, Franz.

Warm greetings to Mother, the three little ones and, Father-in-Law.

See you again.

An additional note:

Dearest wife, I want to answer your short letter about the tax. I would like to advise you to pay the 20 marks. Soon it will be Candlemas.[14] Things will at last change, and you will no longer receive this bill.

I still receive my usual payment from the state, even though I do not perform a civil service apart from eating and drinking. I realize, dearest Fanj, that you will not be angry with me if I give you no other advice.

Many kisses to you and the little ones.

I look forward to a warm reunion.

From Franz to Franziska

Sunday, October 27, 1940

Most beloved wife!

I received with joy your letters from Tuesday and Wednesday. I am grateful for these. Yesterday I sent you my suitcase. You will have to scrape away the solder. I lost the keys. Also, my shoes are not in the suitcase. They have apparently found other feet. Perhaps they will come to light before I travel home for leave. You'll have to hand out the sweets in the suitcase. We received

---

14. On Candlemas, February 2, farmers as civil servants could change their tax status.

thése things with our meals. Otherwise, I have not included anything else. Everything here is very expensive.

Yesterday we had horrible weather, rain with snow. Today the Mühlviertler Mountains, which are not far from us, were completely white. It is hopefully warmer at home. Otherwise, you'll need to tend the furnace, and you'll not be able to work outside. From your letter I can see that you have done a great amount of work in three weeks. When I come home, no more work will remain for me. I'll become a babysitter. We have to endure many tests of our patience here. As a result, I'll manage well with the little ones.

It was too cold for me to take a hike today. Instead, this afternoon I went to Benediction, and of course this morning to Mass. In this way, I can always pick up the strength for the whole week. I feel at home there. We have two churches here, and they are built side by side. If one wants, he can walk from one to the other without going outside. Beside the parish church is the Franciscan church, which has a beautiful Marian altar, especially when it is lit up. One rarely sees such a beautiful altar. Will All Saints' Day be transferred to Sunday at home as will happen here?

I want to describe a little bit for you the area here. The autobahn is being built about five minutes from our military installation. In the surrounding region there are large farms. There are many sugar beets here, for there is a sugar factory in Enns. We are about an hour away from the Danube River. We must often go to the meadow near the river for our military exercises. It is at least a beautiful spot, even with the marching back and forth. It does not matter here what we do. The main question is, will the time pass quickly?

Recently Schmied from Tarsdorf came to our barracks no. 110. We shall hopefully not need to make our way to the air raid shelter tonight as we did last Sunday night. We do not know whether it was a mere practice drill or the real thing. The next day we learned that British airplanes were over Steyr and Linz. But they apparently did nothing. We do not learn much about these matters. We have a radio in our room, but it does not give any information.

I must end my writing for today. I know nothing more. Hopefully, all of you are still well, as I always am, thank God.

Warm greetings from your loving husband, Franz. Warm greetings to Mother, the three little ones, and Father-in-Law.

See you again. Good night.

From Franziska to Franz

Sunday, October 27, 1940

Much beloved husband!

I am again writing you a few sentences today, Sunday. Not much has happened during these days. Yesterday we got some snow, and today it is the same weather. It is raining and snowing. Very disagreeable. Yesterday we finished reaping the grass. There are perhaps a few wagonloads still remaining in the Grünschneider meadow. So we'll soon be done bringing in the grass. I did not think that we would be done so soon.

I sold a few pounds of cabbage at 3 pfennigs per pound. Mari bought 140 pounds. Rachender picked up 30 pounds; he paid 5 pfennigs per pound. Frau Huber, 44 pounds. And Eichelseder, 44 pounds. We still have about 44 pounds for ourselves. When you are home again, you can eat sweet cabbage and potatoes. These two were not unusual for you during your last time home, I believe.

During this week children, ages four to six, from Berlin arrived in St. Radegund. The Wiesers have two boys who are never apart. A girl is with the Schnecks. I do not know about the other children. Kathi Schneider has a girl. There are many in Tarsdorf, too. Almost every day, when these children awake, they cry for their mothers. I think that it would be very hard to have to give up your little loved ones for an indefinite length of time.

All Saints' Day is again on a weekday here. The Mass is scheduled for 7:00 a.m. The visiting of the graves will apparently be on Sunday. It is not certain. All feast days should be abolished, say these H[itler people]. But during war there is still the need for prayer.

The doctor found no little baby in Frau Huber. She has an inflammation in her stomach area. There is nothing on the outside.

A new baby will again come to the Zieher.[15] But when Nani saw a diaper, she said, "I am giving it to Fani." Since Mari could not say anything [about the new baby], she allowed Nani to give me [the diapers]. It was a dumb thing to allow happen.[16] Mari also bought herself a baby carriage because the women in Ach have beautiful baby carriages. But she could still use the carriage that she had for the two previous babies. Today I was with her for an hour because she offered me some meat. I took eleven pounds and gave her apples in exchange.

Franz Tischler must report for military duty tomorrow.

---

15. "Zieher" is the name of the farm of Franziska's family. Franziska is referring here to her sister Maria (1904–75), whose married name was Lenzbauer.

16. Maria Lenzbauer's daughter Anna, also known as Nani, gave the new diapers that she saw in her home to her Aunt Franziska for Loisi. She did not know that her own mother was pregnant.

Were you in church today? We celebrated the feast of Christ the King and Youth Sunday.[17] Our three newlyweds went to communion and many single people as well.

Warm greetings from your Fani, along with your family.

Write again soon.

From Franziska Jägerstätter, Lorenz Schwaninger, and Rosalia Jägerstätter to Franz

Tuesday, October 29

Much beloved husband!

My warm greetings to you. The housekeeper picked up the suitcase today. It took me some time to open it. But it is now open. I want to thank you for the chocolate and the sweets. You could have allowed yourself to have some of them. You are always very austere. We are able to remain at home and enjoy eating everything. You want to give everything to your loved ones. Maridl immediately said, "Father sent us a lot of chocolate!" The two girls would eat everything at once if I would give it to them. However, I'll hide things well so that we'll no longer hear the begging. You know this, their dear father.

Did you receive slippers [from the army]? You sent home the ones that I made. Also, what about soap? Have you received it there, too?

Father finished in the field today. It went quickly with our team [of cows]. Father exerted himself in the field. He also discussed everything with the neighbors.

Today I received a letter from you. Thank you for this. I am always delighted when I receive a letter from you. Warm greetings from the housekeeper! Gasteiger has also been called to military duty. I'll close my letter with many greetings, and I look forward to our reunion soon.

Your loving Fani.

Yesterday Rosi said that I should ride to father on the motorcycle. Greetings from your little rascals.

There follows a note from Franziska's father:

Esteemed son-in-law!

I feel obliged to add a few sentences. Fanö has strongly praised me for my work. I was happy to do it. Your mother and your Fanö fully trust me, and

---

17. Pope Pius XI instituted the feast of Christ the King in 1925 in order to undercut absolutist political claims such as those by Fascism in Italy, Nazism in Germany, and Communism or Bolshevism in the Soviet Union. [RK]

hence the work is a joy. I can say that things go better for me here than at my own home.

I received a letter today from Nanö in Gilgenberg.[18] She has again invited me to do some carpentry there. So I cannot complain about a lack of work.

I enjoy reading your letters. One can truly learn what a deep religious belief you possess. When one joins himself in all things to the will of God, then one has chosen the best part. With all my heart, my wish is that you remain healthy so that you can fulfill the hardships of a soldier's role. Will it soon be time for your leave, or must you wait until Christmas, which is a long time off? I think of writing a formal request to the military corps asking for a leave for you. But when subordinates are patient people, then they can perhaps have good fortune. I know well what it means to have a leave of two weeks with one's family. So good luck! For a reunion soon!

Your father-in-law, Lorenz Schwaninger, who is always favorably disposed to you.

I'll add something more about the weather. This will fill the paper. I always like it when all four sides are completely full. On Saturday we got some snow. On Sunday morning no more snow fell, and so I could ride my bicycle to Tittmoning. It was the feast of my patron saint.[19] So I was delighted to be there. Afterward, at 10:00 a.m., I went to the church of the English Sisters. Then I had done my service. In the afternoon, back to Radegund.

Today (Tuesday) Fanö and I went to Mass and the October rosary. Also, last week we made the Way of the Cross. Every evening, two stations for you soldiers. On Thursday I'll go home for All Saints' Day and All Souls' Day. I'll now end with many greetings.

Your friend, L. Schwaninger.

There follows a note from Franz's mother:

Dear son!

Warm greetings to you. I want to add a couple of sentences. I'm grateful for all of the sweets. You are always in our thoughts at home. We are always with you. Do not get discouraged. We will help you with our prayers. No day passes for the children without them asking for their father and saying that he is not yet home. It will be a joy when your leave comes!

---

18. "Nanö" was Lorenz Schwaninger's daughter Anna (1907–84), whose married name was Neuhauser.

19. The parish church in Tittmoning, which is three miles from St. Radegund, is dedicated to St. Lawrence.

Siegel Moni is at home.[20] He has a three-week leave. And now Rosel would like to write a couple of sentences. Greetings from your mother.

Franz's mother ends her note with statements from his daughters, followed by her own comment:

Dear father, come home soon. Your Rosa and Mari and Loisi. Good night.

It is approaching 10:00 p.m. Good night. No enemy airplanes will come tonight. We can sleep well. A gift from God.

From Franz to Franziska

Enns, October 30, 1940

Much beloved wife!

I have received your loving letter of Sunday. I am very grateful for it. I thought that there would be a photograph of you in it, and I looked forward to it. You have apparently not yet picked it up. Hopefully, I'll receive a copy soon.

Early this morning we got a lot of snow. Probably you did too. Now there are daily wet feet until the weather gets better. It is good that I am free of rheumatism. Hopefully, it will remain this way. Otherwise, I'll always take pavement with me. To be sure, something bad can often lead into something good. Hopefully, winter has not yet seriously begun. It would be too soon. Many farmers here have a lot of their sugar beets still in the fields. Are you happy that we do not cultivate beets?

Dear Fanj, I would like to ask you to send me a couple of handkerchiefs. The ones that I have with me are slowly wearing out. If you find the earmuffs, you could send them too. I am thinking that there is no point to sending only these things. So please include some butter as well. When the weather gets colder, one always needs more food with fat. Not that I suffer from hunger, as you perhaps may believe.

I would like to visit Pastor Karobath. It is difficult to do, however, even though we are only fifteen miles from each other. If one requests a Sunday leave, one must give very significant reasons for it. And these come up mainly when one wants to travel home for his family. This reason I cannot give. One suffers when they catch someone in a lie. They want us to become good Chris-

---

20. "Siegel Moni" is Siegfried Sommerauer, a nephew of Rosalia Jägerstätter.

tians, or so they say! Actions for no good reason! But getting away for an afternoon does not appear promising, and I've already seen the city of Enns. The Lord God will send everything to those who think about him. For today, I must end my letter because I must now polish my shoes.

Warm greetings to you from your loving husband, Franz.

Greetings to Mother, the little ones, and Father-in-Law.

Greetings to the Langs, the Rachetseders, and the Hofbauers.[21]

---

21. Herr Rachetseder administered St. Radegund's tax office.

Chapter 2

Military Training Letters
November 1–December 31, 1940

This chapter begins with Franz's letter to Franziska on the feast of All Saints and concludes with his letter to her on New Year's Eve. It contains twenty letters from Franz and nine letters from Franziska. In their respective letters, Franz and Franziska express their mutual love of the liturgical seasons of Advent and Christmas as well as of the church's religious devotions, especially to the Blessed Mother.

Franz writes, too, about his meetings with three priests who had been pastors until they were forced to resign from church leadership because of their public criticisms of National Socialism. These priests were Leopold Arthofer, Josef Karobath, and Franz Krenns. (See their biographical sketches in the appendix.) Moreover, on December 9 Franz tells Franziska about his entrance into the Third Order of the Franciscans on the previous day. Franz's ties with priest-critics of National Socialism and his growing commitment to the Christian faith nurtured his eventual refusal to take the military oath of unconditional obedience to the Führer and his conscientious objection to the war. [RK]

From Franz to Franziska

Friday, November 1, 1940

Much beloved wife!

I received your letter on Tuesday with joy. Thank you for it. Yesterday I learned from Schmied of Tarsdorf that he may travel home on leave. I have asked him to bring me back some things from home.

On Wednesday I sent you a letter in which I requested these things. I would like a pair of handkerchiefs because mine have slowly worn out. I'd also like to ask you for some butter for I am lacking fat. When I come home in the winter, I'll not have enough lard in me to cut the straw. If you tell me the cost of the butter, I'll pay for it! However, have no anxiety that I am perhaps suffering from hunger. I must simply be responsible for some things. The quality of our food apparently depends upon the weather. As we have had bad weather, the food's quality has worsened.

23

I'd also ask, dear Fanj, that you include two pairs of my old socks. They can be white. These would be good enough. Today no less than two pairs of my socks disappeared. They may perhaps reappear. I had hung them on the furnace to dry, and then I went to get my food. When I came back, I looked around. But they were already gone. They could not yet have been dry. If one leaves something lying around and comes back an hour later, it is gone. One must have luck to get back what he left out. Apparently this is part of being a *Volk* community![1] Hopefully, we shall soon have better weather.

You must bring these things to Schmied before Tuesday night, for he will apparently return here on Wednesday. If he decides to leave earlier, Schmied will make this known to you. Today I found the key to the suitcase. The chief thing is that you have already opened it.

It would be good if I could send you some sweets every week. Then Rosl and Maridl would be the same rascals who would hold out their empty hands to me when I come home. I am already inquisitive about my little darling, Loisie. If only Christmas would come soon! I am looking forward to our reunion.

Warm greetings to you from your loving husband, Franz.

I am grateful to your housekeeper for picking up the suitcase.

Dear Fanj, two pairs of socks are enough. Happily, I received my old socks back today. Someone had picked them up by mistake.

Dear mother, I am grateful for your words. You are always anxious about me. But have no anxiety, mother. Franzl never ends up too short, not even here. Earlier I wrote enough about some things. If no one in the world was less fortunate than I, then there would be no war.

Dear mother, you will also be anxious about the flowers.[2] I have already thought about them. It is good that it has not been too cold for them. On Sunday I shall visit the cemetery here, and also I'll offer my Mass and communion for my dearly departed.

Warm greetings from your son, Franz.

From Franziska to Franz

Sunday, November 3, 1940

Much beloved husband!

Since we still have a lot of work, I am getting to write you today. Thank you for your dear letter. Yes, I shall tell you as soon as possible all that is happening

---

1. FJ is criticizing the N.S. rhetoric concerning the Germanic people becoming a *Volk,* a thriving community based on race and ethnicity. [RK]

2. A frost in late October threatened the chrysanthemums that people brought to the graves of loved ones for the feasts of All Saints and All Souls, November 1 and 2.

here. Also, write right away when you need something. I am delighted when I am able to send something to my most beloved. Although you hoped to receive the photographs last week, I can now tell you that you must be patient for another week. They were promised to me for today. But unfortunately they are not done because other work needed to be done first.

Mother and our housekeeper are in St. Radegund because the feast of All Saints is being celebrated here today. I must remain at home with the three little ones. They are so mischievous at the moment that I am almost not able to write to you. Loisi is a little pest. She always wants to be held.

This morning I went to Tittmoning for Mass at 8:30 in the parish church and at 10:00 in the cloister church. I intend to pray persistently that my dear husband will return home soon in good health to his loving family. I also bought Rosi shoes for 7.50 marks. Everything is very expensive, and the three girls have worn out their clothes. I have already spent a lot of money. Yesterday I received the subsidy of 48 marks. I am receiving only 20 marks for the housekeeper. Each day I receive 2 marks. I have not paid the housekeeper as quickly, and so for this month I shall not spend as much. I gave your mother 15 marks because she must be without her son.

On Thursday I went off to the mill at 11:00 a.m., and in the woods I came upon a car in the middle of the road. The people were loading it with firewood. I could not go around them until they were done, and so I had to wait for half-an-hour. I also took apples with me to Zieher. I gave them to Mari who had paid 7 marks for the meat she had given me. As I wrote in an earlier letter, there were eleven pounds [of apples]. At the mill I also had a long wait, and so I did not arrive home until 5:30 p.m. It was already dark. I was very happy, however, that I was not even later. The cows quickly came into the barn [for milking]. I had taken two sacks of wheat and three sacks of grain. The miller said that he would grind everything right away. I received back a lot of wheat flour, almost two full sacks of bread flour and a half sack of noodle flour. During the past week in the evening we ate rye noodles twice, soup with bread three times, and wheat noodles on Saturday and Sunday.

I just had a small interruption. I had to separate the two older girls. They were arguing terribly with each other.

I had to pay 10 marks and 10 pfennigs for the little bit that I took to the mill, and 1 mark and 50 pfennigs for the wheat of Thomas. As Mari said, they now have enough flour for a whole year. They do not want to suffer from hunger.

The feast of All Saints was celebrated on Friday in Tittmoning and elsewhere around here. Apparently only our bishop made this decision.[3]

You probably laughed about the previous letter in which Rosi wanted to write to her father. Your mother had guided her hand, and now Rosi has been pestering me since I began writing you. She's saying, "I also want to write father." I must permit her this pleasure and direct her hand. You will forgive us if everything is a bit ghastly.

Dear father! I am sending you a big kiss. Greetings from your little Rosi!

I am also sending you a kiss, dear father. Greetings, Maridl!

As you can see, Maridl also had to write you. She would have screamed incessantly if she had not been able to write her father. Loisi is getting bigger. She has a large dress on. You'll see for yourself when you come home.

Many men are now home on military leave. When I see them, I am saddened. Even though they were away longer [than you], I think to myself that if you would request a leave, we would say that your wife has no one to cut the firewood because so many men have been enlisted, and she needs wood for the winter. Don't you want some time, at least two weeks, to help cut the wood? Or do you think that it would be disadvantageous for you if you were to request a leave during your training? I would be enormously delighted if you could come home soon. I have so much to tell you.

Father went home on Thursday. He asked me whether he could come again. He sees that we would not necessarily need him further. I do not know how soon he will come again.

Sailer has come for the calf for Auer from our cow. This morning, as I was picking up the piglets, Sailer was also there. I had not seen the calf for a while. It is now five weeks old and weighs 191 pounds. We think it should have become 220 pounds.

This week I received a bill from the Donau Insurance Company.... (This smudge is Rosi's work. She did it while I had gone to do something.) We must pay 18 marks. Should I send it soon?

I have now received the photographs that Josef Strohhofer developed. We must be satisfied with these at the moment.

Dear husband, come home soon to your Fani who continually thinks of you.

---

3. Bishop Gföllner may have celebrated the holy days during the week in order to defy N.S pressure to move religious feasts to Sundays. [RK]

Your dear children and your mother and your always faithful wife, Fani, send you warm greetings.

See you again, dear father!

Have you received all of my letters? Did the one written on Monday arrive?

From Franz to Franziska

This is a postcard from Tabor in the city of Steyr:

Steyr, November 4, 1940

Dearest wife!

Many warm greetings from your Franz J. in Steyr.

Today we were here for sharpshooting. It was a lovely holiday. Even the weather was glorious.

Of course, I was not best marksman. But it is also not necessary that I be one.

Warm greetings to Mother.

See you again.

From Franz to Franziska

Enns, November 7, 1940

Much beloved wife!

Yesterday I received the box of apples that you gave to Schmied in Tarsdorf. And today I received your letter from Sunday. I am grateful to you for both of these. You have abundantly cared for me. I am delighted. Now I am living as a nobleman.

During this week, I have things easy. In the mornings, a bit of riding on a motorcycle. In the afternoons, some practical stuff. For me it is of course entertaining. The theoretical material is somewhat demanding. For this reason, I'll have little time to write later this week. Next week I must take a test. I would not go much for the dumb jobs. They already have their men for these things. Today we were in Linz and St. Florian.

Dear Fanj, you asked about my military leave. I'd like to advise you to make a request soon. My training could perhaps end sooner than we believe. Speak with the village council. If the council's members agree with you, they should write two formal requests on my behalf for you. [One will go to the Farmers' Association.] If the board of the Farmers' Association will not grant my leave, then I shall speak with the military commander, using the [second] formal request that you'll send me. You have an entirely valid reason: someone must cut the firewood. Perhaps I'll be able to come home for a longer time, and I would be truly delighted.

Your photographs have brought me great joy. Loisi is already quite big. I had been wondering about this. Rosal appears a little bit upset.

I'll now end my writing. Perhaps I'll be able to write more the next time. Today I must finish eating the sausage that you sent me. Tomorrow is Friday.[4] And the sausage may be no longer good on Saturday. It has tasted wonderful to me. Of course, I am now thirsty, and so I'll allow myself a half glass of fresh beer. Perhaps we can soon drink beer together again! So, cheers, dear wife!

Warm greetings to you. See you again. Your loving husband, Franz. Warm greetings to Mother and the little ones. Good night!

Greetings also to the village's leaders. I'll again debate with them if I am able to come home!

From Franz to Franziska

This is a postcard from Wolfern near Steyr with greetings from Pastor Josef Karobath:

Wolfern, November 10, 1940

Dearest wife!

Warm greetings to you from here.

Your husband, Franz.

It is truly beautiful here, just as St. Radegund is.

See you again! Greetings to everyone! Josef Karobath

From Franziska to Franz

Sunday, November 10, 1940

Much beloved husband!

I received your postcard on Tuesday and your letter yesterday. They have delighted me, and I wish to thank you for them.

We worked hard during the past week, spreading the manure. I did not get to write you during the week because I was very tired in the evenings. Also, the children are always demanding my attention. An official from the tax office stopped here on Monday. He wanted us to pay the taxes, for which you had sought a delay in payment. I paid him the 49 marks and 93 pfennigs. This week Pastor Thomas will come here in order to purchase five pounds of

---

4. Following the church regulations at that time, Franz did not eat meat on Fridays. [RK]

butter.[5] Further, the Lokei family is expanding with a baby girl. They will also be baking the cakes for the young mothers.[6] I should now be contributing eggs, butter, flour, lard, etc., to the [N.S.] Women's Association for their packages to soldiers. Unfortunately, I have nothing left to give. Hopefully, you will not be disappointed if you do not receive a package from the Association. I think, however, that there are no exceptions. Perhaps you can come home soon, and then the Association can send more to other soldiers.

Yesterday Lipp brought us the straw machine from Pleikner, who had invited me to use it. Between noon and 3:00 p.m., we were able to separate all of the straw. Father had come here on Thursday, and so we were able to finish the whole job. Everything went smoothly. At least you need not worry about separating of the straw. Also, we let the cows out to pasture on two days, but they did not eat much because there are so many leaves on the ground in the Tiefenhaler meadow. So we've now stopped letting them out.

Our housekeeper bought herself an overcoat in Tittmoning, and I had her bring me the bill. Unfortunately, we have not yet paid it. Today I spent the entire day locked in the house. This afternoon your mother went to visit Moni.[7] Also, father has left. At the moment, the children want to have fun. Today, immediately after Mass, I went to the village council and requested that it write a formal petition for your leave. The council immediately promised to do so. I am very happy that you may come home, hopefully for a longer time. Auer Bote must report for duty on November 19. I do not know what else to write. It is better when I can tell you things face-to-face. I hope that you'll come home soon.

Warm greetings from your loving wife, Fani.

See you again.

From Franz to Franziska

Wednesday, November 13, 1940

Dearly beloved wife!

Today I was delighted to receive your letter of Sunday. Thank you very much. I'll not have any work to do when I come home, now that you have separated the straw. Hopefully, the straw will not run out too early in the spring. You must use it sparingly. We must remain patient for a few weeks until we have our reunion. A formal petition for a leave does not usually move quickly. It is still a good time

---

5. Thomas Huber (1900–1950), who was born in St. Radegund, was FJ's cousin.
6. Neighbors baked cakes for the women who had recently given birth.
7. Monika Sommerauer, née Huber, was Rosalia Jägerstätter's sister.

here, but it will soon be over. Tomorrow I must take a test. Then the marching and the exercises will begin again. It will require simply enduring things.

Last Sunday I visited with Pastor Karobath. By now, you should have received the postcard that we wrote to you. Things are not going badly for him. He cannot easily forget St. Radegund. I also told him that the prospect of him returning soon to St. Radegund is poor. He sees himself superfluous in Wolfern because the parish there is not especially large. There are mostly large farms. You can imagine what this means for religious practice. As long as he has no prospect of a parish, he will not reject the possibility of returning to St. Radegund. Perhaps he will be able to change places with another priest who does not want to remain in his current parish. He was very pleased that I visited him. I requested a Sunday leave since one does not need a reason for this. One needed to travel only thirty miles. On Sunday I left Enns at noon and returned at 9:00 p.m.

I must stop writing for tonight. I must go now and reserve a place for tomorrow morning's test. After the test, I'll immediately write you and say how it went for me. So, for today, good night!

November 14, 1940

Dearest Fanj, it is now the next day, and I have taken the test concerning motorcycles. It was a game for me. It is good that it is done. One could very easily become corrupted by this fraud. Tonight I went to church for the rosary and Benediction. I prefer going to church more than to the cinema. In fact, I have not gone to the cinema here. I have no desire to go to it because you cannot go with me. Instead, you must always be annoyed with the three little rascals. I would love once again to hear your lovely music. It would be dearer to me than what's on the radio here.

Dearest wife, it would be helpful if I could again have some butter next week — if my credit is still good! This week I'll finish what you sent me. Are you wondering, "Does he need butter but not the food that I cook?" Do not send me more sausage. I have not yet finished the apples. Everything has tasted very good to me. Of course, the noodles were also very good. Indeed, these are always my favorite food. You'll have some anxiety about me when I come home because I always have an enormous appetite. Because one has little interest in the work here, one is always thinking about food. It is this way for others here, not only for me. Hopefully, you are in good health, as I always am, thank God.

I'll end my letter now with warm greetings to you and my whole family.

I am looking forward to our reunion soon.

From Franziska to Franz

Wednesday, November 13, 1940

Much beloved husband!

I am grateful for the beautiful postcard that you sent me from Wolfern. I received it yesterday and have enjoyed it. As you can see, I have enclosed with this letter one formal request [for your leave]. The other request I turned in today at noon. Huber gave it his attention and asked for no payment.[8] You yourself can send him a thank-you note if it would help his letter in support of our request. Lw. became troubled when I approached him for his signature. As you can see, he was not able to write his own name properly.

Today the film *Das Edelweiss* (or a similar name) is showing at the Gasthof Hofbauer. Of course, our housekeeper has gone to see it. I wish I could say that this film is wonderful, but I do not yet know. She could have invited me to see it with her. We are busy cutting down the brush. We are having good weather, which we can always use. Loisi continues to try to crawl. When you come home you'll see how big she has become since you left.

Hopefully, you will see us soon. I'll be delighted when you can be with us again, even though soldiers are described as being dangerous. It will not be so bad, though I do have some anxiety. You'll laugh over our stupidity. I'll enlist your help every day, and then you'll sleep well at night. So come home soon. I do not fear you because I have become strong. You know what I mean! Now I'll stop my complaining. I hope that we can occasionally speak alone with one another. With warm greetings to you, your loving wife. Also, with many kisses. For this, one does not need to use postage stamps.

Warm greetings from your Fanj and mother and the little ones. I forgot to tell you that we had a disturbance last night. A steer and four cows broke free. We did not hear them for a while because we were sound asleep, and the wind was very loud.

From Franziska to Franz

Friday, November 15, 1940

Much beloved husband!

Since I now have the time and the children are already in bed, I want to write you a few sentences again. Today we celebrated the feast of St. Leopold.[9] (You were aware of this, I'm sure.) Nevertheless, we were very busy this morning. I

---

8. Ferdinand Huber was St. Radegund's civil registrar.

9. Duke Leopold III (1075–1136) is the patron saint of Austria. Known as a just and kind leader, he founded some monasteries and reformed others. He was canonized in 1485. The feast of St. Leopold was a national holiday in Austria. [RK]

brought home a large bundle of brushwood today as I did yesterday. By midday it began to rain. Now it is raining very hard. Hopefully, this wet weather will not last very long.

Warm greetings to you from Kernpeisser. You should write to him. And also to the Tiefenhaler family, who also often ask how you are doing. Also, write the Schirks if you have not already done so. You may have forgotten them. Yet they are your godparents. Toni St. has received four months in prison because he spoke out, I believe. He opened his mouth too wide. You'll not do the same. Those who speak out do not receive a leave for a long time, I've heard. Toni Strohhofer is already in Poland. The other Lang is in Silesia. There they are receiving very little to eat. The bread is almost inedible.

Tomorrow the ration cards will be given out again. I must again go to the village council's offices.

Max Reiserer has bought a tractor, and is now able to take better care of his horses and himself. I must now stop writing to you. I do not know anything more. Perhaps I'll know more the next time.

Warm greetings from you loving wife, Fani. See you again.

In a different handwriting:

Greetings from your mother. Come home soon. We long to see you.

A postscript from Franziska:

Many greetings from your three girls. The older ones are always asking for you. Each would like to be well behaved so that then father will come home soon, as we tell them. Good night, dearest one!

From Franz to Franziska

Saturday, November 16, 1940

Most beloved wife!

Today I received with joy your dear letter along with the formal request [for my leave]. I am grateful for these. Our training should come to an end within two weeks. I am now wondering whether the [N.S.] Farmers' Association will process my formal request by then. Otherwise, I'll go to the commander with the request that you have sent to me. Huber has surely completed his work. They are good people in St. Radegund. I did not believe that they would write this request for you since I acted against their will in the summer. Most of the men here hope that they will be allowed to go home after this training. All of us have strong longings for our homes. These two weeks will soon be over.

You need not do as much work before then. Otherwise, I'll have no work to do when I come home. Of course, you could continue to cut the brushwood because it will be too cold for me to do it when I get there.

Dearest Fanj, I must stop writing for today, for I must still save some space [in this letter] for tomorrow. And if I have nothing more to write to you, I'll have to go to a tavern! I enjoy every Sunday; these are wonderful days for me here. So, for today, good night!

Sunday, November 17

Dearest wife!

Today I again gathered wealth for eternity. I was able to participate in a few Masses. We do not yet have a priest shortage in Enns, and one can find active Catholics among the soldiers. They are few in number, but they are not eradicated. It is really a joy when one meets Catholics who bear their fate entirely differently from the other men. Tomorrow we shall again travel to Steyr for sharpshooting practice. Hopefully, it will not be very cold, for one quickly gets cold standing around. Hopefully, too, the beautiful weather will at least partially continue until these days of training are over. When I am once again at home, then it can storm very often, and I'll not need to go out of the house. Or will you throw me outside? I'll hope for the best, and also Rosi will defend me, especially if I bring her more chocolate.

How is it going with the cutting of the straw? Hopefully, the animals are not eating too much of it. Have you greased the scythes and already hung them up? I'll end my letter now, for I want to go to Benediction and afterward drink one or two small glasses of beer.

Warm greetings to you from your loving husband, Franz.

Many warm greetings to Mother, the three little ones, Father-in-Law, and the housekeeper.

Greetings also to the neighbors. See you again.

From Franziska to Franz

Sunday, November 17, 1940

Much beloved husband!

Yesterday I again received a letter from you. I am grateful for it. As soon as possible I'll send you the butter. I just returned home from Benediction. In the late morning mother was in Tittmoning, and she brought home the photograph that you now see before you.[10] I almost did not send it to you, for I appear horrible in it. There were many tears on that Sunday. I did not want

---

10. The photograph, taken in October 1940, shows Franziska, Rosalia Jägerstätter, Rosa, and Maria.

the photograph on that day, but mother did not yield to my wishes. Hopefully, this photograph will not frighten you so that you no longer want your Fani and, instead, are happier in the army. You have your children who are truly dear, especially Loisi, who is unfortunately not in the photograph. She had gone on strike, as I wrote to you at that time.

My goddaughter Maral will go to Lichtmess with Pleikner as a house-keeper.[11] They no longer have a housekeeper because she went to Michl Datz.[12] She did not want to work any longer on a farm. Moreover, your god-son has left. He wants to become a locksmith and no longer do farm work. Maral will go to Schnaitl and work as an assistant cook. Her parents immediately agreed to this, since Albert himself would be happy if he could change his job. All of this struck me as a bit vague. So I spoke with Frau Pleikner, who was happy no one had come to them. Schnaitl has recently married, of course, into the Pächter family. He is a first-class pm.[13] I would like Maral to work for a nice boss. Also, since there are many soldiers in Ach, this place could be a bit dangerous for a young woman. I myself am happy that things did not turn out in Ach, even though she is not my daughter.

Thomas Lang wants a new position. Stöcklbreu has money available for the cleaning of the grain seeds. I thought that you at one time paid Habl for this. It has cost 1 mark, 75 pfennigs. Do you still know whether you have already paid for this or not? It is not so expensive that one must contest it with them.

Today Ferdl Moni comes home for a three-day leave.[14] He has been in Krems and will come here from there. I do not know, however, where he will go next. I'll close my letter with many greetings. Your always faithful wife, Fani.

Your three girls and mother send you warm greetings.

See you again!

I would be greatly delighted if I were to receive a photograph of you.[15]

From Franziska and Mother to Franz

Tuesday, November 19, 1940

Much beloved husband!

Today Thomas goes to his new position. He took his bag with him to Ostermiething. I did not go with him because I always have a lot of work. You

---

11. Franziska's goddaughter Maria Dicker (b. 1927) eventually took a job neither with Pleikner nor in the Gasthof but in an unmentioned place. Her married name is Kern.
12. A butcher in Ostermiething.
13. Franziska used "pm" in place of "N.S. party member."
14. "Ferdl Moni" is FJ's cousin Ferdinand Sommerauer.
15. In response to Franziska's request, FJ sent her a photograph of him in his uniform.

must come home soon in order to cut firewood. I have not sent you much butter because it would become too sour for you. Next week you will again receive fresh butter if you do not come home. Mother has worked hard baking noodles. But by the time you receive them, they may not be so good. Many greetings to you, Fani.

In a different handwriting:

Dearest son!

Warm greetings to you at the start of my writing. Moni Ferdl is on leave for three days because his military unit was transferred. Now you will also soon come home so that you'll again have fresh noodles.

Rosl is always asking about you coming home.

Greetings from your mother.

Good night.

From Franz to Franziska

Enns, November 20, 1940

Dearest wife!

Your letters from Friday and Sunday arrived yesterday and today. Also, I've received the lovely photograph, for which I am most grateful. I can still not tell you much [about my possible leave], for we shall soon have our review ceremony for military service. Although it is now the afternoon, there is not much more being asked of us. Unfortunately, I cannot yet send you a photograph. I'll receive it at the end of the month.

On Monday we went through Wolfern, but I could not stop.

Warm greetings to you from your Franz.

See you again.

From Franz to Franziska

Enns, November 22, 1940

Dearest wife!

Yesterday, Thursday, I received your package with delight. I am grateful for it. Of course, I wish to thank my mother, too, for the good noodles. They were still fresh. Yesterday I made a meal of butter and some noodles. An emperor would be envious of my good meal.

Yesterday I had a broken tooth extracted. I believe that dentist felt more pain than I did. Afterward he did not want to release me. He prescribed bed rest for the remainder of the day. I did not anticipate any of this, for I did not feel any pain either before or after. I allowed him to extract it because it cost me nothing.

It would be wonderful if I would be able to come home soon after the butter here runs out. If need be, I'll eat up the butter in a couple of days.

For a few days, we've had thick fog here. Now Thomas [Eckinger] will again be anxious about being drafted, that is, if he were found to be in [physical] shape for the military.

Dear Fanj, you did the right thing offering Maral to Frau Pleikner. It is better to work in a Catholic household than in a Gasthof of the sort you've described. It's wonderful work!

Greetings to you from your husband, Franz.

Once again, many thanks for everything.

Many greetings to Mother and the three little ones.

Warm greetings also to Thomas. I must thank him for bringing the package. Be well.

See you again soon.

From Franziska and Lorenz Schwaninger to Franz

Saturday, November 23, 1940

Much beloved husband!

Your photograph arrived today.[16] I am deeply grateful for it. As you see, I have enclosed a letter to you that came today from Braunau. I do not know what it is about. Tomorrow I'll ask [Ferdinand] Huber about it, and then I'll write to you. Father is again with us for a few days. We always have work for him to do. On rainy days we are always in the cellar, and we always need light. Therefore, I have bought a kerosene lantern. The candles became too difficult. I poured out something from a container which was in the shed. It smells similar to fuel but it did not burn. Do you remember what you bought? A lubricant or a fuel? Please write me about it so that I can buy fuel, if need be.

Besenböck has written and sends you warm greetings. He is at home at the moment. Soon he will be called away for three months. We must send him a goose.

Tomorrow we'll have adoration [of the Blessed Sacrament] throughout the day, as we do every year for November 24. Perhaps you have already thought about this. In Tittmoning it is market day, which does not greatly interest you. Today we could have used you for leading the rosary. Loisi did not want to pray.

---

16. This is a photograph of FJ in his military uniform.

She can be quite troublesome as the other two can also be. You will soon see what a character she is. Rosl now always sleeps in your bed. She does not want to be in her own. So you'll have a sleeping companion when you come home. Hopefully, you will soon travel home. However, the letter that recently came from Braunau has not pleased me.

According to Bachmeier in Ach many things, even gold, were recently stolen from a truck. Bachmeier is also in the military. The thieves were successful because there were no guards. I am always anxious about break-ins here.

On Thursday the Mass was held at the school because the children are now not allowed to go to the church on school days. There were many children at Mass.

I'll end my letter for today. Tomorrow I'll write a bit more. Good night.

In the handwriting of Franz's father-in-law:

Dear son-in-law! Last week I was in Überackern with Lisi. Half of the time we helped her neighbor, whose husband, Hans Meier, is away, and no one had helped her. Many people want to end the war, says the forester who is a member of the Hitler party.

During this week I was with Nanö in Gilgenberg for three days.[17] On Thursday, the feast of the Presentation of the Blessed Mary, I went to Gundertshausen, Geretsberg, and Franking where I hoped to visited with Pastor Lindinger.[18] Unfortunately, he was not at home. He had gone to Eggelsberg for a conference. I would have enjoyed speaking with him. From Franking I rode my bicycle to your wife, mother, and children at your home, which I dearly love. Over the last year, I have spent many weeks with you and your loved ones. There have been no arguments, and I have not been upset by anything.

Franzl, things are no longer good for me at my home. While I enjoy working for my daughters at their homes, I do not like being in my own home. Since August, my daughter-in-law has said nothing to me. And of what am I guilty? On two occasions something unfortunate happened. Once, I spoke nicely to her. However, the second time I was angrier. I did not allow this offense. I should have remained silent. I'll now demand a suitable agreement.[19] With this, I'll end things there because I am so poorly treated.

---

17. "Nanö" was a nickname for Anna Neuhauser, née Schwaninger (1907–84).

18. Josef Lindinger (1884–1971) had been the pastor in Hochburg until 1938, when he criticized the National Socialists there. As a result, they broke the windows in the rectory and forced him to resign from the parish. He became the pastor in Franking.

19. Lorenz Schwaninger is referring to his signing over the family estate to his son and daughter-in-law, an agreement that entailed him receiving payments and certain items from the family home.

Franzl, please give me your thoughts on this matter in your next letter to Fanö. I believe that from a religious perspective I have not acted wrongly. I have to be here during the coming weeks so that your mother can be healthy again. She had the flu. Then she got back to work too soon and developed some chest pains. I bought her some heart pills. Perhaps they will improve things for her, God willing.

Now I'll end with an uplifting story, told to me by the builder's son Lehner, who lives near Rosi.[20] A soldier came to Lehner in his room. He said that he wanted to withdraw from the army. In response to the question why, he said, "Because I cannot tolerate the military way of life." Then he went quickly out the door.

A postscript in Franziska's handwriting:

Unfortunately, I was not able to speak with Huber today, Sunday. It would be best if you would do nothing with the request and instead send it back to me. I'll go to Braunau with it. It would not be so good if I go again to the village council about the request. I have heard that the request would have been more successful earlier because the men who have completed their basic training cannot easily receive a leave. Write me again soon. Warm greetings from Fani and mother and the three little ones. See you again!

From Franz to Franziska

Enns, November 24, 1940

Dearest wife!

Forgive me. I can write only a note today. This afternoon I read for a long time, and now Sunday has passed too quickly for me. I would have traveled to Kronstorf today if the weather had been better. Pastor Karobath would have also gone there. Hopefully, the weather was too miserable for him, too!

Today I ate the last of the noodles. They were very good, though a bit dry, of course. Writing is not easy at the moment, for there is music and dancing here, of course without women. The men can be hungry for dancing! However, in the morning their faces will no longer be so friendly.

Greetings to you, mother and the little ones.

Your Franzl.

See you again.

---

20. Rosa Schwaninger (1914–78), whose married name was Eder.

From Franz to Franziska Jägerstätter and Lorenz Schwaninger

Enns, November 27, 1940

Most beloved wife!

Yesterday I received your dear letter with delight. I am grateful for it. I am happy that you have included for me the statement from the Farmers' Association. However, I cannot send our formal request back to you today because it is with my military commander. Yesterday, as soon as I received your letter, I brought the statement and the request to my platoon leader. He promised me that he would bring this matter to the commander. I cannot tell you today the decision because I have not yet learned what the commander said.

Next week we have the military review ceremony, for there is nothing more for us to learn here. At this point, our basic training will end, and we'll learn what will happen to me. If I can do nothing with our request here, then perhaps you can accomplish a little more with the Farmers' Association. Their statement, which you sent to me, is nothing more than a somewhat sarcastic denial. I can hope for nothing more from these _____ .... [21] Nevertheless, you need not have anxiety that what comes next will necessarily be harder than our basic training. It may be that some people have this view, but they have not gone through basic training. Two single men among us have already taken off their uniforms because they were granted their requests for leaves. Where will the military assign all of these soldiers if after basic training none are permitted to return home? The war is not going to break out in the south or in the east over the winter. Hence, I am not concerned about not being permitted to go home.

Dear wife, do not be worried about me. I have more confidence in the Lord God than in our Farmers' Association. And if things should come about different from what we hope for and would like, they would not be bad because God's will comes about, even when painful.

Dear wife, I'll not make you a bit hungry by telling you about our meal here tonight. It was very good. We received good sausage in a dish of lentils along with a lot of good cocoa. Of course, meals are not this good every day.

The work should be ending for you. It would be good if you could put together some pitch. Apart from this, be done with things! I think often about the butchering of the swine. Hopefully, this will not be difficult!

---

21. FJ deliberately omitted the word.

Now I must end my writing. We have again had a big interruption in our free time. This occurs not infrequently.

Warm greetings to you,

your loving husband, Franz.

Many warm greetings to Mother and the little ones.

See you again.

Good night.

Dear father-in-law!

Thank you for your loving letter. I am saddened by your unfortunate situation. It is very hard to go on when there is disagreement in one's family. Unfortunately, I do not have much time to write to you today.

Dear father-in-law, according to our human thinking and feeling it is always better in many cases to get a little revenge. But according to the Christian view this is not allowed. We must repay evil with good. Christ himself went ahead of us with this example [see Matt. 5:38–42].

And only love is capable of once again establishing peace. Read again the beautiful verses on love. Faith and hope will eventually pass away, but love continues forever [see 1 Cor. 13].

Warm greetings from your son-in-law; do not be angry with me because of what I've written.

See you again.

From Franziska to Franz

St. Radegund, November 30, 1940

During this week I received from you two letters and a card. I am delighted by these, and I wish to thank you for them. I did not get to write sooner because in the evenings I must make some clothes for the little ones, and during the day I always have a lot of work to do. You'll laugh and think that we're always inside in the family room. But no, we have now finished cutting down the brush, and I have already brought it home. I have also cut down the branches and arranged them. Further, if it does not get too dangerous in the snow, we'll cut down some trees, too.

Hopefully, you'll come home soon to help with the tree cutting. This is hard work for two women. But if you are always eating such good food, as you described in your last letter, you'll not quickly leave your military post! However, they will not be able to use you because you will be too fat. Then you'll need to come home. We also have a good kitchen, especially if you were to come home, for then we'd butcher a swine. The swine have become big. We still have the pork from Zieher's sow. We are eating it sparingly so that it will last until you come home.

After I write you a letter, I think about you, wondering whether that letter will be the last one. But one week passes into another, and Franzl does not come home. I would be delighted if you would come home soon.

Yesterday Loisi was put into a safety belt because she is always standing up in the wagon. We must always hang on to her so that she does not fall out. She is getting her teeth, but with much pain. She often cries terribly. I always am concerned about her. Some children die from bad teeth. However, please God, her teeth will soon appear. I feel pain for my Loisi.

They recently brought Hansi Jahrl to the hospital in Salzburg. The poor child cried as his mother left him. It is a great hardship.

Tomorrow Schweiger must report for duty.

Father went home on November 24 because he found no more work here. He said, he must again cheat in order to eat [at home]. Herr Müller says nothing to him. Lenz does not say much.[22] And his daughter-in-law says nothing. It is difficult for him when he is seen to be unpleasant at home. Old people interact poorly when they feel superfluous.

I received a letter from Loisi.[23] She is still in Nürnberg with Herr Franks to whom she became engaged in September. She sends you warm greetings.

Rosl is still always well behaved because her father will come home soon. In a motherly way, she even takes care of her sister Loisi when she wants to do so.

I know nothing more that is new. I also think that I say things better face-to-face, but you are not at home. I would have more to tell you if you were not away.

I must write a few sentences about Frau Kaiser. Her baby arrived on the 25th. But the midwife visited her daily beginning on the 15th. The midwife went there every day because Frau Kaiser was experiencing all kinds of difficulties. Frau Kaiser's new baby is a girl.

Warm greetings to you from your wife, Fani, who is always thinking about you.

Greetings also from your mother and your three little ones.

---

22. "Lenz" is Lorenz Schwaninger's son, whose baptismal name was Lorenz. Lorenz Schwaninger Sr. felt that Lenz, his daughter-in-law, and father-in-law — Herr Müller — were shunning him and making him feel that he should not share in their meals.

23. Loisi is Franziska's friend with whom she worked in Gasthof Reib at Ach.

From Franz to Franziska

Enns, December 1, 1940

Dearest wife!

Receive my warm greetings. Since Tuesday I have received no mail from you. Hopefully, nothing has been lost. You probably thought that your husband would be at home by now, but unfortunately he is still in Enns. The only good thing is that the time is going very quickly here. If no decision is made known this week, I hope it will be next week. I cannot believe that they would tell me that I am not permitted to be with my family for the Christmas holidays. Nevertheless, we have great trust in the Christ child. I believe that when we act properly, he will not abandon us.

Dear wife, we now have the beautiful season of Advent. Think of me every morning at Mass when the *Rorate* is said.[24] I brought in the First Sunday of Advent beautifully. In the morning I went to church, and in the afternoon I was in Kronstorf. Pastor Karobath was also there. He sends you warm greetings. We had a wonderful conversation. The pastor of Kronstorf is a seminary classmate of Karobath.[25] He told us about Theresia Neumann, whom he has visited a few times.[26] He was recently with her. The N[ational Socialists] are not able to control much in Konnersreuth. It should be this way everywhere.

Today I learned that our former parish administrator [Pastor] Krenn is in Enns. I visited with him this evening, which delighted him. He is an organist and cantor here. For this reason, I had not seen him. Perhaps I would not have known him in any case, for he does not appear well. You can imagine what it can do to a priest when he is blamed for actions as he was — actions for which he is blameless. I'll tell you everything when we see each other.

Dear Fanj, go often for the *Rorate*. Also, pray for me so that I can still be there [in spirit] for the *Rorate* in my home parish. Warm greetings to you from your loving husband, Franz.

See you again.

Many greetings to Mother and the little ones. Tell them that their father again has some chocolate for them.

Good night.

---

24. The Masses in Advent began with a verse with the first words *Rorate coeli,* "Let fall from the heavens...." [RK]

25. The pastor of Kronstorf was Pastor Arthofer.

26. Therese Neumann of Konnersreuth (1898–1962) claimed to have mystical visions of the passion of Jesus Christ and is reported to have received the stigmata of Christ beginning in 1926.

From Franziska to Franz

Tuesday, December 3, 1940

Much beloved husband!

Today I received your letter along with the dear photograph, which delights me.[27] I am grateful for these. You have a better kitchen there [than here], for you look very good. Though you also look somewhat sad, and how could it not be otherwise when one must involuntarily leave his loved ones and go to a strange place. I always feel pain for you, dear Franzl, though you always want me to be happy, right? Hopefully, this will happen when you come home. I always think about you and will rejoice when you are at home.

Your photograph is now hanging on our wall. Have you sensed this? You are now in a picture frame and do not look too bad. Rosl hollered at you during dinner. She even wanted to take you to bed with her tonight. You were supposed to sleep beside her. I did not allow her to do this. I told her that when father comes home, he will sleep beside you. She replied that father is already at home. Your photograph has received many kisses from the two little ones. Rosl immediately recognized you when I showed her your photo. But Maridl did not. She simply said, "Man."

Tomorrow we shall bake Christmas cookies for the soldiers. We'll send some to Hansl Adam and Fredl Moni and Toni Strohhofer and Seppi Weber. Up to now I had done nothing. But the Women's Association has baked for the soldiers, and it has brought together many baked goods.

Today I gathered the pitch, and tomorrow we'll stack the logs, which of course must still be cut. Then this work is done, and you can come home without having to work or to cut firewood. We must also deliver 3 yards of firewood and 440 pounds of oats.

Our housekeeper has gone to Dr. Liebl for examinations over the last three weeks because of her poor hearing. She also has a horrible rash over her entire body. I am feeling anxious whether the little ones will contract it. She is receiving injections that make her unable to work throughout most of the day. She also has pain in her feet because the doctor injects her there.

We frequently go to church. I am praying that peace comes soon, and that you are able to remain at home with us. It is so terrible that two people are separated who are always happy together. Now they are pulled far apart. However, with God's help, we'll be able to endure this and not be harmed by it.

---

27. This photograph, taken in the autumn of 1940, shows FJ in uniform.

A controversy surrounding our pastor has again occurred because of the school. On Sunday he preached that parents should send their children to Mass. His words were repeated by the Mittermeier girl to the midwife who then told them to the teacher.[28] Of course, the pastor received a rebuke from the teacher, whom the [N.S.] authorities will not or cannot any longer esteem if the children are always going to church. They hold that the children belong to their teacher. The teacher must now push ahead and instill the new spirit so that he remains in good standing with the authorities. If he does not, then he'll be conscripted into the army. This would be unfortunate, for he is a good fellow. All of this is painful to me, to you (right?), and to most people in St. Radegund.[29] The teacher already brought about the departure of our previous pastor, who had only a good effect on our parish's children. Give my warm greetings to our former pastor if you meet him again. (I accidentally learned from Lidwina that the teacher regularly receives butter from Strohhofer and milk from Woferl.)

So, dear Franzl, come home to us soon. It will be wonderful to have you with us. The children quickly forget when we tell them that their father will not come home if they are always arguing. They are obedient for a few minutes, but their good behavior does not continue for very long. They are like to adults who are not always as well behaved as they could be.

At the moment, everyone here is asleep. I am alone at my desk. I do not know anything else new. So I'll end this letter. I hope that you will be here soon and be allowed to remain at home. If you are not able to come soon, then a letter from you would please me — if you have time to write.

The Tiefenhalers are delighted that you wrote to them. Herr Tiefenhaler told us that he was in Enns for eight months in the last war. At that time, many soldiers were housed with farmers in the surrounding area. The military base had been evacuated because it was being bombarded. It is wonderful that our people were able to stay with unknown farmers. Hopefully, this war will soon come to an end.

Warm greetings to you from your faithful wife, Fani. Again, many thanks for the dear photograph which brings me much delight. I'm sending you many kisses! See you again!

---

28. The midwife was a "trusted person," that is, a Gestapo informer.

29. The resistance of the villagers to the state's suppression of Catholic holy days resembled that of their neighbors in Bavaria, who blocked the Reich from removing crucifixes from the schools' classrooms. [RK]

From Franz to Franziska

Enns, December 5, 1940

Dearly beloved wife!

With joy I received your letter yesterday. Thank you for it. It amazes me that you are already done with the cutting of the brush. If I had been at home, it would definitely not yet be done. There is seldom a loss that does not bring about something worthwhile. There is still much time ahead for the stacking of the logs. It can wait until you receive the help of a man, for it can be dangerous for two women to do.

Winter has already begun here. It is probably not much different where you are, so that you must stay inside. Concerning the butchering of the swine, do not wait for me. I can see from your letter that you have been very sparing with the meat. Otherwise, it would not have lasted you for such a long time.

You need not be concerned about me becoming too fat. I am still very lean! Dear Fanj, I still cannot tell you what's been decided about my leave. I am hoping for something definite next week. Today I am somewhat preoccupied, as you may have already detected in this letter. Today we were to have had the scheduled review of the troops. We were already assembled for this ceremony when the major came to us and said that everything would be postponed. As a result, we must remain on the military base until Monday, and we shall apparently work on Sunday. Everything is by word of mouth. Our maxim here is "only wonder about things but do not argue." With God's help, everything will be okay. I'll end my letter for today. I cannot offer the hope of an imminent reunion.

Warm greetings to you from your husband, Franz, who longs to be at home.
Warm greetings to Mother and my little ones.

From Franz to Franziska

The feast of St. Nicholas, December 6, is an occasion for gift-giving among the German-speaking people. [RK]

Enns, December 6, 1940

Dear wife!

With delight I received your package today. Thank you very much for it. I have already eaten some of it. Everything tastes very good. I must not have behaved too badly, for otherwise St. Nicholas would not have been so good to me. Hopefully, St. Nicholas has also come to you!

I must do military training on the motorcycle every day this week. This morning it snowed. I had to close my eyes, for you couldn't see much with open eyes. Thanks be to God, I was able to return with all of my limbs. Moreover, I have no anxiety about these things.

Hopefully, our well at home has not frozen over.

Warm greetings to you from your husband, Franz.

Greetings to Mother and the little ones.

See you again!

Wait on writing me until you receive my new address. I'll send you a card with it. I've received orders for our company. About sixty of us are going away.

From Franz to Franziska

Enns, December 6, 1940

Dearly beloved wife!

With great joy I received your dear letter today. Thank you very much. However, you will not receive much joy from this letter today. Things will be different from what we have wanted. At midday when I received your package and sent you my letter of thanks, I had no inkling about this. I have just received a sad report. We'll apparently leave here on Monday, but we do not know where we are going. You can imagine what I am feeling! And yet one is not allowed to say anything about how this affects his heart. At such a moment, one would like to creep away so that there can be a reunion with you at Christmas. Let us place all of our concerns and troubles in God's hand. He will guide our destinies for the best. I am not anxious about the future. Schmied in Tarsdorf, with whom I've spoken, is soon going to Poland to work. He is on leave until the 16th of the month because he recently received some new teeth.

Dear Fanj, if it is possible, look for a couple of men to do the stacking of the logs. They could do in a couple of days what would take you perhaps eight days. You know what it is to do heavy lifting, and this is not good for a woman. Do not be concerned about the turning in of the firewood [to the state]. If the need is very pressing, then the village council will issue an order for it. Otherwise, I would prefer that you wait until I come home.

This letter that I am sending to you is coming with all of the things that I am sending home so that I need not carry anything unnecessary with me.

Dear wife, I am delighted that you are sending some things to the soldiers. Please greet all of them for me. It is better to send things this way than if you had given things through the Women's Association. Do not take my situation hard, dear Fanj. Things do not go better for others. Perhaps we shall stay here for a few more days. If so, I'll write.

Greetings to you and also to Mother and the little ones.

See you again. Your Franzl.

From Franz to Franziska and His Mother Rosalia

Monday, December 9, 1940

Dearest wife!

Above all, receive my warm greetings. Today I can still write you from Enns. At 4:00 p.m., we shall apparently learn when we'll depart. For this reason I'll end my letter later tonight. I hope, dear Fanj, that you do not take this recent news too hard. In this difficult time one must be ready for anything. While it appears to us that my reassignment — instead of a leave or a discharge — is unfortunate, it may not in fact be so. It was on Friday, which is dedicated to the Sacred Heart of Jesus, that I received this sad news, and this feast cannot be a day of misfortune for us, at the very least in relation to eternal life. It need not be that everything in this world comes about as we want for ourselves, for we do not see the future. It is perhaps a good thing that we do not know it.

Dear Fanj, yesterday which was the feast of the Immaculate Conception, I was able to share in a Sunday of great grace. In the festively decorated Franciscan church amid a fine celebration, two soldiers were accepted into the Third Order.[30] Dearest wife, one of these two soldiers was your husband. I hope that you are not upset with him for this, for you have — as I hope — the same view of life that I do. It must also be a consolation for you that my faith has not become weaker in the military. If I cannot be helpful to you in your work at home, I hope that I can bring you help through my prayer. During these weeks, I have met here a man with the same outlook as mine.[31] During 1934 he was in Rome and Naples. Now he will remain for a while in Enns. He has applied to work in the kitchen since he is already a trained cook.

Dear Fanj, yesterday in the church it became clear to me that we'll soon have a reunion. It would be a joy if we would at least celebrate Christmas together. Today I received a package with cookies and a packet of cigarettes from the Women's Association of Hochburg-Ach. However, you should not

---

30. On March 7, 2007, Franziska Jägerstätter commented on this decision by her husband: "It is a miracle that he had converted in this way. I did not pressure him into this. All that happened came from within himself."

31. Rudolf Mayer (1906–43) from Raab in Upper Austria. See his biographical sketch on page 248 below.

reproach yourself that you have given nothing to these collections. I have not eaten much from this package. Tonight we're holding a company gathering, and I'll build a *Volk*-community with these things.[32]

Later in the day, Franz added the following:

We must be prepared for departure at 8:00 a.m. tomorrow. We were not told where we are going. It is apparently not far, for we are not bringing much to eat.

Dear wife, write me at the new address. It has brought me much joy that you have gone to so much trouble to write me. Thank you very much for the letters and the packages.

For the last time, I am sending you my warm greetings from Enns. From your husband who is always thinking of you and loves you, Franz.

Be well. See you again!

Greetings to the relatives and the neighbors.

Many k[isses] for you and the little ones.

Dear mother! Warm greetings to you. I hope that you are still in good health, as I always am, thanks be to God. I ask you, dear mother, not to be concerned about me. I believe that things will not go badly for your son in the future. When someone has nothing to fear, then things cannot go badly. Many of our soldiers here are very [spiritually] poor. They would perhaps still go to church but have this harmful human fear. As a result, they do not know how they should begin a Sunday. At the tavern their money does not last long, and then they remain in their room and become apathetic. Pray for us soldiers that it does not go badly for us on the Day of the Last Judgment.

Warm greetings to you from your son Franz.

Be well. See you again.

From Franz to Franziska

This is a postcard:

Obernberg, December 11, 1940

Dear wife!

As you can see, I am now near to you. We are now about twenty miles from Braunau. But there are bad train connections. I'll write more tomorrow.

Warm greetings to everyone.

Your father and husband, Franz Jägerstätter.

---

32. A sarcastic allusion to the N.S. rhetoric. [RK]

From Franz to Franziska

Franz Jägerstätter im Gasthof Schachinger, Number 65,
Obernberg am Inn

Obernberg, December 12, 1940

Dearly beloved wife!

Above all, receive my warm greetings. I hope that you have already received my first message from here. Now things will be easier since you know that I am not so far from home. However, we have such bad train connections from here that I would not be able to begin much work at home during a Sunday leave. I surely hope that I will receive a leave at the end of next week. This would make me very happy.

We do not actually know what we'll do here. I believe that it will surely not be bad here. If you write me, write to the return address that I have given above, even though I'll soon receive a different room. We are very dispersed from one another here. Although there are 250 men here, one can look around the entire market area and see no soldiers.

Warm greetings to you from Frau Besenböck. We had a couple of hours to visit in Linz. I had to make the most of the time. I could not see Toni, who should have lost about forty-four pounds. The little ones appear not bad [in the photo]. Our little Loisi has more life in her now than when I left you.

Allow the logs to sit for a while. I hope that I'll receive a long enough leave so that I can begin this work. Today I shall go to Mass, and I hope to go often to Mass here. Yesterday I made a quick trip to Reichersberg, where there is a large monastery and a very beautiful church.

They knew here three weeks ago that soldiers would be coming to this place. But we learned of our destination only as we reached the train station at Antiesenhofen, the last stop before here. As we left Enns, we were told that we were going to Linz.

As you can imagine, many of us were deeply moved as we were coming here. There are many of us from Upper Austria. We traveled through the villages of some of the men, which was not easy for them.

I must end my writing now, for we must go for the evening meal.

Warm greetings to you from your loving husband, Franz.

Warm greetings to Mother and my little ones.

I look forward to our reunion.

From Franz to Franziska

Obernberg, December 16, 1940

Dear wife!

I am finally able to write you a few sentences. I can tell you that those of us who are married were promised a leave for Christmas. This week will be a long one because in my mind I am already more at home than I am here — especially if it remains cold this entire week, as it was today. You can now write to the new address that I am giving today. I hope that I'll find you in the best of health. Greetings to you and also to Mother and the little ones, your father, Franz.

I look forward to our reunion!

During the Christmas holiday, Franz was at home with Franziska, their three daughters, and his mother. [RK]

From Franz to Franziska

A best-wishes card for the new year:

Saturday, December 28, 1940

Dearest wife!

I arrived back here yesterday at 10:30 p.m. I can tell you that I'll be at home again in mid-January. At that time, I'm supposed to receive my leave of three weeks. I'll come home when the first group returns from their leave. If it is not strenuous here, then I'll look forward to the next leave.

Today I practiced my sharpshooting during the afternoon. Again, I had good luck with this.

Hopefully, mother is healthy again. How are the little ones doing? They will likely be quarreling again.

I wish all of you a good new year, your husband, son, and father.

Franz J. See you again. Good night.

From Franz to Franziska

Obernberg, December 31, 1940

Much beloved wife!

Above all, receive my warm greetings. Almost all of my comrades have gone out to celebrate the start of the new year. So I can write you in peace. I was already at a celebration, namely, in the church with a festive thanksgiving service. The chaplain gave a very meaningful sermon after which came the thanksgiving prayer. It was very beautiful.

Dearest wife, even though I must celebrate the end of the year far away from my loved ones, we still have much to thank God for. We had a blessed year, even though many difficult hours came upon us, especially upon you and mother. Still we can say that the Lord God has guided us for the best. We received God's blessings in rich measure. If we resolve to begin the new year tomorrow morning with the aim of seeking to realize God's will in our lives even more fully, then we need not be anxious for the future, even when it does not seem bright. And if this should be our last year in this world—which we, of course, do not wish but for which we must always be ready—then so be it. We also do not need to be anxious that the Lord God will withdraw his grace from us in the hour of our deaths.

Now, dear wife, be of good cheer in the new year!

I cannot tell you much that is new, for not much has happened since I returned here. We have heard that we should not be here much longer. They are finding us quarters in Ried. I have nothing against this since the train connections for my leaves are at least better there than here. This is something that we must always have in mind. There are some men here who have not yet had a leave.

What is happening with the Besenböcks? Have they written to you? This evening it has begun to rain very hard. Perhaps we have gotten beyond the worst of the cold for now. You'll surely not object to this.

Warm greetings to you from your husband, Franz.

Many warm greetings to Mother and the little ones and also to the housekeeper.

I look forward to our reunion!

Chapter 3

Military Training Letters

January 1–April 8, 1941

This chapter contains twenty-two letters from Franz and twelve letters from Franziska. In his letters, Franz increasingly conveys his frustration with the army's bureaucracy, waste of time, secrecy, deception, and brutality — a frustration that shows itself in his ongoing conflict with his sergeant. Whereas Franz's letters in the autumn conveyed a lightheartedness, these manifest his anger. In her letters, Franziska tells of feeling burdened by the farm's demands as well as by the care of her three daughters. She also repeatedly speaks of her sadness at Franz's absence. [RK]

From Franziska to Franz

St. Radegund, January 1, 1941

I received your card yesterday with thanks and joy. I understand that you will get a longer leave at home. I'll be very happy when you are home again and will help in raising the children. They are especially troublesome today, even Loisi who is again in pain because of her teeth. Two of her teeth have begun to appear. I am happy about this. Perhaps she'll soon feel better.

Yesterday the package from the Besenböcks arrived. They have again sent many things: two sets of toy building blocks, two balls, a jigsaw puzzle, a bead game, and fabric to Mother for a blouse. I have already taken out the balls and the bead game. The children are happy, but they do not yet understand the game. They argue when they play with the building blocks. Rosl would like to do everything alone. You know how she always is. She cannot improve her behavior.

We still have rainy weather. It is probably also the same where you are. On Monday we spread the manure from the sled. On the next day we could not do any more of this because we had many other things to do. Today I have nothing else to write about. So I'll end my letter and send you warm greetings from your loving wife, Fani.

Also, greetings from your mother and Rosl, Maridl, and Loisl.

See you again!

The Hirl family wishes you a happy new year.

From Franz to Franziska

Obernberg, Friday, January 3, 1941

Dearly beloved wife!

Warm greetings to you. I hope that you and all of my loved ones are still in good health, as I am, thanks be to God. I hope that everything is going better for mother! Today it is eight days since I left you. Of course, I already long to be with you. It may be that my next leave will not come as soon as I said in my last letter. Many of us may not be allowed to depart when the men who are on a three-week leave come back. The men who have not had any leave may be allowed to go away first. There are even married men here who have still not had a leave. So I shall come home at the beginning of February. Perhaps I can be of more help at that time than now. Allow more time to pass before working on the firewood. Perhaps I can be at home on a Saturday.

We are having wonderful days here. They would be even better if I were not in the army, especially when I think of my days in Enns. Of course, I would love to be at home.

Let me hear soon about what's happening with you. The train tracks here were destroyed. Hopefully, the trains will run again soon!

Warm greetings to you from your loving husband, Franz.

Many greetings to Mother and my three little ones.

Be well. See you again.

From Franz to Franziska

Obernberg, January 6, 1941

Dearest wife!

Today I received your dear letter. Many thanks for it. I must mention that I shall apparently depart from here tomorrow morning. Of course, I do not know where we're going. It does not bother me, for we'll probably not go far! In the military, things can get worse. I'll let you know when we have moved to our new residence.

Warm greetings to all of you, your Franzl.

Be well. See you again.

Specialist Franz Jägerstätter, Field Post Number 42008.

From Franziska to Franz

St. Radegund, January 6, 1941

Much beloved husband!

I am grateful for your dear letter which I received yesterday. I could not write you yesterday because I had to stay in bed for the whole day. I have come down with the flu. Today things are going somewhat better for me. I can at least send you a postcard. Things are also going better for mother. The three little ones have head colds.

On Saturday, the little daughter of Matilda Mittermeier was buried. She died of diphtheria. Other than this, I do not know anything new here.

The three little ones along with mother and me send you warm greetings, your loving wife, Fanj.

Be well. See you again.

From Franz to Franziska

Utzenaich, January 8, 1941

Dearest wife!

We arrived here safely today at midday, and I received your card. Hopefully, you are healthy again. The good days for our group are behind us. Nevertheless, I hope that things here will be bearable. I hope that we'll soon see each other.

Warm greetings, your Franz.

My new address is: Specialist Franz Jägerstätter, Field Post Number 41326, Utzenaich im Innkreis

From Franz to Franziska

Franz was home on leave between January 8 and January 13. [RK]

Utzenaich, January 13, 1941

Dearly beloved wife!

I hope that my letter finds you in the best of health. I arrived back here yesterday safe and sound at around 10:00 a.m. I had the best time [at home]. Afterward, I met the car in Ach, even though I had to travel fast. Yesterday the car departed earlier than when I returned from leave the last time. I would not have missed much if I had returned today by noon. One should always be a bit omniscient! Today at noon I submitted a request for another leave. However, nothing will be possible for two weeks. The commander is still on leave, and he has already calculated the next leaves. If the possibility exists, I'll be pleased. In any case, you cannot now work with the firewood because it is too cold.

Warm greetings to you and also to Mother and the three little ones, your Franzl.

I am enclosing the ration card for lard. See you again!

From Franz to Franziska

Utzenaich, January 23, 1941

Dearly beloved wife!

With longing and great joy, I received your dear letter. I am grateful for it. I waited each day for mail from you because I am always concerned about you. Something could always go wrong for you. It is always easier for me when I know how things are with you and my other loved ones. It is good that it is warm right now. It is especially good for the water in the well so that it again flows. However, for us soldiers this weather is not the most favorable because our boots are always soaked through with water.

There is nothing happening for me at the moment because I have been in the infirmary since Monday of this week. I do not know when the doctor will explain things to me. I would love to leave this room because the guy next to me flares up as if he is crazy. I have not slept much since I arrived here.

I cannot tell you what is actually wrong with me because even the doctor does not know. He has reached no judgment. He has done everything, and perhaps a different doctor could come up with different results. I already had an enema, and at the same time was on a low fat diet. I can now wear the wedding band again. Today I weighed myself. Over these few days, I had lost approximately eleven pounds, which is not that much. The main issue is whether I can regain my former health. Everything rests in God's hands. A leave for recovery would do me good. Perhaps I'll get some days for this. If so, then good days will follow these bad ones!

With trust in God, I'll close my letter. We have such a small table in this room that there is only one place for writing, and someone else would now like to write a letter.

Warm greetings to you from your loving husband, Franz.

Warm greetings to my little ones.

Dear mother, I am very grateful to you for your good wishes, your son, Franz.

I am already looking forward to our reunion.

From Franziska to Franz

St. Radegund, January 23, 1941

Dearly beloved husband!

I had hoped to receive a letter from you today. Unfortunately you must not have had time to write. Since I have some news for you, I'm writing you now.

Frau Besenböck has sent us 15 marks. One must accept such a generous gift. When convenient, you can thank her. Further, father has written that their farm worker is now away, and that they are promising him a woman worker. On Sunday, the stork brought Zieher a baby girl.[1] You can send congratulations. My sister will return to baking. Also, the poultry continue to lay eggs. One can always find something to do.

Poidl Grüngassler and Peter Pleikner are here on leave. Toni Strohhofer must depart tomorrow. The good time of a leave always passes much too quickly. Hopefully, you will soon receive a longer leave. I am already looking forward to our reunion.

We had another holiday on Monday. It was the feast of St. Sebastian.[2] You will have surely remembered this feast, though it is especially celebrated by women. One should not knit or darn on this day. So I looked for other work and made approximately forty bars of soap. Genuine, good soap is easy to make. You'll see it when you come home. I've also saved some money. Now I do not need to buy soap, and my soap is less expensive to make than the soap that one buys.

I am entirely alone at my desk. Everyone is already asleep, and Lidwina has gone to say good-bye to her brother.[3] So I've already written a letter to Frau Besenböck, thanking her for the money.

Now something about your little women. Loisl is crawling all around and moves very fast. Maridl is always having accidents.[4] She is often falling off the bench. She did so yesterday and landed on her head. She did not breathe for such a long time that I became anxious and alarmed. One cannot be attentive enough. The three children are full of life. One must continually pray that nothing very unfortunate happens to them. Small mishaps occur every day.

Our well is always going on strike, and this is another cause of frustration. However, one can do nothing else other than patiently to carry water home from elsewhere. I hope that you'll not be upset with me when you read this sentence. In any case, perhaps the pump will soon work again because the weather is warmer.

---

1. See Franziska's letter of October 27, 1940 (page 18 above). [RK]

2. St. Sebastian (d. ca. 300), martyred under Diocletian, was pierced with arrows. Mindful of the arrows, many women chose not to work with needles on his feast day. [RK]

3. Her brother was Anton Eckinger, also known as Toni Strohhofer.

4. Maridl (Maria) was born with a physical disability that eventually required surgery. See Zahn, *In Solitary Witness*, 53. [RK]

Please do not laugh at me today for my random thoughts. Although I have not written beautifully, my intention is a good one. "My hand shakes while my heart weeps." This saying has just come to me. I am not in a lighthearted mood. Time passes quickly, thanks be to God!

Warm greetings from your faithful wife, Fani. Be well. See you again.

From Franz to Franziska

Monday, January 26, 1941

Early Saturday I received your dear letter with joy and gratitude. I did not write you because I believed that I'd be able to come home. But I am still in the infirmary, and I cannot report that I am healthy because no doctor has come since Thursday. Otherwise, on Saturday I would have been reported to be healthy, for a human being can seldom endure not working for a long time. Here one must patiently endure things. If I could not come home midweek, then I was hoping for Saturday. [But with no success.] In the military one cannot renounce being indefinite.

Warm greetings to you from your husband, Franz.

Greetings to Mother and my little ones.

From Franz to Franziska

Franz was home for a leave from late January into early February. [RK]

Utzenaich, February 8, 1941

Dearly beloved wife!

Receive my warm greetings. I want to tell you that I arrived here today, Saturday, at 7:00 a.m. I was able to depart from Reib at approximately 8:30 p.m. Then the car had a delay of almost three hours. There was a tedious time of waiting. Then I had to stay overnight in Braunau, and at 5:00 a.m., I departed from Braunau. When I reported to the sergeant early this morning, he did not have much to say.[5] But he asked why I had not arrived last evening. I did not need to lie. I was able to recount the car's delay.

My associate was recalled by a telegram from his leave and arrived here yesterday. They have apparently not yet found the other man who is on leave, for he is not here yet.

---

5. This incident displayed the tension between FJ and his sergeant. [RK]

Dear Fanj, you will be wondering why this sudden call-to-duty occurred. I'll no longer serve as a guard at the stables here in Utzenaich, for in the course of this week we'll depart from here. We do not know where we are going! It seems that it will be a place for troop exercises, for artillery is supposed to arrive here soon. Our journey should take about two weeks. We'll not be transported by train. Rather, we must make our way very slowly with our horses. This will be okay if it does not get colder than it is here today. So we'll become gypsies! All this would be fine, if it would mean that I could claim my deserved leave. But now I must give up hope for a leave.

Because of these thoughts, I have not been entirely here today but much more with you at home! My recent leave at home was wonderful, though short. Perhaps it will be granted us that we'll be able to be together for a long time. The Lord God does not abandon his own, even if things sometimes come about differently from what we want for ourselves. Still it will now be somewhat terrible for me, since I'll receive no news from you for a long time. It is perhaps best that you do not write while we do not have a fixed place. I would receive the mail but perhaps not promptly while we lack a definite location.

I expected to receive three letters today: one from my dear Fanj, one from my sister-in-law Resl[6], and another from [Frau Besenböck in] Linz, which I'll send on to you. I'll write to you every day until we depart from here.

I'll end for today with warm greetings from your loving husband, Franz.

Warm greetings to Mother, my parents-in-law, and the three little ones.

Once again, many thanks for the things that I ate today.

See you again!

From Franz to Lorenz and Maria Schwaninger

Sunday, February 9, 1941

Dear parents-in-law!

Above all, receive my warm greetings. You will be curious about my sudden call-to-duty. In fact, there is nothing urgent. This week we'll depart from here and apparently go to a somewhat distant place for troop exercises. The chief thing is that I am now a guard of the horses. One cannot be upset with this. Perhaps I'll receive a leave before my troop is sent to the front. It would be wonderful to be at home. We cannot give up the hope that joy will again come after suffering.

---

6. Theresia Schwaninger (1918–2007), one of Franziska's sisters, worked on the farm Lichtmess from 1941 until 1954.

I was able to depart from Ach at 8:30 p.m., and then I had to stay overnight in Braunau. The next day, I left from Braunau at 5:00 a.m. Since returning here, not much has occurred that is worth talking about.

Warm greetings to you. See you again! Your son-in-law, Franz. Greetings to my brother-in-law and sister-in-law.

From Franz to Franziska

Tuesday, February 11, 1941

Dearly beloved wife!

Hopefully, all of you are in good health, as I am. I want to mention that we shall depart from here on Saturday of this week. My call-to-duty need not have been so rushed. I also want to tell you that yesterday I assumed responsibility for a pair of horses and a wagon.[7] Apparently the sergeant has taken a more favorable view of me. Since I am a recruit, I enjoy a few good words about me. Now I must be able to do in a few days what others need four to five months to learn in this business. Not saying anything is sometimes hard! These days will pass quickly. And the main thing here is to have the time pass quickly. So can one gain merit for eternal life, especially if one can tolerate everything with great patience.

For today, good night to my loved ones.

Tomorrow I'll write more.

February 12

Dear wife, now I'll continue my letter from yesterday. Today we made a long trip in a military column. Things went well for me. If one does not lose courage, then everything will continue to go well. If you could send me a sack of oats for my horses, then I'd have a bonus for them. They are good-natured fellows.

In my last letter I said that you should hold off writing to me until we were assigned to a definite place. Now I can see that things are different than I expected, and it would be fine for you to write to me during these days. Mail that is not delivered to us while we are traveling is waiting for us at our destination. I would love to receive some letters from you again. For my address, use only my name and the field postal number, and I'll receive it. It would be terrible if you did not write me for a long time. You might forget to tell me much of the news! It would be best not to send me any packages at this time.

---

7. FJ's training with horses and wagons and previously with motorcycles resulted in his being named a "Motor Transport Specialist." [RK]

On Monday I received a package from Linz. In it were baked goods from Frau Besenböck.[8] There were many good things, but what I have received from you tastes much better.

Today we received instructions on our march's route. The commander explained that we are going to Hirschbach, which is in a forest. We'll arrive there around March 5 or 6 and have rest periods between here and there. We were heartened to learn that the mail will be delivered to us on the way. So you can write to me.

I'll now end for today. With warm greetings to you and also to Mother, my sister-in-law, and my dear little ones.

Your father, Franz.

See you again.

From Franz to Franziska

Saturday, February 15, 1941

Today we departed at 7:30 a.m., and went through St. Martin, Geinberg, and Altheim to Helpfau-Uttendorf. A half-hour beyond Helpfau is Ziegelei where there were a couple of empty barns, in which we — ten men and thirteen horses — found accommodations. The barns themselves are not so bad, but the rooms leave much to be desired. We had a strenuous march yesterday. It was especially hard on the horses, since it was about twenty-five miles. I no longer have the horses that I started with. A couple of days before our departure, I received a couple of brown horses that are better than the previous ones. The trip went very well, except that shortly before our destination I [and my horses] slid into a snow-covered ditch in the road. I was not able to get out on my own. Further, we had to retrace our steps because the artillery is situated here, and we have to load boxes from it.

On Wednesday, the 19th, we'll leave here and go through Kremsmünster and Vöcklabruck to Steyr. In Steyr we can pick up our mail if any is waiting for us there.

Sunday, February 16

Today, although there was not much to do, we had no free time in the morning. However, through God's guidance, I was able to attend a Mass. The Lord God

---

8. Along with the baked goods, Hansi Besenböck included a letter (dated January 23, 1941) acknowledging that she had received the meat that Franziska Jägerstätter had sent her for her family.

knows how much strength I need in order to withstand the storms of this time. Indeed, dear wife, such hours of grace are hours of good fortune and joy since one can see clearly that the Lord God does not forget us so long as we do not forget him.

My dear loved ones, use well the hours of grace for you at home. We are swimming in the same stream, even if it is somewhat calmer for you.[9] But who knows for how long! You need not fear that I would do something that would bring you reproach. When someone, because of his diligence for that which is eternally unchanging, can no longer be entirely involved in earthly matters as other people perhaps are, he can still toil and be industrious in earthly matters. One would not go forward if the Lord would not give [it] his blessing.[10]

This afternoon I again had to guard the barns, which I have not done often in recent weeks. I also did it last Sunday afternoon.

Dear wife, it is not a good situation when a man is as close to his loved ones as I am and yet cannot be with them. It is best that I no longer have a motorcycle. If I had one, then nothing would hold me here. In less than one hour, I would be with you, even though I also hope for a reunion with you in three or four weeks.

How are things going for all of you? Hopefully, you are in good health, as I still am, thanks be to God. What is new at home? Rosl and Maridl will now surely wade around in the mud. When the ground soon gets dry, then they can go to Lang's. What about your pile of firewood? Has it gotten smaller? The children must go outside on their own as soon as they will no longer freeze out there.

I'll end for today with warm greetings to you, dear wife, and also to Mother, my sister-in-law, and my three little ones.

Be well. See you again.

I'll not be able to write until the next day of rest. Greetings to our neighbors.

From Franziska to Franz

St. Radegund, February 16, 1941

Much beloved husband!

I can gratefully tell you that yesterday I received your dear letter with delight. I thought that I would not receive a letter from you for another two

---

9. "Stream" (*Strom*) became FJ's metaphor for National Socialism. [RK]

10. FJ is conveying his growing conviction that God is strengthening him as he finds himself disapproving of the Reich, the army, and the war. [RK]

weeks. But you found enough time to send me a few sentences. I am delighted to know that your march is not so terrible. Nevertheless, hopefully, you'll write and tell me when I should send you something to eat. Is the sergeant still with you? I thought he would remain in Utzenaich. But it seems from your letter that he is apparently still at your side. You also have horses. You will now have a high opinion of yourself, for not everyone can handle horses. Unfortunately, I cannot send you oats. I need them for my rabbit. I have gotten a new one. We cannot stretch the hay further, and the rabbit likes the oats. It cost 12 marks. The two older girls enjoy playing with the rabbit, but Loisi is afraid of it. The dear rabbit!

Agatha Afanger was buried on Thursday. Further, Pastor Thomas [Huber] was here this week. You will also recall that Pastor Karobath has donated an expensive sewing machine to the church, for the sacristan's use.

During the week, I received an invitation to a grand wedding celebration, and yesterday Bräumetzger and Anni Kracherlbräu got married. He had received a leave of only ten days, and so he must leave today, Sunday. It will not be good that a new bride must remain alone. Also on leave here are Bürger and Toni Strohhofer, who has again received a leave of three weeks. It angers me that you never receive a leave, even though you are already a long time in the military. How would it be if you were again to ask for a long leave? Perhaps you'd have luck! It would make me very happy. Our little ones are troublesome today. Loisi would like to upset everything. She is a lively little girl. Hopefully, you will receive this letter. I'll again often burden you with my notes, and I hope that I'll often receive them from you.

Warm greetings from your faithful wife, Fani, and from everyone at home.

> The beautiful days are gone.
> Your heart is already mine for a long time,
> and I, filled with yearning, am always thinking of you.
> Good fortune could be even greater.
> Perhaps I shall find that
> you will soon return [and]
> will give me your heart for eternity,
> as you once promised me in good fortune!

Greetings! Fanj

From Franziska to Franz

Tuesday, February 18, 1941

Dearly beloved husband!

I want to tell you about some things in beautiful Radegund. Thanks be to God, all of us are in good health, and we hope that you are, too. We are having beautiful weather. It should also be the same where you are.

Today mother was in Tarsdorf. The elderly Mrs. Meier was buried in Hörndl. Also, the elderly Mrs. Stranzinger died here and will be buried on Thursday.

Today we finished the splitting of the firewood. It took a while because we also had a lot of manure to spread. Moreover, there was the other work that always needs to be done. During all of this, I often thought about you, especially when there were large, long logs that were hard to split. However, everything is now done. One needs only the will, and then everything happens.

They still do not have a housekeeper at Spreiter. Of course, they themselves could do the work. The younger ones should have the energy for it. You know what I mean![11]

Our girls are always busy outside since the weather is now warm. However, they often have accidents, especially Maridl, who too often is kissing the ground. Then she lets out a terrifying scream. You know how she is when she is dirty. Loisi is always funny. She wants to be in every scuffle, though she always gets the worst of it.

Dear Franzl, I do not know anything else. Perhaps I'll have something more intelligent to say the next time.

Warm greetings from your loving wife, Fani

Also from mother and Rosi, Mari, Loisi, and Resi.

From Franziska to Franz

Thursday, February 20, 1941

Much beloved husband!

I received your letter yesterday and am grateful for it. It was very painful to me as I read that you were so near to us and could not visit with us. Where do things stand with your leave? Do you know anything yet? Earlier, you hoped

---

11. Franziska is expressing her frustration about the situation at her family's home, "Spreiter," in Hochburg. The chores that Franziska's sister Resi had done were neglected after Resi went to work at Lichtmess.

to be with us in three or four weeks. Please write us soon, for I am always interested in knowing about your activities.

If you are coming here soon, I have a request. If it is acceptable to you and if it possible, please bring pacifiers for the two littlest ones. These are not superfluous things for our girls, and there are no more for sale here in Radegund. Nor in Tittmoning. And I cannot go elsewhere for them. So, dear father, if they do not cost too much, bring us a few of the kind that can fit over a bottle. You know the kind. However, if this is not possible, do not worry about them.

Today we were in the lower woods gathering firewood. We have brought some of it home. If you could come home soon, you could cut it for us. The weather is now warm. This is the main thing. When you read this letter, you'll again be far away from us. It is painful to me that you cannot be with us. However, one must always dispose oneself to God's will in every situation. It is a comfort to me that you desire to pray and are perhaps enduring everything patiently in this difficult time.

I can sense from your letters that you are not unfortunate, and that you are always finding time to go to church in order to receive comfort and courage. We'll continually pray that you'll come home soon, and that the war will come to an end soon, and that there will truly be peace. Hopefully, you will receive this letter soon. I am always delighted when I get a letter from you. With warm greetings, I am now ending my letter. Your wife, Fani, who is always thinking of you.

Be well. See you again, and write often.

From Franz to Franziska

This is a postcard of the castle and pilgrimage church at Puchheim:

Puchheim, February 21, 1941

All my loved ones!

I am sending you warm greetings from the place we are staying. I put my wagon and horses in this castle's barn, and I am being housed in a guest house about ten minutes away from the castle itself. We are having two days of rest here.

Warm greetings to all of you.

From Franz to Franziska

Sunday, February 23, 1941

Dearly beloved wife!

Today we had to be harnessed up by 5:00 a.m. I had wonderful expectations for this Sunday. I would have had nothing against remaining in Puchheim for a couple more days, for the church was beginning today a Forty Hours devotion.

We were required to engage in a [military] exercise during this march so that we would not reach our destination too early. We went through Schwanenstadt and Lambach to Kremsmünster. In other words, we went about twenty-five miles. In Schwanenstadt where the exercise was undertaken we went to the side of the road. Then a far larger column of soldiers than ours passed us on the road, going in the other direction.

These are the purest of *Volk* treks. They are worthless endeavors in which we simply march down a road. The quarters that we previously had — for example, in Utzenaich — will soon be occupied by the troops who were in Hirschbach and Döllersheim and passed us on the road. Moreover, we must demand almost the impossible from our horses. There is still a lot of snow and ice here. I had a bad day today, and I myself am a bit to blame for this.[12]

Monday, February 24

Today we had to be harnessed up before 5:00 a.m. It did not matter to me for I spent the entire night on guard duty in a barn. We were supposed to have a break in Steyr. This would have been enough. There were twenty miles until Steyr, where there was a brief feeding of the animals. However, we then went another twelve miles farther to St. Johann in Lower Austria. Except for Steyr, the area is very mountainous. In Steyr I had to load on a great amount of oats. At 11:00 p.m., we were allowed to unharness the horses. Of course, my first concern was the horses. My sleeping and eating were secondary. I did not know whether I would find mail waiting for me in Steyr. There was none.

Tuesday, February 25

Today was a day of rest — but only for the horses! It is apparently not necessary for us. Things would be easier to endure [we are told] if we would have more

---

12. FJ said or did something for which he was disciplined by having additional guard duty. [RK]

comradeship. However, one would be impoverished if he had to entrust himself to another soldier here. Today a platoon leader accused me of triviality. It is good that punching someone is severely punished here. Otherwise, I would sometimes not be able to control myself. It sometimes seems that one can no longer act with honor and goodness. The devil works with cunning to bring about a man's ruin.

Wednesday, February 26

Today we went farther, leaving as customary early in the morning and then going until Ulmerfeld. It was not particularly far, hardly twenty miles. The main thing was that we had to wake up very early and depart in the dark. In Ulmerfeld we had to stand around for about four hours and wait until we were permitted to unharness the horses. One must endure everything with patience. With God's help and good will one can bring everything to an end.

Thursday, February 27

Today we departed earlier than usual, and we went hardly more than twenty miles. We made a detour so that we would not arrive too early at our destination of Ybbs. This march entailed the greatest effort from me, for I could hardly make myself fight off sleep. I again had to do guard duty in a barn. We always find barns to accommodate the horses, who sometimes freeze a little!

Ybbs is a beautiful city on the Danube. There is a large mental hospital here, which is filled up. These so-called fools have become smart, and so many of them are no longer brought to this hospital. As you once told me, what happens with these people should be based on the truth. The farmer on whose farm we stayed told us that very sad scenes have played themselves out here.[13]

Friday, February 28

Today we went through Melk to Inning, which is a farm village. The trip was about twenty miles.

Saturday, March 1

Again there was a day of rest for the horses but not for us. It is apparently not necessary for us! Tomorrow morning we shall leave early. In many ways this makes sense because [our military leaders] no longer know what they should do on a Sunday.

---

13. FJ may be alluding to the Reich's euthanasia of people with disabilities. [RK]

I must be brief, for there is little time to write. If I did not know that you long for letters as much as I do, I would not write to you. Hopefully, everyone at home is still healthy, as I am, thank God. Warm greetings to you as well as to Mother, my sister-in-law, and my dear little ones.

Your Franzl

I hope that you have received my letter from last Sunday.

I long for a reunion.

From Franziska to Franz

Sunday, February 23, 1941

Dearly beloved husband!

Today, Shrove Sunday, is a glorious day.[14] We received a lot of snow over the last few days. Hopefully, the snow will melt soon, or we'll not be able to do much work outside. I am always thinking about you, about where you will be today, and about whether you have had a chance to go to church. In Radegund the gathering of the Third Order is this afternoon, to which you were invited. I do not know anything new. I could describe for you the children's good and bad behavior. Yesterday Loisi again had pain from her teeth, but today she is playful again. The other two are always the same rascals.

Yesterday we received meat from Strohhofer so that we'll have good meals during these days before Lent. Here we'll easily pass up the dancing, but we know that you'll again wear out your shoes dancing, dear Franzl! Since we have everything we need, we should have no concerns. Despite the war some people will dance and spend their money, while other people must live through sleepless nights in fear and with troubles.

In recent weeks I've sent you three letters. Have you received them? I'll close my letter with many warm greetings. Your faithful wife, Fani!

Greetings from mother and the three little girls!

From Franziska to Franz

Thursday, February 27, 1941

Dearly beloved husband!

I am deeply grateful for the beautiful postcard which you sent me from Puchheim. You must belong to nobility if you are being allowed into a castle! I am always concerned that no misfortune occur to you on this march, and that you'll be able to travel home for a lengthy leave. This would delight me.

---

14. This is the Sunday before Ash Wednesday and the start of Lent. [RK]

It is unfortunately still cold here. We are always cutting down trees so that we have something for heat. Our Loisi has three new teeth, which came somewhat quickly so that she cried terribly. I feel badly for her because she is a dear girl, and I cannot help her. Also, she can ask for things very nicely as you'll see when you come home! I cannot tell you much good about Rosei and Maridl. They are always the same rascals.

The Gabelmacher girl was here again on Sunday, and Rosei said to her what she has also said to Resi: "We no longer need you here. I like Lidwina more than you. So leave!" She was fresh to the girl because the girl questioned her. Afterward the girl said that, from the outset, she saw that she could not stay here. She has departed because our little ones have hurt her. So we have lost our baby-sitter.

I know nothing more to write to you today. I'll jot down some more things tomorrow.

Sunday, March 2, 1941

Most beloved husband!

The weather is beautiful again today, Sunday. There is some confusion here about your address. Hopefully, you are receiving my letters. I expected to receive a letter from you this week. I hope that you are still healthy, as we still are, thanks be to God.

Radlmacher was required to enlist yesterday. Franzl Nickel had to do the same a while ago, and he must now go to Greece. Everyone is greatly concerned about him. The Mehlharts have gone to Tittmoning into the house at Neuwieser. Kajetan will do work in the Damosers' home, and Marie will be their cook. He said that this is a better situation. On Sunday married couples will have their class on penance. You are invited to it. A priest is coming from Ostermiething to help out. Also, Zilli Steiger will be married in Hochburg this week.

Dear Franzl, we would again have a stack of firewood if you could come home on leave. I'll now work on it. But it would be better if you could come home.

Warm greetings from your loving wife, Fani.

Tuesday, March 4, 1941

Dearly beloved husband!

What is happening to you? Why are you no longer writing to us? I hoped to receive a letter today but unfortunately none came. I am concerned because up until now you have sent at least one letter each week. Have you gotten sick again? Please write us a few sentences soon!

Today I was summoned to the office of our region's farm officials. In the name of the officials, [Ferdinand] Huber asked where things stand with the need for you on the farm, and whether [our request] should be approved and moved ahead. I am anxious about what decision we'll receive. Hopefully, a positive one!

Our Loisi is now crawling and saying some words. She is even able to take a step alone. When she pushes a chair in front of her, she goes around the entire living room. Tomorrow she'll be ten months old. She is crawling sooner than the other two did. Since one must save paper, I have not sent this letter sooner. Also, I did not know whether you would receive my letters during your march. Many greetings from your loved ones at home.

From Franz to Franziska

Sunday, March 2

Dearest wife!

When the first light of dawn appeared on the horizon, we had already put five miles behind us. We have gone for a long distance through the Wachau region. If it had been merely a holiday trip, this stretch would have been the most beautiful days of the march which we've made over these two weeks. However, it happens that sometimes even what is most beautiful does not appear to be so. Our goal today was Stein-Krems. It was twenty-five miles away. We arrived here early because there were very few rests along the way. Our horses are now accustomed to twelve hours with no feeding and always pulling [the wagons].

Monday, March 3

Today turned out to be a day of rest for the horses. Also, we had good quarters. Most importantly, I had the chance to go to Mass, which I prefer on a Sunday. You must pray still more for me because I am having fewer opportunities to go [to Mass].

There is no more snow here, and it is already warm.

Tuesday, March 4

We were allowed to sleep at least a little bit later this morning. We got up at 5:30 a.m. But we had a strenuous march today and were not able to unharness the horses until midnight. Some horses were almost not able to make it. Mine were entirely courageous. Today we stopped at the area for our military exercises, and we brought the artillery that must now remain here. It is very sad to go through this region in which villages are empty and have been abandoned.[15] Many tears must have flowed as these people abandoned their homes.

Wednesday, March 5

Today we reached our final destination, arriving safe and sound in Hirschbach. This is not an especially large town. There is still ice and snow here and a lot of mud, which is even more troublesome for us. I am again quartered in a large room in a Gasthaus. We do not know how long we'll remain here.

Thursday, March 6

Dearest wife!

I'll now bring my daily reports to a conclusion. Hopefully, all of you are well, as I still am, thanks be to God. I wish to tell you that I received two letters from you yesterday, and today I received another. One of these is the letter from Shrove Sunday. I am grateful for these letters. I look forward to the next ones. Even though I am far away from all of you, it does not seem that I am so far away when I receive news from my loved ones. Concerning a leave, I may be able to say something next week. I have not yet heard anything. Perhaps I'll have good fortune and be able to pass some fortunate hours with my loved ones. Now I must end my letter for it is late.

Warm greetings to you as well as to Mother and the little ones and to my sister-in-law.

Your husband, Franz. Be well! See you again!

From Franz to Franziska

This is a postcard from Stein on the Danube:

Stein, March 3, 1941

Dearest wife!

I received with joy your letter of the 18th. Many thanks for it. I am sending you warm greetings from the beautiful Wachau. In a couple of more days we'll reach our destination.

All is going well. Warm greetings to all of you.

Yours, Franzl.

---

15. In order to make the region of Allensteig suitable for military exercises, the army required the residents of many villages to abandon their homes and farms and leave the area.

From Franziska to Franz

Wednesday, March 5, 1941

Much beloved husband!

Each day we have awaited with longing for a letter from you. The last letter we had received from you was from Puchheim on February 24. Today we received a letter and two cards from you, one card from Stein and one from Ybbs. I am very grateful for these. We are again relieved that nothing has happened to you or, to say it better, that you have had no great misfortune. Your letter from Sunday, which you asked about, has not yet landed here. Hopefully, it will soon appear. During these days you have surely been very busy, as I can extract from your letters. I'll continue to pray continually for you, that you may soon be able to travel to your loved ones at home who have a great longing for their dear husband and father and son.

You will be delighted with your children, dear father! I am always pleased with them. The two older ones are sometimes almost too smart, and they think that they do not need to do what I say. Loisi is a dear sparrow. She is always trying new things. She does not go far yet. At most, a step. Then she flutters about and falls. But right away she is up again. She has an adventuresome spirit!

Dearest, are you not coming home soon? You have been gone a long time. Hopefully, we'll see you soon. It will delight me.

Warm greetings from your faithful wife, Fani, as well as from your three girls and mother and Resi.

Be well! Se you again! Write often and much.

From Franz to Franziska

Monday, March 10, 1941

Dearly beloved wife!

Many thanks for your letter, which I received today with great delight. Please forgive me for overlooking your name day.[16] Belatedly, I wish you all the good that you desire. I would also have some wishes that can hardly be fulfilled.[17] My first wish would be to return home soon to all of you. However, it will likely not be before the end of March. A couple more weeks are still ahead of us.

---

16. "Franziska Romana," whose name day is March 9.

17. Given his growing anger, FJ may be referring to his desire to avoid a confrontation with the army. As the next chapter shows, this moment came two years later. [RK]

It would be good if my leave for farm work came through, so that at the very least I would be able to be with you for a longer time than during a normal leave. And perhaps I'll get free from this organization, for they will soon not allow us even to breathe heavily. I had three Saturdays and three Sundays with no free time. Yesterday would have been free, but unfortunately Franzl was assigned to guard duty. Tomorrow I am supposed to give the same service. All of us should help one another, [we are told]. But they are not able to insert their mentality into me.

What we suffer in this world, we need no longer to go through in purgatory. If one often thinks about eternity — which one must do here — then nothing is too difficult. This evening there is a film that we are expected to see. I'll write you, dearest wife, some more sentences later. I must not lose my time for this film-activity. You must celebrate the day of penance [at church] without me. You do not need to postpone it, for when I am home we'll have another celebration of it.[18] I hope that I can celebrate Easter in the company of my loved ones. I am also interested in my little rascals. Of course, I'll have some sweets for them with me. Now I must end with many warm greetings to my dearest wife as well as to Mother, the three little ones and my sister-in-law.

I am looking forward to a joyous reunion.

Do not send me any packages. I'll endure without them during these weeks. We always receive enough bread. One would think, however, that the portions of meat could be larger than they are.

From Franz to Franziska

An undated card:

Best wishes on your name day.
From your husband, Franz.
Forgive me if my wishes arrive late.
See you again!

From Franziska to Franz

Monday, March 10, 1941

Most beloved husband!

At the moment I am home alone with the children and have the time to write you a few sentences. Mother is celebrating this day of penance. She went

---

18. Until 1965, a day of Easter penance and communion was observed in Upper Austria. Villagers would attend a special ceremony at their church, after which they would gather at a Gasthaus.

to Tittmoning because there will be the market there today. Resi has gone to church. Today's preaching is for young women. Tomorrow the visiting priest will leave. It is too bad that we cannot keep this priest.[19] One takes note of his engaging words, not of him. Even his trembling voice is glorious to listen to. If all priests could sing so beautifully, there would be many more people, even lukewarm Christians, at church. Although he is young, he has surely already experienced much in life. He has even been imprisoned. While he is here, the N.S. authorities have stayed out of sight. However, their wives have not, nor has G. Hansl, who is not ashamed of himself.

I have received a card from my friend Loisi in Nürnberg, who sends you warm greetings. I also received a letter from you for which I am very grateful. Further, I have received a written summons from the village council, instructing me to come to its office this evening concerning our request for your leave for agrarian work. You will soon see how obliging these gentlemen are!

Resi has received a letter from a friend who wrote that one group of soldiers departed from Burghausen, leaving behind approximately thirty-five pregnant women. The number may be even higher. More soldiers have now arrived there.

Our Loisi had a great accomplishment today. She walked five steps, though no more. She does other things more often, which are not so pleasant. The stork has brought the Schweigers a baby boy.

Warm greetings to you from your wife, Fani, who is always thinking about you.

Be well. See you again!

From Franz to Franziska

Sunday, March 16, 1941

Dearly beloved wife!

Receive my warmest greetings. Yesterday I received with delight your package and your letter. I am very grateful for these. Although you have made too much food, everything tastes so good to me that I could not stop eating what you sent me. Such fine food is not our usual meal! Today I wanted to use some of our lunch time to write you at least a few sentences. Yesterday afternoon I was not free to so do. Today a few free hours were scheduled for the afternoon,

---

19. Anton Gebetsberger (1910–85) was the parish administrator in Ostermiething from August 20, 1940, until 1944. Earlier, as the parish administrator in Königswiesen, he was arrested on February 3, 1940, because of his criticism of National Socialism. Sentenced to six months in prison, he was released from the prison in Garsten on August 3, 1940.

but unfortunately your husband again had to take guard duty — as I am now accustomed to doing. However, I do not believe that I am unfortunate, for as you know, dear wife, one can transform every minute of service into the service of God. Today I was able to attend Mass. This must be a Christian region. The church was full.

Yesterday our officers arranged an evening of comradeship with dancing. They believed that the people in this region would not observe Lent. But they judged wrongly. Very few of the townspeople showed up, even though all had been invited. The young women who came had bobbed their hair. And the farmers boycotted the dance, which was just as well. I am happy that I am no longer young and am now free of the urge to dance.

Dear wife, I'll send you a small package tomorrow or the following day. For a while, I have had a few oranges for you. I thought that I would bring them to you when I began a leave this week. But now I do not want them to go bad. This would be a shame. I'll also include the pacifiers in the package. I have three of them for you. Of course, it would be most desirable if I could arrive before the package does. But this is not likely. In any case, I hope that we'll have a reunion very soon.

Warm greetings to you and also to Mother and my sister-in-law and my dear little ones. Your loving husband, Franz.

From Franz to Franziska

Thursday, March 20, 1941

Dearly beloved wife!

My warm greetings to everyone. I want to write you a few sentences, for it looks again as though I'll not receive a leave soon. Some men have recently left on their leaves, and this means that everyone else will still need to get a leave. Today a man with a farm left, having received an agrarian leave of only two weeks. Perhaps it is best that I wait patiently until our requested leave comes through, especially if it would allow for a long period of time. Hopefully, this will happen soon. Tomorrow evening the replacement troops will arrive. There should not be many of them. Fourteen men will leave for Holland tomorrow to pick up horses. We believed that things would be easier after they finished the military inspection, which occurred yesterday. But this will apparently not be so. They are again requiring us to engage in early morning sports. They want to make the older men young again.

After the inspection I was fortunate. Five of us were told to head off to Raab with nine sick horses. It was no sport. We had to march twenty-two miles. But it seemed like a holiday to me because we were in charge of ourselves and also because I was away for a full day from this tango. Raab is a lovely town. Unfortunately, I did not have the time to send you a card. As soon as we were free of the horses, we had to go immediately to the train station. In order to return here as soon as possible, we took a train that got us here at 11:30 p.m.

Hopefully, all of you are in good health, as I am, thanks be to God. I have not yet given up the hope of seeing you soon.

Warm greetings to you from your husband, Franz.

Greetings also to Mother, my sister-in-law, and my dear little ones.

From Franziska to Franz

St. Radegund, March 25, 1941

Most beloved husband!

Above all, warm greetings to you! I thought that I did not need you to write any more since you would be coming home soon on leave. But I could tell from your last letter that your leave is not yet in sight. I had been very delighted about your leave, but now I am hoping that you can celebrate Easter with us.

Also, I want to thank you for the package and for the recent letters. The oranges were very good. Even Loisi enjoyed them. However, you yourself could have eaten the oranges, especially since you are engaged in a great deal of exertion. I am also happy about the pacifiers. Maridl cannot be without hers, and you cannot find them here.

Today I received a letter from Frau Besenböck. She wrote that her husband has left the military service and gone into the police force. He can remain in Linz. Further, she asked whether her daughter Inge could do her land service with us. What do you think? I shall not write to her until I receive an answer from you. I think that she would not help us much, and that she would have to be paid. Mother shares my concerns.

Hohenauer is now at home on leave. He received merely twelve days.

Forgive me for not writing you for a while. Each day I hoped that you would come home. We have looked for you since the 15th. The days have gone slowly. Perhaps you will still be able to travel home this week. We are longing to see you. I have much to tell you. I am ending my letter, and I hope for our reunion very soon.

Many greetings to you from your loving wife, Fani, and from everyone here!

Thank you for your note, which delighted me. I'm sending you many kisses!

From Franz to Franziska

Hirschbach, March 27, 1941

Dearly beloved wife!

I hope that all of you are still healthy, as I also am, thanks be to God. Since I myself cannot come right now, I want again to write you. Today I spoke with the first lieutenant concerning my leave. I could no longer wait, and I wanted to make use of this time during which the sergeant has been sick for two days. Unfortunately, the first lieutenant was not able to help me because there is currently a ban on leaves. We do not know the reasons for this prohibition. Only eight men were allowed to depart for a Sunday leave. However, I am not entirely without hope. The first lieutenant told me that the [papers concerning an] agrarian leave have in fact arrived for me, and that he has sent them up the ladder to military headquarters. As of today, no decision has yet been sent back. We can hope for the best!

Dearest wife, go ahead and cultivate the oats without me. I would surely like to be with you for this. But while the weather remains beautiful, it is better that you do not wait for me. It would also be good if you could exchange a few sacks of oats so that we could get other seeds. Perhaps you can speak with Schirk or Hirl. They have the best oats. Whether our oats are also among the best is a good question!

How are you doing with the hay? It appears to be not a favorable time for the straw.

Here there is not much that is new. The same tango is always going on. We must continue to remember that after hardship there always follows joy. Perhaps we can expected a joyous Easter. I'll end my letter now with warm greetings to you, my dear wife.

Greetings also to Mother, my sister-in-law, and my dear little ones.

Your husband, Franz.

I am looking forward to our reunion.

From Franz to Franziska

Friday, March 28, 1941

Dearest wife!

Warm greetings to all of you.

I hope that you have received the letter that I wrote yesterday. Today I want to tell you that I learned from my group's commander this evening that the transfer papers have arrived: I am being sent to Enns. I believe that this will not be bad for us, for I can be in position there to receive my agrarian leave more easily.

I am sending you warm greetings perhaps for the last time from here. Your Franz.

From Franziska to Franz

Monday, March 31, 1941

Dearly beloved husband!

Above all, warm greetings to you. Today I received two letters from you. But they did not bring me especially great joy because I have hoped every day for the last three weeks that you would be coming home. But unfortunately I must be satisfied with your letters since you are not able to come home, which would have delighted me. But a small spark of hope did come out of your letters: everything would be different if you would be able to remain home for a few months rather than for only two weeks, during which we'd live with the anxiety that you could receive a telegram calling you immediately back to service.

Today I went to Shirk about the oats. As he had promised me, we hauled out three 110 pound sacks, and I went to exchange them. Tomorrow I'll do the cultivating.[20] Hopefully, I'll hit no hard spots, for I have an awful fear of such places.

I would have been happy if you could have come home so that I could have no shame if something were to go awry. I hope that I'll receive no great rebuke if something not so good should happen. However, we'll undertake things so that you can be at least half pleased with our work. To put you at ease, I can tell you that we finished the straw a long time ago. Pleikner's machine made it possible for us to get the job done quickly. Morever, we already brought home three cartloads of leaves. We need the area for the straw from the meadows. The neighbors are already raking diligently. But I think that it is still too early for this work. In any case, we did not have time for it because we had to cultivate the soil without the cultivator himself. But it initially seemed more difficult than it was in reality. Further, you do not need to be concerned about the hay. We still have an abundance of hay. Of course, we have saved enough work for you. But if you cannot come, we can handle it ourselves.

Further, we have also brought in some wagonloads of brush from the forest. I have already brought in two loads or, to be more accurate, three. You

---

20. Men usually did the demanding work of planting the oats by hand.

know how things go: if one takes too much, more work follows.[21] It is a cross when persons of the weaker gender must do everything. But someone of the stronger gender came along, namely, the forester. But after a few minutes he slipped away.

I'll end my letter now because I have no more space. There are many stories I could tell you. Forgive me for my scribbling. I am terribly tired today. Because I am looking forward with delight to our reunion very soon, I am sending you additional kisses. But when you come home, you must give them back to me. Okay? Greetings, Fani.

From Franz to Franziska

Enns, April 1, 1941

Dearly beloved wife!

Above all, receive my warm greetings. I wish to tell you that I have been here in Enns since Sunday night. Things are not difficult for me here, but this waiting is very painful for me. I am not allowed to travel home until my papers and my agrarian-leave permission are sent from Hirschbach. They want to irritate me a little bit more. Hopefully, I can nevertheless come home this week. I'll telephone you when you should come to Enns with my civilian clothes. Also bring some pieces of smoked meat for Pastor Krenn, and do not forget the ration card for the beef. Warm greetings to you and also to Mother, my sister-in-law, and my little ones.

Your Franz. I am looking forward to seeing you.

From Franz to Franziska

Franz had been at home on leave for a couple of days. [RK]

Enns, April 8, 1941

Dearest wife!

I returned here yesterday at 9:30 p.m. Unfortunately, no papers have yet arrived for me. I was assigned to guard duty today. I do not know what is happening. I must wait patiently and not give up hope. Do not send me anything unless I write to you.

It snowed here today throughout the morning. It must have done the same at home. Perhaps I'll get home to you before this card reaches you.

Warm greetings to everyone. Franz

Your most recent letter has still not arrived here.

---

21. A load would often fall off the wagon and need to be reloaded.

On April 6, hence two days before Franz sent the letter above to Franziska, the Wehrmacht seized Yugoslavia and Greece. With the momentum of these victories, the Führer ordered the attack of the Soviet Union on June 22, 1941 — thereby violating the nonaggression pact between the Reich and the Soviet Union. Soon afterward, people in Germany and Austria learned by word of mouth about the deaths of the Wehrmacht's soldiers on their eastern front and also about the atrocities by Hitler's "elite" troops, the SS. As these reports increased over the next twenty-two months, Franz clarified and strengthened his moral convictions against National Socialism, the Third Reich, and the war. [RK]

Chapter 4

Linz Prison Letters

March 1–May 4, 1943

The tide of the war turned against the Third Reich during Franz Jägerstätter's leave at home. The United States entered the war after the bombing of Pearl Harbor on December 7, 1941. In October 1942, General Montgomery and his British forces routed General Rommel and the Reich's soldiers at Alamein, North Africa. Three months later, on February 2, 1943, General Zhukov and the Soviet army defeated General Paulus and the Sixth Army at Stalingrad (Volgograd). After telling the public of the humiliating and devastating defeat of five hundred thousand soldiers at Stalingrad, Hitler and his inner circle ordered the conscription of more men. At the same time, they tightened their grip on the Reich by executing anyone who questioned the war or seemingly threatened the Führer's rule.

On February 22, 1943, Franz Jägerstätter received notice that he should report for military duty at Enns on February 25.[1] At the end of February, knowing that he would likely never return home, Franz bid farewell to Franziska, his daughters, and his mother, and he walked into the induction center at Enns on March 1. He had to return the next day because of the long line of men ahead of him. On March 2, he declared his refusal to fight, was arrested, and was incarcerated at Linz from March 2 until May 4, when he was taken by train to Berlin.

This fourth chapter consists of fifteen letters from Franz to Franziska and sixteen letters from Franziska to Franz. The first was written by Franz on March 1 from Enns, and the last in this chapter was written by Franz on May 4 from the train station in Regensburg. In his letters, Franz tells his wife of his hope that he might resolve his conflict with the Reich while remaining true to his conscience. In her letters, Franziska keeps her husband informed about their family, farm, friends, and neighbors. Both of them are painfully aware on April 9 that it is their seventh wedding anniversary. They are cautious in what they say, however, because of the censoring of their letters by prison officials. Moreover, they both know what Franz

---

1. For FJ's letter of February 22, 1943, to Pastor Karobath, see Zahn, *In Solitary Witness*, 59. [RK]

wrote in his essays during his twenty-two months at home — the essays contained in this book's second part. [RK]

From Franz to Franziska

Enns, March 1, 1943

Dear wife!

Warm greetings once again from me. Today I shall dare to take this difficult step. Yesterday and this morning, I stayed with the Krenn family, except for the time that I spent in church. I would have stayed another week at home so that I could have participated in many Masses. If I had no friends here in Enns, I would have found things easier. I did not say anything to them about what I intend to do. They will first learn about it through a letter. There would have been a quarrel. I would have found no understanding here. Do not lose heart. Even if one would speak in the spirit of penance and renunciation, one would not find much more understanding. Krenn now receives a civil service salary of 100 marks per month.

Dearest wife, I am once again grateful for all of the love and faithfulness and sacrifice that you have shown me and the whole family — and that you are continuing to show me. It will also be a difficult sacrifice not to have someone with whom you can be angry and perhaps not to have anyone who will hurt you. Love requires it, always striving for more perfection. It will become easier for you. At least you know to whom you can entrust your hurts, the One who has understanding for this and can help you. Even Christ prayed on the Mount of Olives to the heavenly Father. He would have allowed the cup of suffering to pass from him, and we must never forget his request: Lord, not my will be done but yours (see Mark 14:36). Continue to help the poor for as long as you can. Care for the children and also for your father. Do not be angry with mother if even she does not understand us.

Should it be God's will that I do not see you again in this world, then we hope that we shall see each other soon in heaven.

Your husband.

Greetings from me to the children. Speak with them often about the child Jesus and heaven.

Another letter was attached to the first:

To all my loved ones!

I would like to send all of you warm greetings while I am still free.

Become a family that loves one another and forgives one another, then come what will. Readily forgive everyone, including me if you undergo suffering because of me.[2]

Be well. See you again.

Warm greetings to you from your husband, son, father, and son-in-law, Franz.

From Franz to Franziska

Enns, March 2, 1943

Dearest wife!

It is possible for a short moment to send you a few sentences. I reported in yesterday evening. But no bed could be found for me. So I came back again this morning. Think of me [at Mass]. Before noon I reported in, and soon the interrogation got underway. The company commander was not here. A second lieutenant, who followed the protocol, was somewhat critical. He critically presented the whole matter to me, but there was no shouting. Now I'll be transported to Linz. Of course, people are curious. Our pastor spoke about this.[3]

Warm greetings to you from your husband, Franz.

Greetings to my dear little ones, mother, and Resie.

Perhaps things seem worse than they will be.

From Franz to Franziska

Garrison Headquarters
Department I b
Freiheitsstrasse 30, Linz
March 3, 1943

Dearest wife!

Warmest greetings from my new residence. I already have behind me twenty-four hours in this place. I shall be here for the duration of my interrogation. So far it has not been bad. There are five of us in this cell.[4] The food is not bad and sufficient. There is no need to be concerned about my physical well-being. Only do not forget me in prayer. When we submit ourselves fully

---

2. FJ was concerned that Franziska, his daughters, and mother would be ostracized because of his decision. He was also aware that the state might seize his family's home and farm. [RK]

3. FJ had discussed his decision with Pastor Ferdinand Fürthauer at St. Radegund.

4. FJ was incarcerated with four men from the Lorraine region: Lucien Weyland from Metzing, Gregor Breit from Forbach, Emil Bour from Sarregemines, and Albert Boul from Geblingen. For letters written by FJ's cellmates, see Zahn, *In Solitary Witness*, 77–79. [RK]

to God's will, everything will turn out for the good. May things come about as God wants. If only things go well for you!

How are the little ones doing? I wish you the very best on your name-day. May God give you what you yourself wish so long as it does not keep you from eternal salvation. This world's suffering will quickly pass.

Warmest greetings to you from your loving husband, Franz.

Greetings to my three little ones as well as to Mother and Resie.

May God protect all of you. See you again!

Write soon.

Dearest wife, send me a shirt and dress pants. Nothing white. Also, a toothbrush and a clothes brush. But no food. With your next letter, send me a pamphlet on the Mother of God's apparitions in Portugal.[5]

You can also include a bar of soap.

From Franz to Franziska

Linz, March 5, 1943

Dearest wife!

First of all, my warmest greetings. Since this letter will leave here this morning with a cellmate who is being released, it will come to you without being censored. I want to write a few sentences to you. Perhaps you will receive a visit from this fellow who was in our cell and will go free today.

You should not give any testimony to anyone. I advise you to say only one thing if someone asks you whether you agree with my decision not to fight. Honestly say how it has been most difficult for you. I believe that you cannot lighten things for me.

I have no great terror before the lying and cheating [of N.S. officials]. If I did, I would not be sitting here. I want to save my life but not through lies. Officers in Enns wanted to trap me by means of trick questions and so to make me once again into a soldier. It was not easy to stick with my decision. It may become even more difficult. But I trust in God to let me know if it would be better for me to do something different.

I was of course asked what the pastor had said. I had to remain silent concerning his words, however, or he would no longer be free. So I calmly said that he had advised me to report for military service so that then I would do what's best. One comes to saying this when one considers what it would

---

5. New literature on the apparitions of Our Lady of Fatima appeared in 1941–42. The apparitions themselves had occurred in 1917. [RK]

mean for a priest if one were to say something different when asked about the priest's words.

I want also to tell you that there is a farm woman in Enns who has not allowed her children to join the H[itler] Y[outh]. This is a rarity. Yet one does hear that there are people in other places who are not being pulled along by the crowd. I want to say further that I hope that in this cell I shall have a greater religious awareness than I would have in the army. There are many men here to be comforted. One encounters here bitter disillusioned men. I am with men who broke various kinds of laws. What all of them recount is horrible. What people have gone through over these five years and what they have suffered [is terrible]![6] For the slightest offense, people are imprisoned for months. But months and years [of possible imprisonment] are reduced if one agrees to combat duty on the front. What does one offer to people with bitter disillusionments? If they would undergo a conversion, it would be appropriate. There are SS men who have undergone a conversion before dying.

Give my greetings to our pastor, and tell him that people are not often as bad as one may believe. However, they err because of religious ignorance. The pastor should give the greatest energy to Christian teachings, even when the attendance is lacking and when the effects seem empty. In any case, he will save his soul [by teaching the faith].

Warm greetings to you, your husband.

From Franziska to Franz

St. Radegund, March 7, 1943

Much beloved husband!

I received your letter yesterday. I am very grateful for it. Approximately two years have passed since I last needed to write a letter to you. At that time, I was sad of heart that you could not be at home with us. But then I had the anticipation of seeing you again during your leave. However, writing to you now in your current situation makes me terribly sad.

To be sure we know that the loving God and his heavenly Mother will not spare from suffering even those who are pure and without sin. So we sinful human beings should not grumble when the suffering which God sends us becomes greater. We do not refuse it, but trust in the loving God. He will guide everything for the best so that we attain heaven most easily. We do God's will even when it brings sadness. We do God's will even when we do not understand it. I had still a small hope that you would change your decision during your

---

6. FJ is referring to what had occurred in Austria after Hitler's "annexation" of it on March 12, 1938. [RK]

trip [to Enns] because you have compassion for me and [know that] I cannot help [being as I am]. I shall pray to the loving Mother of God that she will bring you back to us at home if it is God's will.

Your three girls are always asking about you. Little Loisi harmlessly asks, "When will Father come home again?" She assumes it to be obvious that you will come home soon and bring sausage with you. The two older girls understand a bit better that you cannot come home so quickly from military duty. Maridi always readily prays [for you]. Rosl even makes small sacrifices for the child Jesus so that our loving Father will allow you to come home. On some occasions she does not eat meat (and you know how much she loves meat). For her, this is a great accomplishment. I do not buy meat for her. Even other things that she enjoys eating she has refused many times. She prays often during the day. For your delight, I can write about only the good things that your children do. You already know well their lesser traits.

Rosi is also concerned about you. She wanted to know everything that was in the letter that you recently sent. We have not yet told the children that you are imprisoned. The villagers of Radegund still believe that you are with the troops. I have told only the pastor about your situation. Karobath and Krenn have written to me, and I have told them where you are being held. They are also rightly concerned about you, and that you have taken on something so difficult. I would have written a letter to you in Enns on Sunday. Karobath and Krenn will perhaps send letters to you when they know your address. What about your letters? Can someone write to you at any time? Are the letters opened?

Breinbauer died on March 1. Tomorrow his mother will travel to Braunau. Schoschl Lobauer is in the hospital. He has suffered as Breinbauer did. Frau Breinbauer will take my letter and packet for you with her so that you will get both of them soon.

Today I have thought with sadness about you. It is the feast of the Sacred Heart of Jesus. There were celebrations in all of the churches. For us, Mass was at 7:00 a.m., because the firing of guns began at 9:00 a.m., after which no one wanted to go out of their houses.[7] The blessing will occur at 7:00 tonight.

How do you find yourself spiritually? Are you experiencing solace? I always fear that when you are no longer. . . .[8] You do not need to be concerned. Everything is going well. I hope that you will receive this letter and the packet. The

---

7. On some religious feasts in German-speaking lands, people gathered for sharpshooting contests, games, and other festivities. [RK]

8. Part of the letter is missing here.

return address on your letter was not easy to read. I'll end my letter with many warm greetings from your loving wife, Fani!

Many greetings from mother, Resi, and your three darlings.

May God protect you. See you again! I shall constantly pray for you.

From Franz to Franziska

Linz, March 11, 1943

Dearest wife!

Hopefully all of you are in good health, as I always am. I want to write you a few sentences, even though I do not know much. I fear that you suffer much because of me. Forgive me for everything if I have done wrong.

I also want to say that I am ready to serve as a military medic, for in this work a person can actually do good and exercise Christian love of neighbor in concrete ways.[9] Doing this would not disturb my conscience. I would also receive punishment [by doing this work]. It would resolve everything, if God wills it. We would see each other again in this world.

How are our little ones doing? Could they sometimes send me something to take up their time? Otherwise, you need not be concerned about me. The food and the conditions here are good.

Warm greetings to you, your husband, Franz.

Many greetings to my dear little ones as well as to Mother, and Resie.

From Franziska to Franz

St. Radegund, March 14, 1943

Much beloved husband!

First of all, the most loving Sunday greetings! Yesterday I received a letter from you, for which I am truly grateful. Hopefully, you have received the package and the letter that I sent to you last Sunday. Perhaps you forgot about these because you said nothing about them. I hope that you received both of them.

With my whole heart, I wish you good luck with your decision that you could do the work of God [as a military medic]. Most of all, I look forward to seeing you again if this is God's will. Your little ones are enthusiastic about

---

9. FJ proposed serving in the medical corps in March, but he may have changed his mind by July. According to his military-appointed defense attorney Friedrich Leo Feldmann, FJ might have avoided execution if he had agreed to noncombatant service as late as the morning of August 9. See Zahn, *In Solitary Witness*, 84–107. However, according to Franziska Jägerstätter, her husband's request for the medical corps was denied. See Erna Putz, "Franz Jägerstätter verweigert den Militärdienst: Gründe, Reichskriegsgericht, Sanitätsdienst," in *Franz Jägerstätter: Christlicher Glaube und Politisches Gewissen*, ed. Alfons Riedl and Josef Schwabeneder (Thaur: Druck-und Verlagshaus Thaur, 1997), 25–41, esp. 38–40. The sticking point was likely FJ's refusal to take the military oath of unconditional obedience to the Führer. See texts no. 85 and no. 87 (pages 235 and 240 below). [RK]

you throughout the day. They pray readily and diligently that the loving God will protect you in every situation, and that you may come home to us again.

We are having beautiful weather. We could use you here for the work, especially to break in the calf. Twice it was harnessed to the dung spreader and pulled it here and there. When there's no one else, one must think about everything. If only you could come home to cultivate the oats, to rake the hay, and to plant the potatoes! You know the large and difficult projects for which we could use you. We have not yet gathered the brushwood. Some neighbors have already obtained two wagonloads. The forester is very nice and does not want to overwhelm us with too much work.[10] Although mother is in pain, she can also work satisfactorily.

Greetings from Frau Schweighofer. She told me that she is also praying for you. Herr Wachter from Ach, whom you perhaps remember, has died in battle. I'll end my letter with a thousand greetings. I remain your faithful wife, Fani.

Greetings also from your three girls, mother and Resi. I'll tell Krenn about your decision [about the medical corps]. The children and I send blessings and are praying for you. See you again!

From Franziska to Franz

St. Radegund, March 18, 1943

Most beloved husband!

First of all, warm greetings!

I received your dear letter with joy. I am deeply grateful for it. Thanks be to God, we are still in good health and hope you are too. Frau Mayer has written.[11] Because the military postal address of her husband has changed, every letter that she wrote him was returned to her. As a result, for a long time he received no mail from her.

Yesterday I went to Stemmer for treatment.[12] Of course, he asked about you and sends you warm greetings. Greetings too from Lid Hofbauer.

Over the past two weeks our well has run out of water. We must carry the water with buckets. If you could come home to improve things, there would be need. Thomas does not trust himself in the well, and so the mud remains down there. We already need rain for the cultivation of the oats; things are dry.

Greetings from your three little women. Maridi says that she will soon go to you and help you fight the Russians so that you can return sooner to us.

---

10. Appointed by the state, a forester supervised the use of land and its resources. [RK]
11. Frau Mayer was the wife of Rudolf Mayer. See Mayer's biographical sketch on page 248 below. [RK]
12. Herr Stemmer was the dentist in Ostermiething.

I'll end my letter with many warm greetings, your faithful wife, Fani.

Greetings from mother and Resi.

Be well. See you again!

Mother went this morning to the Mass in Fridolfing. Obermeier, whom you perhaps knew, has died in battle.

From Franz to Franziska

Linz, March 19, 1943

Most beloved wife!

Yesterday I received your letter with great joy. Thank you for this. I cannot recall whether I also thanked you for the letter that you sent on the preceding Sunday. Hopefully, all of you are well. Thanks be to God, I remain well.

I can see that things are not the best for you, my dear wife. With troubles and concerns, also with all of the work. If we could sometime change places for a week, the rest here would be good for you, and I could help with the work at home. I am placing my future in God's hands. He will direct everything as it is best for us. This means fearing God more than human beings.

St. Joseph — whom we implore for his intercession during this month and especially today when we celebrate his feast — will surely come to help us, though this help may not come as we hope. For the people who enjoy freedom there is, I believe, no more beautiful feast for St. Joseph than today's.

Dear wife, I wish to ask something of you. Would it be possible to put some pieces of edelweiss in the next letter? A cellmate here requested that I get him edelweiss. He is a young Frenchman who was condemned to death a few weeks ago. He would like to send edelweiss to his beloved as a farewell gift. She loves flowers.

If you have not yet sent me envelopes, then do not do so for the time being. I have bought some military stationery.

My three girls will already be running barefoot and picking flowers. It must be truly lovely at home now. What is new otherwise in Radegund? I knew Wachter from Ach. So one man after another must lose his life in battle. Is Franz Pate still in Braunau?[13] I'll end my letter for today with warmest greetings. Your loving husband, Franz

Many greetings to my little ones as well as to Mother and Resie.

Do not forget me in your prayers. See you again!

---

13. Franz Pate was drafted into the army in the winter of 1942 and was wounded at Stalingrad on September 9, 1942. After recuperating in field hospitals, he was stationed in Braunau beginning in January 1943.

From Franziska to Franz

St. Radegund, March 21, 1943

Greetings in God! Most beloved husband!

Our little ones have insisted that I write you about them, telling of course only the good things that they are doing. I am making my report to you. I would not surprise you by telling you about their daily lapses that would bring you no joy. Rosi, Maridi and even little Loisi said to send you rich greetings. They want you to come home soon. They pray constantly for you. [They say that] if you come home, they wouldn't quarrel anymore. It would indeed be wonderful if you would come home again. For Loisi, it has gone on too long. Today she did not want me to lock the door to the house [at night]. In tears she said that Father will come home, but will not be able to get in.

Dear husband, our girls are full of hope for your return soon, and I would rejoice with them if it would be God's will to include you again soon in our family circle. However, one does not know God's eternal puzzles, and one must accept everything with gratitude that God sends us. The loving God will not send us a cross and more suffering than we can bear. He will lead us so that we do not forget him, so that we will attain the proper goal in heaven for which God has created us, and so that we may rejoice together with him eternally.

Dear husband, I would like to ask you to write a few words directly to our children. They are always asking whether you have written anything for them. I'll end my letter with warm greetings, your loving wife, Fani.

Also, many greetings from mother, Resi, and the children!

Also, greetings from Hirl. Be well. See you again.

> To heaven I must go.
> I have definitely decided this.
> May it cost what it will.
> For heaven, there is nothing that is too much for me!

From Franziska to Franz

St. Radegund, March 24, 1943

Dearest husband!

I received today your letter of March 19. Thank you for this. Today we finished the cultivation of the oats. The calf now walks with such ease that it can be with the cows. You have received an invitation to the major celebration of the men in the [Marian] Congregation on Sunday, March 28, at Burghausen.[14] I would love you to be there.

Since March 1, the upper mill is closed. However, the owner hopes that he will soon be able to mill again.[15] He may be a bit naive. Further, the apartment building in Holzhauser has been taken down. A new one will be built. The butter vats and the centrifuge have been closed to those farmers who have produced no milk or too little milk. A son of the Schober family in Tarsdorf has died in battle, and a son of the Hofbauers is missing. Lakei must now report for military duty. Herr Mayer has sent a letter to you.

Rosl has asked me to tell you that she is doing some of the chores here. So too are her two sisters. The three girls send you many greetings and kisses, and they hope that you will come home soon. We know that you will do so as soon as you are able to do so, dear Father. We are in good health, and hope that you are, too. I'll end my writing, for I have nothing more worthwhile to tell you. Please forgive me. I am tired. The weather is continually lovely, and so we have much to do. I have not yet said all of my daily prayers. I remain continually concerned about you.

Warm greetings from your loving wife, Fani! Many greetings, too, from mother, Resi, and the children! Be well. See you again!

> Mary with the child Jesus love [us].
> Give to us all of your blessings.

Franz Pate is still at Braunau.

From Franz to Franziska

Linz, March 25, 1943

Most beloved wife!

Warmest thanks for your letter of March 18, which I received yesterday with great joy. I am in good health, and I hope that you are as well. I have thought a lot about what's going on with the water. Perhaps it will rain soon. I wish that I could take a leave in order to clean out the well. Have you already brought in the straw from the pasture? If the weather holds out, perhaps you could have the green fodder already by Easter. Yesterday we saw apricot buds already blooming in our garden. These would be wonderful for our children.

---

14. FJ and Franziska were members of the Marian Congregation, a Jesuit-sponsored religious association for laity, dedicated to the service of others and devotions to Mary.

15. The Jägerstätters brought their grain to the mill in Ach. The owner often returned more milled grain to Franziska than she had actually brought. Franziska has recalled, "He was a devout man and not a Nazi."

I believe that it would be better to tell the children where their father is rather than always to fib to them. Although one has almost no activities here, it is not necessary to waste the day so long as one can pray. For this, there is plenty of time, and then life is not for nothing.

What about the celebration with the Congregation? Did the invitation arrive? Today is a beautiful day for the feast of the Annunciation when Christ took on human form out of love for us. The king of heaven and earth has done so much for us sinful human beings. We may call ourselves Christian, yet out of pride we cannot bring ourselves to forgive our fellow human beings. When something difficult comes about, whoever remains in love will receive everything for the best.

Dear wife, be so good as to write down the communion petition for the month of April in your next letter.[16] I am grateful for the envelopes and the pad of paper. I have still not received the letter from Krenn. I do not know whether he knows my address. I have written to no one from here other than to you and Lang. The most important thing for me is to remain in contact with my dear family.

Fortunately, I left a little room here. I had hoped that I would receive still today a letter from you. And it arrived at the evening meal. I am very grateful for this.

And now to my little ones! Dear Rosl, Maridl, and Loisi, I am very grateful for your dear greetings which you sent me and which have brought me great joy. I am very grateful, too, that you pray often for me, and that, as I hope, you are being well behaved. I think of you often, and also pray for you. It will bring me great joy if I am able to see you again soon. I want to urge you not to quarrel. Also, do not lie.[17] And at meals be content with what you receive. Then, I believe, the heavenly Father will bring it about that I shall come home to you. Since this will not happen soon, Mother must be able to lock the door at night. I shall come home during the day. I ask you to obey your mother and also your grandmother and Resie. Warm greetings to my three dear girls. I pray that the child Jesus and the loving heavenly Mother will watch over you until we see each other again.

Many warm greetings also to you my dear wife as well as to Mother and Resie.

---

16. In keeping their devotion to the Sacred Heart of Jesus, Catholics were encouraged to receive communion once each month in the spirit of atonement and simultaneously to have in mind the pope's intentions.

17. During the final weeks of his life, FJ reiterated the Commandment against lying (Exod. 20:7, 16) as he explained why he could not take the oath of loyalty to the Führer. [RK]

From Franziska to Franz

St. Radegund, March 28, 1943

Greetings in God to you, dearest husband!

A beautiful, though lonely Sunday is almost over. For you the days pass even more silently. For us the children are always fun. During the whole day, they were in the meadow and busily picking flowers — so many flowers that we have filled up all of our vases. They had a wonderful time with the flowers.

Today I visited Frau Wiese. She does not have much hope for her current condition. One illness gives way to another. She again has rheumatism in her bones. She has great pain and can no longer move. Her husband must lift her and gently put her down. Yet he has much to do. He has received help from Vevi Schneck, for his own daughter is rarely at home.

Gasthaus Hofbauer has been closed. Lidwina told me that the Hofbauers tried everything [to stay open]. They even made big contributions.[18] Nevertheless, they were forced to close. Meanwhile, Gasthaus Habl is still open, even though no one ever went there. A result of their contributions, one must guess, and also of their business jealousy.

The well went dry on Thursday. On Friday we dug it out, and now we need a good rain. At the moment we must carry home all of our water. The first time we did this we did not of course bring enough. You can imagine why. The second time we poured in hot water. On the same day Lang also had to begin redigging his well, and things have still not gone better for him. He should have dug out his well more often.

Warm greetings to you from Mari Damoser. Rosl brought me some violets to put into this letter. When you receive this letter, you will not see much [of the violets]. I should also put in some primroses. But these too would be dead by the time you would receive them. Your little ones think of you throughout almost the whole day. When they see beautiful flowers, they immediately say that they want to send them to their father who will laugh when he receives them and will be delighted by them. Many greetings from your loving children and from your loving wife, Fani.

Also from mother and Resi.

Be well. See you again.

---

18. The N.S. Party may have punished the Hofbauers because their son, Pastor Johann ("Pleikner") Hofbauer Jr., had publicly criticized National Socialism, for which he was imprisoned. See his biographical sketch on page 248 below. [RK]

From Franziska to Franz

St. Radegund, March 31, 1943

Greetings to you in God, most beloved husband!

We have received your dear letter with gratitude and great joy. All of us are in good health, thanks be to God, and we hope that you are too.

Father arrived yesterday and feels already at home with us. Your loving sentences that you wrote to the three girls have brought them great joy. Rosl in particular is always interested in your letters. I must read everything to her. Yesterday Strohhofer from the mill drove us to Bachmeier in Tittmoning. More people from our village are driving there. We received wonderful flour, as good as anything available since the war began. One must therefore be satisfied. You should be grateful to Strohhofer for driving us there and back. He did not demand any payment and would not accept any money.

Mother also received your letter today and is grateful for it. She will not, however, write you because of the censoring. I'll close my letter now, and I'll write more next time.

Many greetings from your loving wife, Fani. Also from mother, the children, Resi, and father. Be well. See you again.

From Franzsika to Franz

St. Radegund, April 1, 1943

Greetings to you in God, most beloved husband!

We had true April weather today. So there's a lot of water in the well, and we have less work. We had already brought home the straw in March.[19] We had used Schmid's haying machine, which cuts up everything. We got quite a lot done because we did it together.

We have received a new price for electricity, a basic tax. Energy should be less expensive, especially for the people who have many electrical machines. The change will not make much difference for us. Those on military leave are here. Gänshänger. Also Josef Strohhofer and Toni Kohlbacher.

Rosi's husband [Lehner] again had some good fortune. For a long time he was in a hospital in Munich, and he recently returned home. The other day the arrogant British flew over Munich and caused much destruction. They killed many people. They even bombed the hospital that Lehner had left a few days earlier. There were two hundred dead at the hospital. What these people must have undergone!

---

19. Sedge grass from the Salzach-Au area.

Dearest, yesterday I paid our pastor the stipend for a Mass that he will say on the 9th of this month in remembrance of us, in gratitude for our [seventh] wedding anniversary, and for our intentions. How sad that we cannot celebrate our anniversary together.

> Heart of Jesus, dwelling place of righteousness and love,
> bestow on us wisdom, righteousness, temperance, and courage.
> Amen.[20]

Warm greetings from your loving wife, Fani, as well as from [my] father, [your] mother, Resi, Rosl, Maridl, and Loisl.

Be well. See you again.

> Mary with your child love us,
> give us all your blessings.

From Franziska to Franz

[undated]

Dear husband!

Our relatives are telling me that I should visit you so that I have certainty about your situation. Many think that things are not going well for you. Although I cannot help you and can send you nothing, I would very much like to visit you. But I do not know whether I may visit at all or only for a few minutes. So I would like to ask you, what do you think?

It is very painful for both of us. I believe that you do not feel as unfortunate as many here think, for you have — as I hope — a great trust in our loving Lord Jesus and in his heavenly Mother. They will also send us what is best for us.

Many greetings from your faithful wife, Fani.

> Mary with your child love [us],
> give us all your blessings!

From Franz to Franziska

Linz, April 4, 1943

Most beloved wife!

Many thanks for your dear letters of March 23 and 28, which I have received with joy. Soon we shall come to the end of the second Sunday, dedicated to the Sacred Heart of Jesus, that I have had to spend here.

---

20. A communion prayer from Mass.

Concerning your visiting me, which you wrote about, I would like to advise you not to do so at this time. Perhaps at Easter, for by then something will be decided about me. My case has still received no trial.

I readily believe that most people are of the view that things are bad for me here. But it is not the same in every prison. Here we get enough to eat every day. Also everything is well prepared so that a person can have an appetite. Our cooks are the cloistered nuns since this was a convent of the Ursuline Sisters. You do not get fat with these meals, as you can easily imagine. They did not lock us up in order to make us fat. But things could be much worse.

You know, dear wife, that I do not engage in this struggle in order to make my life wonderful. As long as God's grace does not abandon me and I do not lose my faith, nothing can be unfortunate. If our hearts are often sad, nevertheless we know indeed that our sadness will be changed to joy. If we could extend our lives to one hundred years, this would still not be half a second in relation to eternity. Yet we human beings sometimes act as though the opposite were the case.

Concerning your visiting me, I can also mention that a visit cannot extend beyond fifteen minutes. You could ask Pleikner about the details. Seeing you again would clearly bring me great joy. Yet I would like to advise you to wait for a while. Dearest wife, we now patiently carry our crosses farther until God will take them from us.

This week you will receive a package with my shirt and pants and three oranges. I ask that you send me another shirt and a pair of pants. It would be better if you would send me a shirt without a collar, perhaps one of the blue workshirts.

Thanks be to God that you again have water so that at least you do not need to carry it. I believe that you already have enough work. Hopefully, all of you at home are in good health as I am, thanks be to God.

And now my dear little ones, I am grateful to you that you think so often about your father and pray for him. Unfortunately, I have not seen the flowers that your mother included in her letter. You must also arrange your flowers beautifully for your heavenly Father. Today receive beautiful greetings from your father.

Dear wife, I would like to advise you to buy a pair of scythes. So you will at least have one sharp blade for reaping.

Warm greetings to you. Your husband, Fr.

Best greetings to Mother and Resie.

Greetings also to those who have asked you to give me greetings.

From Franziska to Franz

St. Radegund, April 4, 1943

Greetings in God, most beloved husband!

Today we are having a glorious Sunday. The first days of April were stormy and cold. This weather does not suit my lungs.

This afternoon there is the talk on penance for married couples. You are warmly invited to attend. On Tuesday, the talk will be for the village's young women. It was held last Wednesday for the young men because some of them were required to depart yesterday for military training and will not return home before Easter.

Mother went to Tarsdorf today. There was a Mass for Josef Hörndlbauer, thirty-three years old, who died in the war. Perhaps you knew him. Also, Ferdl Som was shot in the chest.[21] He is now in Warsaw. Moni does not yet know how it occurred. Herr Höft and Hans Wolfpauli are home on leave. Schossl Lohbauer came home on Friday from the hospital in Braunau. He was operated on and still has a large swelling. He'll need a long time to recover.

Maridi and Loisi have picked violets, which I again must send you in a letter. Warm greetings from Frau Adam. Thomas Schirk is in Poland. Frau Schirk is still not in entirely good health and must remain inside. Franz Jahrl is also in Poland. Because today's weather is so good, all of us could go together to church. The three girls are delighted when they can come along. You surely know that today is dedicated to the Sacred Heart of Jesus.

I am closing this letter with many greetings, your loving wife, Fani. Also, greetings from your three girls. Loisi has told me to write that you should come home soon to play. Also, greetings from mother and Resi. Father went home on Saturday and will return in better weather to help with the work. In bad weather he does very little work but does not want to remain inside because the children are too playful for him.

Be well. See you again!

From Franziska to Franz

St. Radegund, April 7, 1943

Greetings in God, most beloved husband!

We have received your dear letter with great joy. Many thanks. Our days with talks on penance are behind us. Many people participated. We received help from a very nice Capuchin [friar]. The talk on Christian life went for an

---

21. FJ's cousin, Ferdinand Sommerauer ("Ferdl Som"), died from this wound.

hour. It is too bad that the people who need to hear these words always fail to attend the talks.

We had a very sad death here. Mari Damoser's thirty-three-year-old daughter, Kathi—her only daughter—died after a short illness. Perhaps you knew her. Amid a large gathering, she was buried on Wednesday in Radegund. She had the grippe. In this bad condition, she had resumed her work. Among other things, she had to spread the chemical fertilizer. Then she came down with blood poisoning and was unconscious for a few days. The pastor gave her communion. She died without regaining consciousness. She had worked with Mayer in Schmidham and died with Frau Damoser at her side. She was waked there and prayed for with Damoser. Thomas Jahrl is here; he said the Requiem Mass.

I am closing my letter with many greetings, your loving wife, Fani. Also, many greetings from M, R, R, M, L, and V.[22]

From Franz to Franziska

Linz, April 9, 1943

Greetings in God! Dearest wife!

Above all, my deepest thanks for the three letters which I have received from you with great joy during this week. Despite all of the work that you have, you remain concerned to give your husband joy, which I perhaps do not deserve. I have a great interest in every sentence that you write to me. Please forgive me for not writing to you more often, for I cannot tell you much that is new here. I have still not received a trial.

Dearest wife, it was seven years ago today that we promised each other love and faithfulness before God and the priest, and I believe that we have faithfully kept this promise. Moreover, I believe that God still confers his grace on us, even if we must live apart, so that we can be faithful to this promise until the end of our lives. When I look back and observe all the good fortune and the many graces that have come to us during these seven years, I see that many things often border on being miracles. If someone were to say to me that there is no God or God has no love for us, and, if I were to believe this, I would no longer understand what has happened to me.

Dearest wife, if we should find ourselves anxious about the future, we must not forget the thought that God has preserved us and favored us and will not abandon us, and we must not grow weary of our struggle for heaven. Then our good fortune will continue into eternity. While I sit now behind prison walls,

---

22. Greetings from "mother, Resie, Rosi, Maridi, Loisi, and father." [RK]

I believe I can build further on your love and faithfulness. And if I should be cut off from this life before you are, look beyond my grave and know that I sat here not as a criminal.[23]

It delights me very much that you are having a Mass celebrated today for us. I know that you have thought especially about me.

Your husband warmly greets you. Indeed, if human beings renew themselves every seven years, then today you have a new husband! The best of greetings also to Mother, my parents-in-law, and Resie. Greetings also to our pastor. See you again.

My dear children, I am grateful for the violets which you sent to me. I can see that you do not forget your father who does not forget you and would love to be with you. However, the heavenly Father wants to have it otherwise. We shall always be able to rejoice together in heaven if you become well-behaved children.

Dear children, we must give thanks to the heavenly Father because he has sent a good wife to me and a mother to you. Always have love for your mother, and you can do this only by being obedient to your mother. If you are obedient to your mother, she will not die soon but will become even healthier. There are many children who no longer have a father and a mother or not a good mother as you have. At the moment you cannot run outside with bare feet. Early today we had snow here. It may soon become warmer for you. Greetings to you from your father who frequently thinks of you.

Dearest wife, if you still are interested in the new motor, you could ask Zelbak about it.

Greetings to our neighbor. My thanks to him for the card.

From Franz to Franziska

Linz, April 11, 1943

Greetings in God, dearest wife!

Another sad Sunday comes to an end. But I do not want it to end without me writing a few sentences to you. Yesterday morning I asked whether I could go to church on Sundays. In the evening I received the decision that it would not be allowed because two men must accompany me. I'll try again at Easter. Perhaps I'll have good luck then. It would not be too much for me to walk even

---

23. FJ reiterated this point during the final weeks of his life. See text no. 85, page 235 below. Church teachings, especially since the Congress of Vienna (September 1814–June 1815), had stressed obedience to civil authorities as well as to ecclesiastical authorities. As a result, it was widely assumed that civil disobedience was sinful. [RK]

sixty miles in order to attend the sacrifice of the Mass. This situation requires patience and reconciling oneself to one's God-given fate.

The words which Christ said are true: my yoke is sweet, and my burden is light [see Matt. 11:30]. When I see my cross and suffering in relation to the suffering of other people, I must say to myself that God has laid on me one of the smallest crosses.

Books were distributed in the cells last Sunday, and I had great luck. Among these books was a beautiful one, in which there are the sermons of John Chrysostom and other saints. Although most of the men here gladly read in order to kill time, they also gladly left this book for me. In this situation one can recognize the value of our faith. We pray diligently that the light of faith does not die out in us.

Dearest wife, you have had difficult days because of this weather. Hopefully, it will be beautiful soon. How are things going for you with the haying? Has Wagner already begun [to help] with the wagon?

Warm greetings to you from your loving husband, Franz. Best greetings to Mother and Resie. Also, greetings to my three little ones! See you again!

Perhaps you again have a few envelopes available. I'll soon be out of them.

From Franziska to Franz

St. Radegund, April 11, 1943

Greetings in God, dearest husband!

Your package arrived. The girls are grateful to you for the oranges. They are delighted with them. They are saving them for their pussy willow branches.[24] Rosi has set aside a beautiful apple, which I am supposed to send to you if it is okay to do so. We cannot imagine how you obtained these oranges. You should have eaten them. We still have apples.

Should I once again send you handkerchiefs, or can you wash the ones you have? Our three little girls went today with Resi to see the pony at the Schirks. They recently obtained this pony. It is lively and energetic. Afterward, we went to church.

I send you warm greetings. Also, greetings from our children. And greetings from mother and Resi.

Your loving wife, Fani.

Be well. See you again!

---

24. In the procession on Palm Sunday, villagers carried pussy willow branches decorated with ribbons, fruit, and cookies.

From Franz to Franziska

Linz, April 18, 1943

Greetings in God! Dearest wife!

I received this week your package with its contents. I am grateful for this. I am in good health, and I hope that all of you are too. With great joy our little ones will go to church today [Palm Sunday] with the pussy willow branches. No one could wish, I believe, for more beautiful weather. The fresh green of the grass is good for a person, especially if you pay attention to it. Someone with freedom may not notice it.

This week enables us to bear our destiny more easily with courage and strength. What is our small suffering in relation to what Christ suffered during this Holy Week. Whoever does not suffer with and for Christ will not also rise to new life with Christ [see Rom. 6:8]. While the cross that God or we ourselves place on ourselves sometimes presses on us a little, it will never become as hard and difficult as that which Satan often lays on his followers. How many people break under this burden and then take their own lives! We may condemn only the act of suicide, but never the person who commits suicide.[25]

I cannot tell you anything about my future. I again had no trial this week. Dearest wife, if I cannot celebrate a joyful Easter with you, I can at least wish you from afar a joyful and peaceful Easter celebration. Even if there exists no glimpse of a peaceful Easter, nevertheless we must not lose hope. If it is God's will that we can no longer celebrate together in the trusted family circle a joyful Easter in this world, then we await with full confidence the day when the eternal Easter Sunday morning breaks. Then no one from our family will be missing, and we can rejoice together forever.

Concerning your visiting here, I would like to advise you against it at this time. As long as I receive no trial, I'll not be quickly transferred to a different prison.

You do not need to send me handkerchiefs. I can wash them here myself. How do things look there with the fruit trees? Which ones are blooming? I'm ending for today with heartfelt greetings to you, dear wife, as well as to Mother and Resi.

See you again!

My dear children! You are now delighted that it is so warm. You can again pick flowers, and at Easter roll eggs.[26] Of course, eat them when they break.

---

25. This statement, along with his statement on April 11 concerning "another sad Sunday," suggests that FJ may have struggled with depression during his incarceration. [RK]

26. According to this Easter custom, colored hard-boiled eggs are rolled on a flat surface. The winner is the one whose egg goes the farthest.

Dear Rosl, thank you for the beautiful apple which you sent me. I am saving it today and eating it tonight with great reverence. Hopefully, the oranges are still good, for I had already saved them for a while. Be good so that your mother does not get angry with you.

Warm greetings to you from your father.

From Franziska to Franz

I often think with love about you!

St. Radegund, April 18, 1943

Greetings in God, most beloved husband!

Today I have an opportunity to write you a brief letter. Please forgive me for not writing you for a whole week. We had a lot of work, and so I did not get to write. This week we finished the raking and gathered wonderful straw. Father also helped us, even though the work was terribly hard for him. During these days, Mother has whitewashed the family room, the kitchen, the front of the house, and the entry. All of which now look beautiful.

On Friday I went to Burghausen and bought flowers. I purchased eight zinnias, which are large and very beautiful. The woman gardener knew me from previous years, and I received the most beautiful flowers because they will go into the church. Mari Thomas gave me 10 marks for shopping. Our primroses are almost completely dried up. Also, some other flowers no longer look good. In May I'll buy some more flowers. It is unfortunate that you are not here to arrange everything. You are much better at this!

The pastor requested that we always take care of these matters, and I promised him that we would. On Tuesday and Wednesday we'll clean the church. You are invited to help us. Warm greetings to you from Thomas Jahrl. Mari's aunt Maria is visiting us this week and sends you greetings. I tried to convert her but my words were not effective.[27] This is too bad. Maria is so deluded that she thinks we're dumb. It would be a miracle if she would get more intelligent. Of course, nothing is impossible for God. Her son Hans is now locked up. He apparently became a dissenter and was imprisoned. For how long, I do not know. Maria's daughter-in-law Rosi Zauner is not much smarter. She cannot be consoled. She was briefly here and said that things are getting worse. She was inconsolable.

---

27. Maria Huber and her son Hans belonged to the Jehovah's Witnesses, which the National Socialists were intent on persecuting.

On Wednesday we had a marriage ceremony. Mari Überreiter married a certain (Kärntner) Brandstätter. He is on military leave until Good Friday, then he returns to Russia. It will be a painful farewell for the newlyweds.

Franz Pate has left Braunau. He is again on the move. Where they have sent him is wherever one may guess. We are easily finishing with the haying. It is always so warm that one can already see the green fodder. Tomorrow the sow will be butchered. I am happy about this because she has become more and more difficult. She would not eat the grain.

Today we were in the church in the early afternoon. It was Palm Sunday, which our little ones have looked forward to. Each held a pussy willow branch to which a lovely orange was attached. They went in the procession with the other children. Even Loisi is no longer very shy.

I am grateful for the two letters that I received from you this week.

Today I was with Jungwirt and received the promised pound [of butter]. They have new building projects: another stall, and also the side of the house to finish with Hansl Kreil. In general, they are overwhelmed with work.

I'll close my letter with many warm greetings, your loving wife, Fani. Also, many greetings from your children and from Father, Mother and Resi. Also, I wish you a happy, peaceful Easter day. Be well. See you again!

From Franziska to Franz

St. Radegund, April 21, 1943

Greetings in God, dearest husband!

I am sending you a few sentences, even though I do not have much to tell you. Krenn wrote to me and sends greetings to you. Krenn is truly an empathetic person. Tonight the Tiefenhaler cow gave birth. It did so without our assistance as happens most times. Thanks be to God, nothing went wrong. Now there's a female calf, which is important to me since you cannot be at home to buy one.

Lang also has a cow that gave birth on Sunday. However, the calf was crosswise. Jungwirt turned it with great trouble, and seven or eight people had to pull it out with much effort. Neither the cow nor the calf are doing well at the moment.

Dearest, our fruit garden is becoming glorious. The pear and plum trees are already in full bloom, and the apple trees are partially so. It is unfortunate that you cannot be here. I wish you a good, peaceful, and happy Easter day. Also, our children and Mother wish you a happy Easter! Also, Father and Resi wish you all the best. Warmest greetings to you from your loving wife, Fani.

Be well. See you again!

From Franz to Franziska

Linz, April 25, 1943

Greetings in God, most beloved wife!

Above all, thank you for your letter with the envelopes, which I received with joy on Thursday. I can no longer write you as often because we are now allowed to send something out only on Mondays. We may still receive mail as often it comes.

"Christ has risen, alleluia!" So the church rejoices today. When we have to endure hard times, we must and can rejoice with the church. What is more joyful than that Christ has again risen and gone forth as the victor over death and hell. What can give us Christians more comfort than that we no longer have to fear death.

Dearest wife, you can well imagine how these days of grace are for me in prison. However, with God's help one can overcome everything. One need not always think about what one cannot have at the moment. I believe that even if our sufferings in this world were to become great, the poor souls in purgatory would still like to change places with us at any time. So we should help them as much as we can.

Dearest wife, I can tell you the joy of these days. I am still a fortunate child. Early on Holy Thursday I requested to go to church on Easter. I was not permitted to do so. However, I was promised a priest who in fact came that same day at 3:00 p.m.[28] So I was able to fulfill my Easter duty, for the priest had brought the Blessed Sacrament with him. On Friday some others asked to speak with a priest, and so early on Saturday I was again able to receive Holy Communion. There were seven of us.

Otherwise, not much is new here. Up until now I have not been sick, and I am entirely well. So one week passes into another. The chief thing is only that when no more days pass, death would not necessarily mean eternal life for us.

It delights me, my beloved, that you are still making sacrifices for our dear house of God, even though you have much work to do at home. But no sacrifices should be too great for us for the eternal reward. If athletes want to attain their prizes, they must undergo great sacrifices and troubles.

The graves must again be glorious.[29] There are already many flowers in bloom. In a few days you will again adorn the Marian altar in order to honor our dear Mother of God. She will definitely not abandon us.

---

28. The priest was Pastor Franz Baldinger. For his letter concerning FJ, see Zahn, *In Solitary Witness*, 75–77. [RK]

29. During Holy Week, people commemorated the burial of the crucified Jesus by placing flowers and candles at the graves of family and friends.

Now this Easter Sunday comes slowly to an end. How many must still come to an end until there will be an Easter Sunday with peace? It is good that one cannot see into the future. So we accept each day as God sends it to us.

I am closing my letter with many warm Easter greetings to you, dear wife, as well as to Mother, Father-in-Law, Resie, and friends. Be well. See you again.

My dear children, how did things go for you with the Easter eggs? Were you so strong that you broke a lot of them during the egg rolling? Now you will not be able to pick all of the flowers. Now Mother or Resie will scold you when you roll around too much in the grass.

Your father warmly greets you.

Do not forget me.

From Franziska to Franz

St. Radegund, April 25, 1943

Greetings in God, most beloved husband!

Now is the most holy Easter day almost over. This morning as well as this afternoon all of us, including the little ones, were in church. There was beautiful weather today. It was also beautiful on Good Friday when Resi and I rode our bicycles to Altötting to visit the graves.[30] All were beautifully adorned. I did not forget you in my prayer. Also, I would have sent you a card from there, but I brought it home because I forgot to mail it there. I could have used you here with us to adorn the graves. The Habl boy was not aware of things, and I did not know much. The pastor had little concern for it. He left it to us because he is so forgetful.

Franzl Pate has a three-day leave. He and the others are quartered in private homes in Mattighofen. They have little to do. Greetings to you from him.

I would like to ask you to thank Father for his work here. He is always with us. Only on Saturday did he ride home. He accepts no payment. He can clearly no longer do much, but you know how the older people are. A written greeting from you would delight him, and I would be grateful to you, too. Father reads everything you write to me.

All those whom you invited here for Christmas were again our guests here today.[31] Also, Franzl Pate.

I am closing with many greetings, your loving wife, Fanj. Also, greetings from your children, and from mother and Resi.

---

30. Altötting is a pilgrimage center for devotions to the Blessed Mother. It is located approximately sixty miles east of Munich. [RK]

31. Among the guests for Easter dinner was FJ's daughter Hildegard Auer.

From Franziska to Franz

St. Radegund, April 30, 1943

Greetings in God, most beloved husband!

We received your Easter Sunday letter with great joy. Thank you very much for it. I thought about you continually during the day, [wondering] whether you had received a few hours of free time. I did not forget you in my prayers.

Tomorrow is already May 1. There is the first of the May devotions. You will be thinking every evening of these devotions with deep longing. How joyful it is in all churches in order to honor our heavenly Queen most worthily! You should bear everything patiently, and then in your cell you can gain merit for eternity.

Our fruit trees — the pear and the apple as well as the plum — are blossoming here more strongly than ever before, at least since I have been here. I see how beautiful it is when I go walking with the children. But it is also sad that you cannot be with us to marvel at the beauty of nature. If you were, it would be doubly beautiful.

Gänshänger was most unfortunate during his military leave. On Easter Monday, he cut off four fingers in the feed grinder, similar to what Frau Jahrl did. On such a high feast day he should not have been working. God has often punished such things. Of course, the police arrived. He is now under suspicion for self-mutilation. People are speaking much about all of this. In my view, he is a poor individual whether he did it to himself or not.

On Sunday there is a Mass for the Fröhlichs' son. I am sure you knew him.

Today, the last day of April, we have begun to cut the hay. We finished planting the potatoes on Wednesday. Frau Grün Schuster has an acre with us. She asked if she could do this. The poor woman.

I send you greetings from Fani Jahrl, Kathi Bäcker, Lidwina Hofbauer, and Frau Breinbäur.

Since no mail goes out on Saturday and Sunday, I have not yet mailed this letter. So, I will add more to it. Today — Sunday, May 2 — was dedicated to the Sacred Heart of Jesus. It was also First Communion Sunday for us. There were three girls and four boys for their First Holy Communion. We took our three girls to church. Rosi took a great interest in everything, which she had never before seen or heard. Hopefully, she will become a good Christian.

The people here who own sheep must turn over [to the Reich] 3.3 pounds of every pile of wool and can keep only 1.1 pounds for themselves. If they have large sheep, they receive 4.4 pounds in a year. It is good that we no longer have sheep.

Krenn has written to me that Mayer is now with the Panzer division and is already on the front. Also, warm greetings from Krenn.

I am closing my letter with many greetings, your loving wife, Fanj. Greetings too from your children, from Father, Mother, and Resi.

> Heart of Jesus, you are the source of all virtue.
> Adorn us with yourself and
> with all of the virtues for our situation! Amen

Be well. See you again!

From Franz to Franziska

Linz, May 2, 1943

Greetings in God, most beloved wife!

Many thanks for your two letters, which I received with joy during the past week. Reading between the lines, I sense that you are well. And I too am always well. We have the third Sunday dedicated to the Sacred Heart of Jesus, which I cannot celebrate in my home. Now the days of the Easter celebration have passed. Hopefully, our little ones have become masters of the Easter eggs, yes?

I still cannot say how my future will unfold. There are some men here who have been here longer than I, and they have still not had a trial. This means that one must wait patiently. What comes next is seldom better.

Now there begins the beautiful month of May, which is the most beautiful month, especially for those who live on the land because there is usually not as much work as there is during the other summer months. Nature does not notice the misery that has now come upon people. Even though I cannot see much here, I can nevertheless imagine that everything is a more beautiful green and blossoming more than in past years. There is hardly a day that begins gray. One can hear blackbirds loudly singing outside our windows. Even the birds have, it seems, more peace and joy—although they are not rational animals—than we human beings who have the gift of understanding.

We know what great reward awaits us after this short earthly existence. It should not sadden us very much if we must do without many things now and renounce what our hearts desire now for we shall be rewarded a thousandfold in eternal life. If we shall be content with what we are able to have at the moment, we will no longer belong with those—spoken of in the Gospels—whose God is their stomachs [see Phil. 3:19]. Our desires and concerns are directed no longer toward food, drink, and enjoyment but to the eternal goods. Today has probably been the celebration of First Communion among you.

Dearest wife, write down in your next letter the communion petitions for the months of May and June. Consistently attend the May devotions so that there is brought to you what is not possible for me here. Mary has always helped, and she will continue to help. It would be lovely for me if I could hear the lovely Marian hymns as we hear the pop tunes that one can usually hear in the cells.

You have written that new life has again come to you in the barn. I wish you much good luck and blessings that have not abandoned you, I believe. One can always and in general use God's blessings. You could ask Schmied about a new rotating plowshare, for it could do some necessary things for our plowing. How does the grain look? You see, I am no less curious in how everything is at home. One remains interested when one loves his home.

I am closing for today with warm greetings to you, dear wife, as well as to Mother and Resie. Additional greetings to my little heart throbs.

Be well. See you again.

Greetings to Franz Pate.

Greetings also to neighbors and friends.

From Franz to Franziska

Linz, May 4, 1943

Dearest wife! And all my love ones! I am sending you greetings from Linz's train station. I am leaving for Berlin at 10:13 a.m.

You can write me at this address: Wehrmacht Investigation Prison, Branch Office, Seidelstrasse 39, Berlin Tegel. Have no concerns about me. The Lord God will not abandon me.

Warm greetings to you from your husband, son, and father.

Many greetings and kisses to my little ones.

Be well. See you again.

Greetings to my parents-in-law, relatives, and friends.

From Franz to Franziska

Regensburg at 2:00 p.m., May 4, 1943

Most beloved wife!

I want to write you a few sentences from here. I hope that you have received my letter from this morning. This departure came as a complete surprise. We had no time even to say goodbye to our companions. Accompanied by an officer from Berlin, I am departing for Berlin at 2:30 p.m. He is a very pleasant man.

Concerning my decision, I can tell you that I have come to no different decision as a result of the process that has played itself out. I am resolved to act no differently. During the interrogations, they wanted me to deny everything, [e.g., to deny] that National Socialism goes against the church.

This morning a man whose father is a general told me that someone in a position higher than a general has said: "One must first fight against our enemies outside and afterward against our enemy inside, namely the C[hurch]."[32]

Concerning the state of my soul, you need not be concerned. If things in Berlin should go bad for me, have no concern. I must now close, for it is almost time for the train's departure.

Once again warm greetings from your loving husband.

I am resolved about everything.

Many greetings to Mother, Father-in-Law, Resie, and the little ones.

See you again.

Pray for me.

---

32. Statements similar to this were made by the Reich's minister of propaganda, Joseph Goebbels. [RK]

Chapter 5

Berlin-Tegel Prison Letters

May 7–September 5, 1943

Franz Jägerstätter arrived by train in Berlin on the evening of May 4, 1943, and was immediately taken to the prison at Tegel, a suburb of Berlin. It was there that he marked his thirty-sixth birthday on May 20. On July 6, he was brought before the Reich's Military Tribunal, interrogated, and convicted of "the demoralization of the armed forces." For this, he was sentenced to death. At the request of Franz's defense attorney, Franziska Jägerstätter and Pastor Ferdinand Fürthauer traveled from St. Radegund to Berlin and visited for twenty minutes with Franz on July 13. On August 9, Franz was taken before dawn to the prison at Brandenburg and executed by the guillotine at 4:00 p.m.

This chapter contains Franz's letters to Franziska on May 7, June 6, July 8, August 8, and August 9. (He was permitted to write only one letter each month.) Over the thirteen weeks, Franziska wrote at least twelve letters to Franz. Of those letters, missing is her letter of July 25. Among the letters below, Franziska's last letter to her husband is that of July 13, which she wrongly dated July 12. The chapter ends with Franziska's letter of September 5 to Pastor Heinrich Kreutzberg, thanking him for ministering to her husband at Berlin-Tegel prison.

The Third Reich's execution of Franz Jägerstätter was not an isolated incident, but one of numerous executions that occurred as Hitler and his officials eliminated their critics and opponents. For example, soon after the Sixth Army's defeat at Stalingrad, the state executed the students Sophie and Hans Scholl and other members of the "White Rose" resistance group. However, the Reich's Christian martyrs courageously lived and died with an unflinching belief in Christ's resurrection from the dead. Each prized St. Paul's words: "But if we have died with Christ, we believe that we will also live with him" (Rom. 6:8). In this spirit, Franz Jägerstätter assured Franziska on August 9 that "we shall see each other again soon in heaven!" [RK]

From Franz to Franziska

Motor Transport Specialist Franz Jägerstätter
Wehrmacht Investigation Prison, Branch Office
Seidelstrasse 39, Berlin-Tegel
May 7, 1943

Greetings in God! Dearest wife!

I arrived safely in Berlin on May 4 at 11:00 p.m. If it had been a vacation, it would have indeed been a lovely train ride, for the farms and villages through which we traveled were indeed extremely beautiful. Although I am removed farther from you, have no heavy heart because of me, for you know under what [divine] protection I exist.

Moreover, all goes well for me here. To be sure, it is a little different in some ways than at Linz, as far as I can now see. As at Linz, a person here need not suffer from hunger, and I find many things better here. In my cell, I have a very nice small closet of my own. It is surely not difficult for me that I had to come here.[1] God does not want us to be lost, but fortunately to be with him in eternity. If one has vindictiveness against no one and can forgive all people, if one dismisses an occasional harsh word, then one's heart remains at peace. There is nothing more beautiful in this world than peace. So we pray to God that a true and lasting peace will soon move into the world.

Dearest wife, something difficult will happen to you now. Here we may write one short letter only once every four weeks. We can however receive mail as often as it comes. Mailed packages of food are also not allowed. If I cannot be with you on June 6, then perhaps other good things can come about.[2] It delights me that you are engaging in this good activity at Easter. If I would have had an inkling that I would be taken from Linz without a trial, I would have invited you there for a visit. A trip to Berlin would be too demanding on you. If it is God's will, we shall have a reunion with each other again in this world. If not, then we hope for it in the next world where the visiting time will be somewhat longer than fifteen to thirty minutes.

Dearest wife, be so good as to send a card with my mailing address (above) to my friend Alfred [*sic*] Boul so that he knows this address and can give my

---

1. Dietrich Bonhoeffer, who was incarcerated in Berlin-Tegel prison while FJ was there, told his family that the guards brutally treated the prisoners, especially during their first days at the prison.

2. On June 6, the parish in St. Radegund held special religious devotions, after which families would gather for lavish meals.

warm greetings to my other friends.[3] Greetings also to brother Mayer, if he still writes to you, and to Franz Pate.

Your loving husband, Franz, sends warm greetings to you. Greetings also to Mother as well as to my sister-in-law, father and Resie. Greetings also to our relatives, neighbors and friends.

My dear children, receive my warmest greetings. Now your father may not write you very often, and I am far away from you. Nevertheless, I can still be near you in thought. I can also still pray for you. I shall constantly do this so that you will become well-behaved children. Be obedient to your mother and also to your grandmother and Resie. Then the heavenly Father and heavenly Mother will love you and may bring about what you ask for. Also, do not forget your father and pray for him. I commend you to the protection of the loving Mother of Heaven. Loving greetings to you from your father who always loves you.

Be well. See you again!

"Motor Transport Specialist," which stands in front of my name in the return address, has no significance.

From Franziska to Franz

St. Radegund, May 10, 1943

Greetings in God, most beloved husband!

Your two letters of May 4 have arrived. Many thanks for these. We are all concerned about you. Hopefully, things are not going poorly for you. We are praying for you, that everything again goes well. Our loving Lord Jesus and the loving Mother of Heaven will surely not abandon you.

I do not know whether you will receive this letter, and for this reason I shall not write much today. I do not even know whether you have yet received my letter of Sunday, May 2. Thanks be to God, we are still in good health, and we hope that you are as well. That you are so far from us is very painful to me, especially since there is no prospect that I can visit you. I'll end this letter with many warm greetings, your loving wife, Fani. Also, many greetings from Mother, Resi, and your parents-in-law. Father is grateful for the letter that you included for him. Also, the three girls send greetings and kisses which, Loisi says, they give you together.

Be well. See you again! Write soon.

---

3. Albert Boul (his first name was not Alfred) never received Franziska's card. He and the other men from Lorraine who were at Linz's prison with FJ did not learn of FJ's fate until after the war when Franziska told them.

From Franziska to Franz

St. Radegund, May 16, 1943

Greetings in God, dearly beloved husband!

Your letter of July [*sic*] 14 has arrived. Many thanks for this. It is very painful to me that I no longer have the possibility of visiting you at Linz. It must be God's will. It is also very painful to me that I can look forward to very few letters from you. But one must submit to God's will. I have already written to your friend Boul.

A week of prayer will occur in the coming week, or at least it is supposed to come about. A Capuchin from Burghauser has arrived to give assistance. It is a so-called mission, as it was called in the past. Every evening there is a May adoration with preaching, and in the morning there are two Masses and a short sermon. Of course, the first Mass is at 6:30 a.m. We have very little time. But since there are troubles and concerns, we also think about praying. We cannot thank God enough for the weather. It is always warm, and almost no day passes without rain. The grass and the clover are beautiful. In general, the grain is magnificent. Hopefully, no hail will destroy it. However, the British are to be feared with their firebombs. An official spoke about this at an air-raid meeting that Resi attended. He said that [British bombers] are flying over the countryside in order to destroy our grain. It would be terrible since we would have nothing to eat. So we must always constantly pray. Then this year will go well, for God will not abandon us. If only we do not forget to pray, which unfortunately is often the case.

Hans Lang is home for two weeks. He was in Holland....[4] Mother is in Altötting today. She went there yesterday, Saturday. An invitation from Altötting came to the parishes here so that many people would participate. The bishop will be there. There is a devotion to the loving Mother of Heaven. We are hoping that she will intercede with God for peace. It is sad that she is not honored by many people, since the loving Mother of Heaven has always helped people. She will not abandon us, dear husband, if we constantly call out to her.

It is unfortunate that you cannot participate in May devotions. They are always very beautiful. It will certainly be painful for you. Our children are full of joy when they can go to church. The May procession occurred last Sunday. By mid-day it was raining, and so I remained at home with the two younger

---

4. A piece of the letter is missing at this point.

ones. Rosl no longer stays at home, even if the weather is bad. Hopefully, she will still find great joy in going to church in a few years.

From Thursday night to Friday morning we had a small interruption in our sleep. A cow cried out. Mother went to see what had occurred and saw to her shock that the two larger one-year-old calves were no longer in the barn. The door to the ox's stall was open, and the two were nowhere to be seen or heard. You can imagine how upset we were. We immediately began the search with the neighbors and discovered them at Strohhofers. It is terrifying to have to search for animals at night. Hopefully, this will not happen again. Everything ended well. Something more horrible could have happened if we would have had to go into the woods.

In my previous letter, I wrote down for you the May communion petition. But I do not know whether you received it.

> Heart of Jesus, you are the source of all virtues.
> Adorn us with yourself,
> and with all of the virtues for our station in life! Amen!

Our June petition is:

> Heart of Jesus, in which exist all of the treasures of wisdom and knowledge, enrich us with the gifts and fruits of the Holy Spirit. Amen!

I'll now close my letter with many greetings and hope that this letter will find you in the best health. I am always in pain for you. I keep you in my love, and you are so far away. . . . I send you many kisses. Also, my little ones would have. . . .[5]

From Franziska to Franz

St. Radegund, May 23, 1943

Greetings in God, most beloved husband!

First of all, most loving greetings on this Sunday. Now how are you doing? What do you do all day long?

I would give you much work to do if you were at home. You know the scythe with which we have had terrible bad luck.[6] Father can no longer [sharpen] it. Resi and Mother have also tried to do it. No one can sharpen it as well as you can. One can always go to Lang, but he is always in hurry.

---

5. The end of this letter is missing.
6. A scythe was sharpened by means of a hammer.

Today in the afternoon there was the concluding celebration for the week of prayer. There were many people present. It was very beautiful. It was also very painful to me that you were not able to join the celebration. The priest touched the people of Radegund with his preaching. Out of necessity, he brought humor to everything. So he could say much more, and people could oppose him on nothing. Every night there were many people there. He preached on the value of the Mass. We should include even the deceased in the Mass, and Mass occurs often because it gives meaning to everything. The whole Mass is significant. We must pray [during Mass] and make the sign of the cross and genuflect. He spoke about many things. It was, so to say, a kind of school on prayer. Such instruction should occur often. During these days, our pastor made the effort to pray more slowly. Even the acolytes held their hands together more beautifully. We'll see how long all of this lasts. When the Capuchin is no longer with us, a lot will soon be forgotten, as always happens.

During this week we were in the forest. Together we cut down the dry brushwood because we have received no more [from the state]. It is similar to the stuff we gathered two years ago. However, we must be happy because we use so much wood. For some time we in Radegund have worked together with the community at Ostermiething. We have gathered the signatures of a large number of farmers and sent them to the council, [saying] that we do not agree [with the state's policy]. However, this has helped nothing.

I received a letter from Mayer this week. He asked about what is happening with [you], his good brother. He always has bad luck with the mail. He is with the combat troops. He no longer wants this. He thought that he may still go to the infantry. Also, he wrote me very comforting words. Among them were these: "Allow no suffering to upset you. Consider that we can never suffer what Christ suffered for us. This short earthly life is not the main thing. When you think about the eternally true joy in heaven, then you can endure everything."

I must also write something about your three darlings who have urged me many times to tell you about everything here. However, one cannot write about every little thing. Most of all, [they send] many greetings and kisses and the wish that you return home soon. Loisi, in particular, cannot understand why you are away for so long. They persistently pray for you and are well behaved. I would like to ask that when you are able to write, write down the dates of my letters so that I know which ones you have received.

I'll close my letter with many warm greetings, your loving wife, Fani.

Also, truly warm greetings from Mother and Resi and your parents-in-law. Be well. See you again!

> If we would know what God knows,
> then we would want what God wants!
> (The Capuchin's words.)

From Franziska to Franz

St. Radegund, May 30, 1943

Greetings in God, most beloved husband!

First of all, most loving greetings on this Sunday. As you can see, I have for you today a small surprise. On Easter Sunday I allowed your three darlings to snip flowers at Schirks, and I had a photograph of them made this week.[7] Surely you can see how much they have grown, even Loisi. Can you still recognize them? Loisi seems to have so many eggs in her basket that she cannot carry any more. Their baskets came from Rosi Zauner. The girls had a great time with them.

With the approach of your name day, I wish you every good, health, peace, and the wish that you may come home to us if it is God's will. During these weeks there are the Rogation Days.[8] Every night there are the rosary and the Rogation Mass, which is not in the morning because no one has time then. There are too few people to do all of the work. Nevertheless, most will pray that our dear Lord God again gives us a rich harvest and protects it from hail and other misfortunes.

On Thursday I brought home a piglet from Zieher. One must still feed it for three months or more. I'll do this even longer since butchering in the summer is too risky if one wants to preserve the meat. I also got small piglets from Moosbauer. They are four weeks old. I did not get any for a long time. Because for a while there were very few of them [available], they were very expensive. Now I have paid 100 for the pair. Not bad, right? For the children I bought young rabbits, 2 marks for each rabbit. The children are having great fun with them. The breeding of rabbits can also be profitable. Frau Huber bought a mother rabbit with ten little ones and paid 120 marks. Not a low price, right? Though more than a calf. Some rabbits are even more expensive. People are paying between 200 and 300 marks for one breeding rabbit of any kind.

---

7. In this photograph, the three little girls are wearing their Easter dresses, holding Easter baskets, and are standing next to a large sign that reads, "Dear Father, come [home] soon!" [RK]

8. The Rogation Days included religious processions with intercessory prayers and blessings for fields, crops, and livestock. [RK]

On Thursday at 3:00 a.m., we received a calf from Lang's cow. Father helped me. I did not wake up the others, for they were already somewhat ill. Resl had a toothache. Mother a bad cold and had also cut herself. The cut is already better. Now there are two calves, both of them very cute. However, I must sell one of them soon because they eat too much. They have already eaten everything in the orchard and also the clover. This week is already time for reaping the hay. I already am having some anxiety about all the work. If only you could be home!

I have again bought four hydrangea from Bergmann in Burghausen. Beautiful white flowers. They could have many blossoms, but are so far not lavish. We have snowballs in bloom at the church. Until Corpus Christi, we'll not have many white flowers, only a few. The red ones are already beautiful. This week we had some rain and planted the kohlrabi.

Perhaps you knew the husband of Ottilie Hirnschrots, Herr Reigassner from Hochburg. In any case, he has died in battle. He had married her during his military leave, which was two weeks long. He was apparently on the front for a long time. Now he is not coming home. She had a husband for only two weeks, as I said. What a great blow!

Warm greetings from Frau Zieher. Also, many greetings from your children who are always asking for you. They send you many kisses. Many greetings from your parents-in-law, from Resi and Mother and your loving wife, Fani.

Be well. See you again! I wish I could invite you to be here next Sunday, June 6. We still have some apples which you have always enjoyed eating. I do not have much of an appetite because you cannot be here. You cannot be here and must suffer from hunger. With greetings, Fani!

Soon after arriving at the Berlin-Tegel prison, Franz Jägerstätter began to write down in a notebook his thoughts on the Christian life. Consisting of reflections on biblical texts, this notebook, which is included in this volume as chapter 11, expresses ideas implicit in his last letters to Franziska. [RK]

From Franz to Franziska

Berlin, June 6, 1943

Greetings in God! Most beloved wife and mother!

Above all, thank you for your dear letters, which I have received with much longing and great joy. I received the letter of May 29, and there is also the one that you wrote on May 16. Four weeks passed without a message from you. Then, on May 2, I received the three other letters: one of May 30, one of

May 10, and also the one from Father. Thank God that all of you are healthy, and that everything is apparently going well. I can imagine that you are surely working hard.

I continue to find my situation very satisfactory. My stomach is sometimes a bit of a rascal, but otherwise I feel healthy, thank God. My stomach's small disturbances are easy to put up with, for it could easily be worse. Otherwise, it is in all things better here for me than at Linz. I am still alone in my cell. Almost daily we have half-an-hour to move about freely. Also, one can work in his cell as much as he wants, making envelopes for [military] letters. It would surely be better for me if I could lessen your difficult work. This free choice is not possible since nothing has changed. At least I can still pray for you. It is also a grace of God when one can suffer for his faith. Here I can make the most beautiful retreat. If I were at home, I would give myself hardly a week for this time which means that I would keep putting it off.

About the future I still cannot tell you anything. Perhaps in the next letter. On May 24, I appeared before the Reich's Military Tribunal for interrogation. It was a somewhat long ride by car because the Tribunal is in Berlin itself, and Tegel is somewhat outside the city. On the way, I caught a small glimpse of the vastness of this city.

You must be already busy with the haying. Will Rosl and Maridl already be helpful in this? Hopefully, you received more rain there in May than we did here. Otherwise, it will be likely disastrous for the fruit. You can imagine that it was painful for me [to hear] about the beautiful May devotions. As a substitute for them, I held a May devotion every day in my cell at night. In place of a statue of Mary, I used the dried violet from Rosl that you sent me. Surely it is more beautiful when a father can join with his entire family in the devotion. Let us pray in this month to the Sacred Heart of Jesus that he will soon bring peace to the world when all people also want it. The month of June is one of the most beautiful months of the church year.

Dearest wife, if it is God's will, there will still occur in this life an opportunity for us to have a reunion. I believe that each of us longs for this. Be at peace! Let us love one another and readily forgive each other. Most people embitter their lives by their lack of reconciliation.

Frau Kirsch wrote to me.[9] I should send her a confirmation of my military unit so that she will receive her benefits. She apparently received my address

_____

9. Theresia Auer Kirsch was the mother of Franz's daughter Hildegard Auer.

from you. I do not know where the whole thing stands and whether it is still paid to her. If it is possible, I would ask you, dear wife, to pay her for the time being. One does not know how things will work after my case is decided and whether she will receive something from the state. If she wants official confirmation of my military unit, she needs to write to the unit itself. The address would be the following: "To the branch of the Motor Transportation Division, Department 17, in Enns."

And now, my dear children, have you forgotten your father because he has not written you for a long time and has not come home? You are once again picking strawberries and blueberries. Soon you will be looking for cherries at Lang's. Loisie is already haying. If you are well behaved and obedient children, then the loving God will make everything right again.

I warmly greet you, my dearest wife, as well as mother and my dear little ones. Your father, husband, and son, Franz.

From Franziska to Franz

St. Radegund, June 9, 1943

Greetings in God, most beloved husband!

I come at last to writing a few sentences to you. We have a lot of work, and I did not have the time on Sunday. Also, we had visitors. My mother, Rosi, and your oldest daughter [Hildegard] whom I had invited. She came on Saturday evening, and her mother picked her up on Monday. The three little ones interacted very well with her. I've sent you a little something. Hopefully, you will receive it while it is still edible. We would readily be haying now, but we seldom have good weather. We have brought in the hay from the first meadow. My mother has stayed since Sunday to help. On Saturday I sold a calf, and it was picked up on Tuesday. We received 630 marks. It went to Handenberg. Today I fetched the piglets from Moosbauer. Together they weigh no more than thirty-two pounds, and they cost 80 marks. Not bad? You get them with difficulty, and so you cannot say anything [about the price]. You can be happy that you can buy them.

Konrad Gabelmacher was here on leave for two weeks and brought a farm woman with him. They have not yet married, for the time was too short. He can rely on her for the work at home. She is the oldest daughter of Grundner in Hochburg and was attracted to him. But she has not yet allowed a ceremony at church. She does not yet want to marry because she knows no one here. She should be a capable business woman. This is the main thing.

Soon Pentecost will be here. I wish you a joyful holy day and hope that you can be at peace with your difficult situation. Hopefully, you will soon again write a few sentences, for we are always concerned about you.

I send you greetings from Frau Zieher and from Rosi, from Peter Hofbauer (senior) and from my sister Nani as well as from my sister Kathi, from your parents-in-law, Resi, mother, and your three girls. Also, warm greetings from your faithful wife, Fani. Be well. See you again! Write soon.

From Franziska to Franz

Sunday, June 13, 1943

Greetings in God, most beloved husband!

With fretful concern we awaited a letter from you, and finally your letter arrived today. I am truly grateful for it. That you also have received no mail from us will make you anxious. We are relatively well and hope you are too. The work is often too much for us. My lungs are weak, and mother's feet are often hurting. So it is, and yet there is always more work. I have terrifying anxiety about the grain harvest. Father can no longer bear the heat, and his energy for work has become an issue. The grain is magnificent for reaping. I could necessarily use you, for my very weak lungs no longer hold up for grain harvesting. If you could come home for at least four weeks! Many people in St. Radegund are sick. The work has become too much for most of them. The old men and the weaker sex do not hold up well. Also, there is much to endure. Fourteen to sixteen hours of work each day is no small thing, and there is concern for the dear ones outside. That peace comes soon is surely the wish of everyone.

Also, there is still the yearning for marriage. Ferdl Schirk celebrated his marriage yesterday in Vienna. Tini, Pepi and Rupert went there. On Tuesday, they will celebrate the marriage here. Fani Hohenauer married a widower in Freilassing. Johann Hofbauer went into the military and is now in an ammunitions factory. The twenty-six-year-olds are being called up. Even Leonhart Adam was retained. Franz is now in Greece, and Hans is in Russia. Frau Adam is very concerned, and Schweiger is not around. She has made requests, but Herr Adam does not come home. She can no longer do the work with so few people.

It was joyous in our little church today for Pentecost Sunday. It saddens me that you cannot be with us. A beautiful sermon was given. There were many people present. There are always more than usual on an important feast day. In the afternoon we were with our children. Many greetings from your children, and they have many kisses for you, which they send to you in this short letter. Loisi cannot believe that you have stayed away so long and that you do not come to tell her stories. She is very smart and takes note of many things. Rosl must begin school in a couple of months, and she already has terrible anxiety about it. Her concerns get increasingly greater.

I paid the benefits for March. Then Frau Kirsch came, and she said I should not pay any more. She will receive them when she applies [to the state]. Later I sent her your address.

Your loving wife, Fani, sends you truly warm greetings and many kisses. Be well. See you again.

Also, many greetings from your parents-in-law, from Mother and Resi. Warm greetings, too, from Krenn and Karobath. They remain concerned about you.

From Franziska Jägerstätter
and Lorenz Schwaninger to Franz

St. Radegund, June 20, 1943

Greetings in God, dearly beloved husband!

This Sunday is almost over. It was a somewhat beautiful day. We have had so many rainy days that we could not do the haying. Hopefully, this week will have beautiful weather. We could surely use you for the hay harvest. We are in good health and hope you are too. Frau Adam had asked [the authorities] for her husband for her hay harvest. Then she sent him to us for our work. However, he did not come until today. There are always some men on leave here.

On Monday, Wimmer picked up the calf from Lang's cow. It was not yet three weeks old. Yet it weighs 176 pounds. It cost 1 mark. We may not keep it any longer because of the milk supply. We can deliver twenty liters each day. A great output? It is unfortunate that you cannot be at home. At the moment, one cannot be happy.

This week Frau Jahrl gave birth to a small son, Thomas. They already have three sons. They would have liked a girl. But one cannot arrange this, as you know, my dearest! One must accept with joy what God gives us. Today Wagner was here and selected the wooden strips for the dung wagon. Until today we had no wagon. He had had no time. He has so much to do. I had to borrow the wagon from Lang. Ours was broken.

Your three girls greet you warmly. They are always asking for you and have many kisses for you. Loisi said that when Father returns, she will no longer sleep with me but always with Father. I'd gladly lose her if you could be at home. I'd like to send you something to eat in case you found yourself hungry.

I do not know. I hope that your situation is satisfactory. You must tell me if I can send you something. Since this month is almost past, I am writing down for you the communion petition for July:

Heart of Jesus, you who are the king and center of all hearts, give to us the knowledge, love, and peace of your kingdom and kingship! Amen!

I'll end this letter with many warm greetings, your loving wife, Fani. Also, many greetings from Mother and from your parents-in-law, Resi and especially from your three little ones. Be well. See you again!

The words below are in a different handwriting:

Dear son-in-law, dear Franz! Since some space remains, I'll add a few sentences. Today for Holy Trinity Sunday I was in Tittmoning at 9:00 a.m. It was truly beautiful. During the consecration I prayed for you to the loving God, asking that we see you again soon and that we come together in good health. At 10:30 a.m., there was the children's Mass. I was there also, for I find it to be the loveliest church. My brother wrote the same. He served in Metz with the Eighth Infantry.

On Monday morning we'll be haying, for the weather should be beautiful. I'll certainly not push your family. I am simply happy if I can still come along. I'll end now. Stay in good health. Receive my greetings. Your loving father-in-law, Lorenz Schwaninger. See you again.

The envelope of June 20 included a piece of paper with the words below from Franziska:

Mayer wrote again this week. He said: "I am with the fighting troops. Every night I went without sleep in a military trench. I prayed the rosary many times." He said, too, that he does not forget you in his prayers and asked that you not forget him. Through prayer you are a medic to the suffering souls who are waiting for something better.

Many greetings from your faithful wife, Fani!

From Franziska to Franz

St. Radegund, June 27, 1943

Greetings in God, my dearest husband!

This Sunday is almost over. We brought some beauty into it. Today was the Corpus Christi procession. There were many people. Our children had a great delight that they were able to participate. The weather was glorious.

It is unfortunate that you could not be with us. Schweiger received a Sunday leave. He is harvesting hay with a farmer. We could surely use him at home. We had it very hard this week. Every day we awoke by 3:00 a.m. We have brought in wonderful hay, though very little. There was very little rain in April and May. We have received help from Mari Adam. Also, Frau Sterz has helped us a few times. On Friday we harvested the whole Grünschneider meadow. There were seven of us because Fani Grabner also helped us. It was not as bad as I had anticipated. You receive help from others when you are a good person. On Saturday we harvested the Leite meadow. There were six persons. Leonhart Adam helped us, and so we are already done with the harvesting.

Thursday was the feast of Corpus Christi. Fani Grabner and I awoke on Wednesday at 11:30 p.m. She had slept with us. We wanted to go to Altötting. At midnight we left the house, and we reached Altötting at 6:00 a.m. We were quite tired. Coming home, we found a ride in a car to Burghausen. We would not have done this if we had more harvesting to do.

Frau Wieser was buried on Thursday. She had been in the hospital in Salzburg and died there last Sunday. She had endured terrible suffering. She must have had a bone disease. She could no longer move because her bones easily broke. Her feet as well as her arms had broken a few times when she was moved to a different bed. In her healthy days she was always very funny and had decorated her house very beautifully. However, God wished something else.

Today Hans Adam came home on leave. This is a joy for the family. Maier [sic] has written me again.[10] He is near Moscow in a very dangerous situation because of the partisans. There seem to be many of them.

Our health is satisfactory. It could be much worse. A person must have some suffering so that one does not forget God.

Hopefully, you are also still in good health. It is very hard now that I receive so few letters from you. I am always with you in thought.

I'll end my letter with many greetings from your loving wife, Fani.

Also, many greetings from your children. They have learned a little prayer. Your girls are well behaved and also very smart. Even Loisl learns things very easily. Also, many greetings from Mother, your parents-in-law, and sisters-in-law Rosa and Resl. Be well. See you again.

---

10. Franziska is referring to Rudolf Mayer. [RK]

From Franziska to Franz

St. Radegund, July 4, 1943

Greetings in God, dearest husband.

Another week has passed. Today we celebrated the feast of the Sacred Heart of Jesus. It was very joyous in the church. All of us went to church, including the children, who do not want to stay at home in this beautiful weather. After the Mass, I went with Rosa to the school to enroll her. She begins on September 6. This will be a struggle. I hope it is for the best. She is smart. On Monday we brought home the last of the hay. Then on Tuesday we celebrated the feast of St. Peter and St. Paul. Most people had to work because the weather was beautiful. In the morning there were very few people at church. However, there were more in the evening for the Mass, which was very joyous.

On Monday I went to the mill at Tittmoning. Strohhofer still had hay to bring in. So, I went alone and did not say anything. There were not many there. It is not as far as Ach. We now must rake the leaves because we need straw. Frau Grüner often helps us with this work. She often helped us with the haying, too. She can still do quite a bit, and she is happy that she can do this work "instead of just eating." She is a funny person.

Herr and Frau Kuster have arrived. They are taking their vacation again in Radegund with the Hofbauers. Ferdl Schirk and his wife are assisting the Hofbauers in their home. Frau Schirk helps each day with Schirk. They work as long as they can. It is expected of them. She is a Viennese woman.

Nussbaumer is still in Vienna. Also, Franz Pate wrote this week and sends greetings to you. I also received a letter this week from Breit Gregori. He asked about you, and I have told him about your situation. I do not know whether you will receive a letter from him. He is still in Braunau with a branch of the First Battalion. He has become outspoken.

Yesterday Aunt Marie arrived to pick blackberries. She will stay here for a few days. The poor thing spent the whole day in the woods. She is full of life. As she reported, she was in the forest from morning on. The blackberries are not yet ripe. But people can wait no longer. The harvest gets nearer. If only you could receive a leave. We are in good health and hope that you are too.

I am ending my letter with many greetings, your loving wife, Fani.

Also, many greetings from your three girls, your parents-in-law, Mother, and Resi! Be well. See you again!

From Franz to Franziska

Franz Jägerstätter wrote the letter below two days after the Reich's Military Tribunal condemned him to death. Although he knew this verdict, he did not explicitly mention it in this letter. Aware that the Tribunal would eventually review his case, he implicitly refers to the verdict of July 6 and to its review by the Tribunal when he states that in his next letter he will inform Franziska of "the final decision." Along with writing the letter below, Franz continued to write in his notebook and also began to express his last thoughts in essays on odd pieces of paper. See chapters 11 and 12. [RK]

Tegel, July 8, 1943

Greetings in God! My dearest wife and mother and also my dear children!

Finally the day is here when I am again allowed to write you a few sentences. Above all, my deepest thanks for your letters, which I have received with great joy and which I look forward to with great longing. Warm thanks too for the lovely photographs which have brought me great joy and also tears. I would no longer recognize Loisie. As the picture shows, she is all energy. It would be a great joy if during life's few days one could share in the circle of a fortunate family. However, if the loving God has chosen something else for us, this is also good.

It is a joy to be able to suffer for Jesus and our faith. We have the joyful hope that the few days in this life when we have been separated will be replaced by thousands of days in eternity, where we shall rejoice with God and our heavenly Mother in untroubled joy and good fortune. If we can only remain in the love of God when difficult tests of our faith come to us. We do not know in this life whether we are being spoken of when it says that the most righteous will be saved.

I am thankful for my dear wife's excellent baked goods, which I received on Pentecost Saturday. They served as my dessert for two meals. Although they tasted very good and delighted me, I ask that you not send me food. It is not permitted here. Someone with good will allowed me to receive what you sent. I believe in your love for me and also know that you are also concerned about me. I believe that it is not as difficult for me here as everyone at home may imagine. Also, I remain in good health, thank God, and hope that you do too.

Dearest wife and mother, I continually fear that all of this summer's work has weakened the health of each of you. I know how much work there is at home when everything is done right. If you became shopkeepers, everything would be easier. Yet I have no expectation that this will happen. As I see from your letters, you will receive no award for idleness. So much to do is often very dangerous. Yet one needs the money.

Dear mother, thank you for your sentences, which have delighted me. I hope that you are no longer angry with me for my disobedience. I also ask that you not be concerned about my physical well-being. If something difficult were to come upon me, it would not matter. The loving God will not send me more than I can bear.

Now I must give you the dates of the letters that I have received from you since I last wrote to you. The dates are: May 23, May 25, May 30, June 9, June 13, and June 20. I believe that I have received every letter that you have sent me.

Dear father-in-law, I am very grateful for your letter with the loving sentences that you included in it. In my last letter, I inserted a separate sheet of paper for you. But I can see from your letter that you did not receive this sheet. So this time I am putting everything into this one letter. I hope that you are in even better health than I can imagine. The Lord God sends the weather with seemingly little regard for the people who must sweat to do the haying. If you have had no better weather than we have had here, you must not be done yet with the harvesting of hay. Right? It has not rained a great deal here. Yet I believe that in all of June there were hardly two beautiful sunny days in a row. July has not begun any better. Hopefully, the weather will now be better for the harvest. It is good if you do not push my family too much about the work. It is important that a little time remain for thinking and praying.

All of you are interested in knowing whether my future has yet been decided. Please be patient until my next letter. I hope to include something then about the final decision.

Dearest wife, for a long time I have been very fortunate. You need have no heavy heart about me. Do not forget me in your prayers as I am not forgetting you. Remember me especially during the Holy Sacrifice of the Mass. I can share my joy with you that yesterday a priest visited me.[11] Next Tuesday he will come with the Blessed Sacrament. One is not abandoned by God here.

---

11. This priest was Pastor Heinrich Kreutzberg, to whom Franziska Jägerstätter wrote her letter of gratitude on September 5, 1943. Kreutzberg wrote to Franziska on February 18, 1946, and spoke about his conversation with her husband concerning the Tyrolean priest Franz Reinisch, a priest in the Pallotine order, whom the Reich had executed on August 21, 1942, because of his refusal to take the military oath of allegiance. Kreutzberg recalled that as he discussed Reinisch's life and death Franz became increasingly calm. In Kreutzberg's words: "I have seen no more fortunate man in prison than your husband after my few words about Franz Reinisch." See Zahn, *In Solitary Witness,* 81–107. [RK]

Warm greetings to you from your husband, Franz, who is always think-ing of you with love. Also, warm greetings to you, dear mother, and also to my parents-in-law and Resie. Greetings to all the people who have sent me greetings, especially to Brother Mayer as well as to Franz Pate, and to Krenn, Karobath, and Fürthauer, and also to our neighbors and friends.[12]

Now also warm greetings to my dear little ones. The photographs of you have brought me great joy. It would be most lovely for me if I could see you again face-to-face. Do not lose heart if your father does not come to tell you stories. Today there are many children whose fathers cannot come to them now or will never come to them again. It brings me joy that, as your mother has written to me, you are always praying. I believe that you are well-behaved and obedient. It would bring me great joy if you would remain well-behaved children. On Corpus Christi Sunday, I thought about you throughout the day. I would have loved to see you wearing the lovely garlands on your heads. From far away your loving father sends you warm greetings. Remain healthy, and be well. See you again!

Many thanks, dearest wife, for your letter of June 27, which I recently received.

From Franziska to Franz

At the request of Franz Jägerstätter's defense attorney Friedrich Leo Feld-mann, Franziska Jägerstätter and Pastor Fürthauer arrived in Berlin on the morning of July 13, 1943. Franz Jägerstätter did not know that his wife and pastor would be visiting him. On July 13, he was taken to a visiting room at the Berlin-Charlottenburg prison, where he found Frau Jägerstätter and Pastor Fürthauer waiting for him. He listened as his wife and pastor— as advised by Attorney Feldmann—asked Franz to sign a statement saying that he would serve in the Wehrmacht. In response, Franz likely explained his refusal for taking the oath of allegiance, and said that, as a result of his conversation with Pastor Kreutzberg, he had reached an "inner peace."[13] At one point, however, Franz became annoyed with Pastor Fürthauer. After twenty minutes, prison guards ended the meeting. Only a few hours later,

---

12. Franz likely wrote these words of farewell to his family and friends because he did not know when he would be executed. From July 7 until August 9, he awoke each morning wondering whether this would be his last day. [RK]

13. See Zahn, *In Solitary Witness*, 93–96. [RK]

Franziska — who was surely upset and exhausted — wrote the letter below to Franz, putting the wrong date on it.[14] [RK]

July 12 [*sic*], 1943

Greetings in God, dearest husband!

We decided to travel home today, Monday, since we do not have a room anywhere and since a train departs at 10:00 p.m. We are with your defense attorney, and I hope that with God's help everything will be made right. I had intended to tell you so many stories about life at home, but I forgot so much. You yourself were annoyed. But the pastor had meant well. I'll surely pray a great deal for you, and please do not lose heart in your difficult situation.

Truly warm greetings to you from your loving wife, Fani, who is concerned about you.

[*A postscript from the pastor:*] Best wishes.

Yours, F. Fürthauer.

[*A postscript from Franziska:*] Also, many kisses. Be well. See you again.

From Franz to Franziska

As already noted, Franziska's letter of July 25 is missing. Franz refers to it in his last two letters to Franziska. Along with these letters, Franz addressed to Franziska the five essays contained in chapter 12. [RK]

Tegel, August 8, 1943

Dearest wife and all of my loved ones!

First of all, receive my warmest greetings. And my warmest thanks for your letters, for the letters of July 13 and July 25, which I received with joy. I hope that you have received my letter from last month.

Dearest wife, you once again made a great sacrifice for me [by coming here]. Tomorrow it will be four weeks since we saw each other. It would have saved you much pain if my defense attorney had not written to you. I still have not received a statement that my death sentence has been reconfirmed. You must offer to God your effort and great expense [in coming here], which would not otherwise have come about [if the defense attorney had not contacted you].

To be sure, I received great joy from our reunion, but not from the fact that you had to make such a great sacrifice. It brought me pain that I could speak so

14. For the chronology, see Kurt Benesch, *Die Suche nach Jägerstätter* (Graz: Styria, 1993), 295–97. Having received defense attorney Feldmann's letter on Saturday, July 11, Pastor Fürthauer and Frau Jägerstätter boarded a train in the early afternoon on July 12. They arrived in Berlin on the morning of Monday, July 13, and met with FJ in the afternoon. That night, at 10:00 p.m., they boarded a train and went back to Austria. [RK]

briefly with you. I am not angry with the pastor. I have asked his forgiveness for all of my unnecessary words to him, which perhaps hurt him and only brought me regret. I did not want to bring pain with my words, just as the pastor did want to do so with his. I wanted to spare you this suffering that you have borne for me.

However, you know Christ's words: "Whoever comes to me and does not hate father and mother, wife and children, brothers and sisters, yes, even life itself, cannot be my disciple" [Luke 14:26]. How it must have brought Christ much heartache as he inflicted pain on his mother through his suffering, which is not comparable with our suffering! And Jesus endured all of this only out of love for us sinners.

Do you believe that all would go well for me if I were to tell a lie in order to prolong my life?[15] I sensed your pain in your words about me sinning against the Fourth Commandment. How our final hours will be, we do not know. Nor do we know what struggles we must still pass through. That I have great trust in God's compassion, that my dear Savior will not abandon me in the final hours — who has not abandoned me up until now — this you can believe with me. Our dear heavenly Mother will also not [abandon me], for not a few "Hail Marys" flow from my lips. This you can also consider.

Dearest wife, consider what Jesus has promised to those who make the Nine First Fridays.[16] Everything will become clear on the Day of Judgment, if not sooner, as to why so many people are struggling today. With my heart, I apologize to you and to everyone else if some of these words that reach your ears are not kind. Did our dear Savior not mean everything? And should we be exempted from his words? For the riches of eternity will not be less if I am defamed by many people. The chief thing is only that the Lord not be ashamed of me for eternity. God the Lord wants to come to us in our final hours, not as our Judge but as our Redeemer.

Do not be overly concerned about earthly things. The Lord indeed knows what we need as long as we are pilgrims in this world. When so much can change and so much goes differently from what we would like, we know nevertheless what we can atone for here on this earth. In the next life we need suffer no longer. And the greater the suffering here, the greater the joy there.

---

15. As already noted, FJ judged that it would be a lie if he were to make the oath of loyalty to the Führer, and he could not bring himself to lie. See text no. 87, page 240 below. [RK]

16. According to St. Mary Margaret Alacoque (d. 1690), God promises special graces for the hour of death to those who receive the Eucharist on the first Friday of the month for nine consecutive months. [RK]

I have recently received a very comforting letter from Brother Mayer. I am very grateful for this. Please send him warm greetings. It is very possible that he will be called into eternity before I am.[17] How many others have already gone into eternity?

Franz's letter of August 8 ends without his signature. It would have been put in the mail on the morning of August 9, a few hours before Franz's execution. Franz's farewell letter of August 9 below has obvious similarities to his letter of August 8.

From Franz to Franziska

Brandenburg, August 9, 1943

Greetings in God! Dearest wife! And all my loved ones!

Your letters of July 13 and July 25 still bring me joy. I am very grateful for them. Four weeks ago today we saw each other on this earth for the last time. This morning, at approximately 5:30, I had to get dressed immediately for a car was waiting. I went with other condemned prisoners on the ride from Tegel to Brandenburg. We do not know what will happen to us. At noon someone told me that the verdict would be confirmed at 2:00 p.m., and that it would be fully enacted at 4:00 p.m.

I want to write all of you a few words of farewell. Dearest wife and mother, I am deeply grateful for everything that you have done for me in my life, for all of the love and sacrifices which you have shown me. And I ask you once again to forgive me for everything that I have made you suffer and feel hurt. You have surely been forgiven by me for everything. I ask everyone else, whom I at some time may have pained and hurt, to forgive me. Especially the pastor if I have perhaps hurt him with my words as he visited with me. I forgive everyone from my heart. May God accept my life as a sin offering not merely for my sins but also for others' sins [see 4 Macc. 6:28–29].

Dearest wife and mother, it was not possible for me to free both of you from the sorrows that you have suffered for me. How hard it must have been for our dear Lord that he had given his dear mother such great sorrow through his suffering and death! And she suffered everything out of love for us sinners. I thank our Savior that I could suffer for him and may die for him. I trust in

17. Frau Maria Mayer wrote to Franziska Jägerstätter that her husband Rudolf Mayer was missing in action beginning on August 12, 1943. He could have gone unharmed into a Russian prison. However, Frau Mayer never again heard from her husband. He may have died a few days after FJ.

his infinite compassion. I trust that God forgives me everything and will not abandon me in the last hour.

Dearest wife, consider what Jesus has promised to those who make the Nine First Fridays. Also, consider that Jesus will come to me in Holy Communion and strengthen me for the journey into eternity. In Tegel prison, I received the grace of the Blessed Sacrament four times.

Give my warm greetings to my dear children. If I am soon in heaven, I shall ask the loving God to prepare a place for all of you. Over the past weeks, I have prayed often to the heavenly Mother that if it is God's will that I die soon, that I celebrate the feast of Mary's Assumption in heaven.[18]

Many greetings also to my parents-in-law, my sisters-in-law, and all relatives and friends. Give my greetings to Brother Mayer. I am grateful for his letter, which has brought me great joy. I am also thankful to Karobath for his letter.

And now all my loved ones, be well. And do not forget me in your prayers. Keep the Commandments, and we shall see each other again soon in heaven!

Warm greetings to my godson.

Greetings to all of you before his last journey from your husband, son, and father, son-in-law, and brother-in-law.

> Heart of Jesus, heart of Mary,
> and my heart be one heart
> bound for time and eternity.
> Mary, love [us] with your child,
> give us all of your blessings![19]

From Franziska Jägerstätter to Pastor Heinrich Kreutzberg

On August 21, 1943, Pastor Heinrich Kreutzberg sent a letter to Franziska Jägerstätter in which he said that prison officials had cremated her husband's body and placed his ashes in an urn that was buried in a Berlin cemetery on

---

18. The feast of the Assumption is celebrated on August 15. [RK]

19. On August 9, Pastor Albert Jochmann accompanied FJ to his execution. A few hours later, Jochmann told the Austrian sisters, who were working at Berlin's Catholic Charities Hospital, that FJ did not want him to read the Bible aloud to him, but preferred to sit in silence. Moreover, he saw that Franz remained at peace throughout his final hours. In Jochmann's judgment, Franz Jägerstätter was the one true saint whom he had ever met. Franziska Jägerstätter has said that, although she did not know the day on which Franz would be executed, she herself felt an intense personal communion with her husband at 4:00 p.m., on August 9, 1943. This sense was so strong that she made a mental note of the day and hour. (For further details, see Zahn, *In Solitary Witness*, 106–7. [RK])

August 17.[20] *In response, Frau Jägerstätter wrote the following letter to the prison chaplain.* [RK]

St. Radegund, September 5, 1943

Your Eminence!

Your dear letter with the comforting words has arrived. Many thanks for this. I thank you with my whole heart especially for your frequent visits to my dear husband in prison. It surely brought him joy that he received comforting words in his cell from Christ's representative and was also often able to receive the dear Jesus in Holy Communion. He was always concerned to follow the Commandments. So it was no great sin that he did not obey the state, and I hope that with God's help he surely will have reached his eternal goal.

This is painful for me because I have lost a good husband and an exemplary father for my children. I can assure you that our marriage was one of the happiest in our parish. Many people envied us. However, the loving God had ordained things to be otherwise, and our beautiful union was lost. I already look forward to our reunion in heaven where no war can any longer separate us.

Once again, from the depths of my heart, I wish you God's reward for everything that you have done for my dear husband.

With the greatest respect, I send you greetings.

Gratefully yours,

Franziska Jägerstätter

St. Radegund

Post Ostermiething Ob Donau

Shortly after the war, Sister Georgia — one of the Austrian nuns who had worked at the Catholic Charities Hospital in Berlin — brought the urn containing Franz's ashes from Berlin to St. Radegund. Franziska Jägerstätter and Franz's mother and daughters as well as his family and friends buried Franz Jägerstätter's ashes in St. Radegund's cemetery on August 9, 1946. Through the efforts of Pastor Karobath, Franz Jägerstätter's name was engraved into a memorial stone honoring villagers who died in war.[21] [RK]

---

20. See Zahn, *In Solitary Witness,* 107. [RK]
21. See Zahn, *In Solitary Witness,* 144–45.

Franz Jägerstätter in his late teens.

Franz on his motorcycle in 1932. From left to right, Aloisia Sommerauer (Franz's cousin/foster-sister), Rosalia Jägerstätter (Franz's mother), Heinrich Jägerstätter (Franz's stepfather).

Franziska Schwaninger in 1935, approximately one year before marrying Franz.

The wedding photograph of Franziska Schwaninger and Franz
Jägerstätter in April or May 1936, taken after they had returned
from their honeymoon in Rome.

Maria, Loisi, and Rosi holding Angora rabbits.

Franziska in October 1940 with Maria on her lap and with Rosa standing beside her grandmother, Rosalia Jägerstätter.

Franz's postcard of the motor-transport barracks in Enns, where he did his basic training.

Franz in his army uniform during his basic training in Enns.

Franz (third from the left) during his motorcycle training.

Franz's mother, Rosalia, and Franziska Jägerstätter with the children in the spring of 1941.

The first page of Franz's last essay, Text no. 88, which begins with the famous sentence: "Now I'll write down a few words as they come to me from my heart. Although I am writing them with my hands in chains, this is still much better than if my will were in chains." See chapter 12.

Maria, Loisi, and Rosi Jägerstätter, probably in 1942.

Loisi, Rosi, and Maria with their Easter baskets in April 1943.
Their sign reads: "Dear Father, come [home] soon." At this time,
Franz was incarcerated in Linz.

Part Two

Early Writings and Essays

Chapter 6

Early Writings

1932 and 1935

Although Franz Jägerstätter received his formal education only until his fourteenth birthday, he continued to educate himself through his reading, discussions with priests, neighbors and associates, and his critical reflection on the Christian faith. At an early age, he fell in love with the library of his step-grandfather. As an adult, he took it upon himself to read newspapers, journals, and books on a variety of topics. Inspired by the writings of others, Franz himself dared to write down his own thoughts. This chapter consists of two poems by Franz and also a long letter that he wrote to his cousin and godson Franz Huber. In it, the future martyr writes: "People who do not read will never be able to think for themselves, and hence they will become playground balls that others will kick around." These poems and letter show that — because of his wide reading, persistent writing, independent thinking, and vibrant Christian faith — Franz Jägerstätter would never allow others to kick him around. [RK]

Two Poems

Franz Jägerstätter wrote the first poem below on the back of an advertisement:

October 3, 1932:

Be not so proud, you rich man;
you too will die someday.
Give up the evil class struggle,
for God's Son was also not rich on earth.
Ah, how painful our days often are
during our short street-car rides
on which we travel unequal distances
until the day when the train de-rails.
Now I ask you, you proud man,

whether riches personally satisfy you
as long as God gives you health
and no suffering presses upon you.
Health and intelligence would be the most wonderful gifts;
also being attractive and having money
are right when one has [them].
But all of these wonderful gifts do not bring you your hoped for good
      fortune
if love is lacking in your heart;
for it is a masterpiece.
Also, peace and love do not continue for long
if you do not believe in your God
and eternal life.

December 1932:

@@Christmas joy, Christmas spirit
will now soon be renewed.
Every year, in remembrance,
young and old always rejoice.

Happy the hearts, full of love,
as they should be at Christmas time.
Give up the hostility, agree to a new peace,
leave aside politics, cultivate unity.

Also, do not forget all of our poor
who, often blamelessly, are oppressed by need.
Open up hearts, have compassion;
God pays back to you everything worthwhile.

For this reason, Christmas peace now stirs again
in all hearts.
Now lay down hate and pride;
as a result, you will be truly fortunate.

Then, like the shepherds for the first time many years ago,
we shall be drawn to the crib
so that we, too, are once again fortunately traveling
to God, to the child Jesus.

Franz Jägerstätter's Letter to His Godson Franz Huber, 1935

Franz Huber, born in 1923, was the seventh of Johann and Anna Huber's ten children, and a nephew of Rosalia (Huber) Jägerstätter. When Franz Huber was baptized, he received — at his father's request — Franz Jägerstätter as his godfather. After Johann Huber's death in 1932, Franz Huber moved into the home of his Aunt Rosalia and his cousin / godfather Franz. However, after three years, he was advised by a physician to move to a different home when his cousin Loisi became ill with tuberculosis. As was the custom in this region of Austria, Franz Jägerstätter wrote his godson a long letter on the occasion of Franz Huber's completion of his formal education in 1935.

Dear Franz!

Since your father is deceased, it is a godparent's duty according to the church to instruct his godchild. So I would like to give you in a few plain sentences a pathfinder as you make your way through the turbulent years of youth.

We often read in the newspaper that a fifteen- or sixteen-year-old has taken his or her own life and that the teenager did this because of feeling rejected in love or because of doing poorly at school. Yet if we were to dig deeper, we would find — I believe — that these suicides were also related to a crisis of faith. Few people would attain the age of thirty if misplaced love were the chief cause of the taking of one's life. We learn in school that a human being has a mind and a free will. It is the latter, I judge, that shapes whether we desire to become eternally fortunate or eternally miserable.

You know that when we want a sapling to grow into a beautiful, strong tree, we must give it adequate support so that it is not bent or uprooted by strong winds. Such is the case, too, with young people. They need good support in order not to be uprooted from their Catholic faith. These good supports should primarily be their parents. For this reason, I am gladly ready to assume the role of your deceased father, especially since a mother alone is often too weak to provide this moral guidance.

When temptations become so strong that you believe you must sin, think about eternal life. Because of a few seconds of desire, people often jeopardize their temporal and eternal well-being! We never know whether we shall have an opportunity to confess our sins and also whether God will give us the grace to repent of our sins. Death can surprise us at any moment. When people face misfortune, they seldom have the time to awaken their regret and sorrow for their mistakes. I know this from my own experience.

You surely want to become a strong adult, and you will succeed in this. Many people believe that athletes, such as award-winning boxers, are the strongest among us. But this is not true, for these individuals often cannot control themselves amid the smallest hardships and temptations. Therefore, the strongest among us are those people who can direct themselves amid the strongest temptations. There exist in each of us hidden inclinations to every possible vice such as acting out sexually, cursing, drinking, gambling, and so forth. Controlling these foes requires training during one's youth. If we want to succeed, we must not fear conflict.

Many people say that there is always more time to act properly. They say that young people "must sow their wild oats." These people overlook, however, the importance of acting properly. If we want to take charge of a foe within us, we must do this during our early years because during our later years we will lack the physical and intellectual-spiritual energy for this challenge.

Contrary to what some people say, our faith does not discourage us from being passionate in our youth. A young man with a pure conscience definitely has no reason to be in the dumps, for he can be truly passionate from his heart. He has nothing to fear, even if he were to face death. However, some people can be passionate only when they are inebriated or are agitated, for it is only in one of these states that they can silence, at least somewhat, their troubled consciences.

Why are so many people tainted at an early age? One reason is that the devil is always at work among us, doing what he can to lead us as soon as possible to a downward path. A second reason is that very few youth read good literature. Human beings need not only physical nourishment but also intellectual-spiritual nourishment. Moreover, we do not always have opportunities to hear good, beautiful preaching. Not all priests possess the talent to be able to preach well.

We can receive literature of poor quality from many people, and we can be satisfied to be dumber than we in fact are. There are many people who read a great deal, but they read mostly romance novels and crime stories. These books may be well written and enjoyable to read, but they have little or no value for one's intellectual and religious development. Moreover, a book of poor quality can bring about confusion and distress in one's life. Therefore, young people should ask their spiritual leaders and teachers what they should read. Even when we lack the zeal to read, we can at least read a little bit on long winter evenings. People who do not read will never be able to think for themselves, and hence they will become playground balls that others will kick around.

How should parents try to educate their children when they themselves do not truly know what is right and wrong? Parents often wait to speak with their children about their values until after they learn that their young adult has already fallen in love and that this love is not entirely pure. Then the parents summon their son or daughter and speak harshly: "You will not be happy about this, but I am punishing you. And if you do not want to obey us even in the smallest matters, then you can move out and go off on your own. But if you move out, then do not ever again seek help from us." In reaction, the son or daughter says, "Well fine! I'll go about my life and have nothing to do with you, even if I fail." As a result, young adults pull away from their parents before they are truly ready to enter into the world. In other words, parents' late efforts to enlighten their teenagers bear little or no fruit. If parents have no better way of communicating with their children, then they would do better to say nothing.

The love that God has planted in the hearts of young people is wonderful and sacred, and it must be respected so that it does not get distorted into filth and smut. If sexual intercourse outside of marriage were not sinful, as some people insist today, then it would not be punished by God as a violation of the Sixth Commandment. God does not call everyone to marriage. Moreover, God has not established marriage so that the married couple can have no limits on their sexual urges as they relate to one another. Rather, God intends for the couple to attain sexual maturity within their marriage. Young people who cannot control their sexual desires outside of marriage will not do better inside marriage, and everything is not permissible inside marriage.

I once had an opportunity to view a public exhibit on human hygiene. There were wax models of the sexual organs of human beings, and there were also images of how sexual diseases afflict human beings. As a result, one could see how sexual promiscuity can be unhealthy for people. For example, there are young men who were robbed of their full powers during their youth because of their lack of chastity alone. It is difficult to anticipate what these bad habits will lead to because Satan often controls them. People can become so morally weak that they lose their free will.

What and who are to blame for the corruption of young people? Responsibility often rests on the loose speech of the lukewarm or superficial Christians. There are various people whom we perceive to be entirely good Christians. They go to church conscientiously on Sundays because it is the custom of our society. They are entirely respectable because they fear being arrested. These are the people whom we see as upright and worthy of our trust. However, if we have a chance to get to know these people and to speak with them about this or that — even about the Sixth Commandment [Exod. 20:14] — we can find ourselves wondering about them and the authenticity of their faith. They may say: "Well, if the Sixth Commandment cannot in fact be lived as it is presented by our spiritual leaders and in the catechism, who will get to heaven? What human nature requires of us cannot of course be a sin. And as most doctors would agree, sexual activity is a part of human life. Therefore, it is not accurate to say that the sexual drive is bad."

We can hear these words or ones similar to them spoken by people whom we regard to be entirely good Catholics. When we do, we must ask ourselves: "Are people capable of doing more than nature asks of them?" There are of course prostitutes and other individuals who are paid for sexual encounters. Is the Sixth Commandment easy for people to uphold?

Along with these lukewarm Christians, there are still other people who publicly mock anyone who takes seriously the Commandments, especially the Sixth Commandment. They say, "That person must not trust himself, or he has received no love, or he is perhaps not capable of something." When these mockers learn that the person himself has broken the Sixth Commandment — which they themselves ridicule because of their own conduct — they become even more outspoken.[1] "Look at this bigot," they say. "Although he himself is filthy, he sees himself better than others. These lowlifes; these phony saints."

This attitude, taken by those who laugh about the Sixth Commandment, is itself a great crime and in itself sinful. Here is the devil in human form. These people disseminate ideas that appear to be pure sugar and honey. But when one bites into them, one finds that they are poison. For this reason, we must be less critical of lukewarm Christians than of nonbelievers and free-thinkers.

When one enters a bit into the world and takes an interest into how things are in most families, one can see families in which faith is taken only lightly and also families in which faith has been thrown completely overboard. While these families may have many possessions and a lot of money, they also live lives similar to life in hell, where there is not love but hate, disagreement, and conflict. Observing these families, many people say, "If there is a Lord God, he must see what motivates people today."

I believe that God has reached out and will continue to reach out to the people who disregard his Commandments. God's punishing hand is perhaps closer to us than we imagine. So we must direct all of our powers so that we are

---

1. FJ is likely referring to how other people viewed him because of his having conceived a child, Hildegard Auer, outside of marriage.

moving toward our eternal home and maintaining a good conscience. Then our enemies can attack us with their forces, but they cannot take our heavenly home away from us. If we must daily undergo hardships and earn very little reward in this world, we could still become richer than millionaires, for the richest and most fortunate people are those who need not fear death.

This heavenly kingdom lies before our free will. When we come before God, we shall not be able to use the excuse that we perhaps did not know what sin is. For we still have the good fortune of receiving a good religious education. Since in the course of time we may have forgotten some of what we learned in religious education, it is no shame for us if we often now take the catechism in our hands and read a little of it. The catechism should always be our best comrade and guide [*Führer*] for all of life.

If the doubts of faith should come to you — and usually no one is exempted from questions concerning the truths of our faith — then think about the miracles and our saints that come in no other faith as they do in Catholicism. Since the death of Christ, the persecution of Christians has occurred in almost every century. And there have emerged Christian heroes and martyrs who have offered their lives for Christ and their faith — often through horrible martyrdoms. If we want to reach our goal, we must become heroes of faith. As long as we fear other human beings more than God, we shall never attain the green branch of victory.

Oh, this cowardly human fear of other human beings! Just because of a few mocking words from our neighbors, we are often ready to throw our good intentions overboard. The most courageous and best Christians can and will fall, but they will not remain in the filth of sin. Rather they will get themselves up and receive the fresh power of the sacraments of penance and the altar, and so they will move toward their goal. Even if terrifying days come over us, if we believers are pressed down with the burden of suffering, then we shall recall that God invites none of us to carry a cross that is too difficult for us to bear.

> Consider two things. From where? To where?
> Then your life will have its proper meaning.
> Whoever goes on a journey without a goal
> wanders poor and weary.
> Whoever lives life without a goal
> has flourished in vain.
>
> Your godfather, Franz J.

Chapter 7

Notebook I

Summer 1941–Winter 1942

After returning home in May 1941, Franz Jägerstätter began to write down his reflections on the Christian life and the moral dilemma of Christians in the Third Reich. He did so in order to decide what he should do when he was again summoned to military duty. Over twenty-two months, he fashioned his views into essays that he gradually put into three notebooks and some on separate sheets of paper. Franz addressed these essays to his family. As a result, he gave them a conversational tone similar to the style of his letter to his godson Franz Huber, in 1935.

This first notebook contains fourteen essays, all of which — except the last — concern essential elements of the Christian life. They are entitled:

- *"On Faith"*
- *"On Humility"*
- *"On Prayer"*
- *"On the Our Father"*
- *"On Sin"*
- *"On the Four Last Things"*
- *"A Person's Character Shows Itself in Suffering"*
- *"On Our Fear of Other People"*
- *"On the Blessed Sacrament"*
- *"On the Feast of the Holy Family"*
- *"We Must Always Be Children before God"*
- *"On Love"*
- *"On Reading"*
- *"A Brief Reflection on the Current Era"*

As the titles show, these essays express the spiritual foundation from which Franz would reflect on specific political, social, and ecclesiastical issues in his subsequent essays. [RK]

To my loved ones:

All of these words and sentences which I am leaving behind for you in this notebook should bring you good fortune in this life and in eternity.

> Whoever goes on a journey without a goal
> wanders poor and weary.
> Whoever lives life without a goal
> has flourished in vain.

On Faith

"Heart of Jesus, lavish for all people who call on you, bestow on us a living faith and good will."

Christ has said that whoever believes becomes blessed, and whoever does not believe will be condemned [see Mark 16:16]. Most people with weak faith would respond: "We believe without reservation that there is a God." That there is a higher essence most heathens also believe. But we must believe as Christians. And this means that we must hold to be true what God has revealed and what the Catholic Church presents for belief.

We often hear Christians say, "Ah, if everything is so sinful and so wrong, as our spiritual leaders tell us, who can attain heaven?" Yet we should also wonder about things when no improvements come about among Christians who receive the sacrament of penance. How could some people express a remorseful confession to the priest and the Lord God when they also regard their failed steps not as sins. While someone could confess his or her sins a hundred times, things may in fact be otherwise. For when faith lacks an awareness of sin, no true repentance can come about and there can be no resolve to improve oneself.

We must have the faith of children. If someone is smart, he or she can still be the most unbelieving person in the world. Faith is therefore a matter not of the mind but of the will. God has given us free will. Therefore, no one has the right to say, "I cannot believe." Instead the person should say, "I shall not believe." No human being can remain exempted from the doubts of faith.

However, we must defend ourselves from and fight against evil. Heaven will be sent to no one. Even if we ponder and study, what can our weak human understanding grasp of the supernatural? We come to know God as we believe and serve and submit ourselves to God and his church. According to Sacred Scripture, Lucifer was one of the smartest angels but did not want to serve God [see Rev. 12:7–9]. Therefore, God banished him eternally to hell. So God will proceed with us human beings if we fall into arrogance and do not submit ourselves to God's Commandments and also to his church.

We can take no steps toward God if we do not believe. A faith marked by error and misunderstanding influences Christians who do not want to believe properly in God's truths and revelations.

Ordinary things can convey a seeming transcendent power — a power that we may experience as equal to God's omnipotence. Let us reflect on this experience.[1] Most people say: "[This power] has brought us good results in many cases. Hence, we should not question it." Yet the devil can bring about many things among people. And for this reason, the church assumes that the evil foe has had a hand in many cases of an apparent transcendent power affecting people's lives. The devil apparently delights when someone persists in having an unsure faith in God.

"We should pray to whomever has power," some people say.[2] However, are these people associating prayer with an earthly power? From what source comes their salvation? Why do they take seriously all possible so-called religious accounts and factors? Do they believe that God is so weak that he needs the help of these ambiguous elements? Do they believe then that people of unsure faith can nevertheless pray so devoutly and trustingly that God would immediately send help in response to their prayers?

Many people have in fact received help from God through their trusting prayer. However, do we as faithful Christians pray with such trust that we always remain confident in God's help? There are very few Christians who possess purity of faith. All of us must strive therefore to become like children [before God] while also being adults.

---

1. FJ is referring to forms of pagan worship. In particular, he is probably speaking about the idolizing of the Führer that N.S. leaders promoted as they made use of ancient symbols (e.g., the swastika), mythologies (e.g., the "Nibelungenlied"), and rituals (e.g., the Nuremberg rallies). [RK]

2. The members of the German Faith movement held that Hitler possessed quasi-divine powers. Hence, they encouraged Germans to invoke Hitler's name in order to obtain a divine favor such as good health, rain for the crops, or victory in battle. The N.S. salute *Heil Hitler* connotes that Hitler is the bearer of *Heil,* that is, of "salvation" and "well-being." [RK]

On Humility

Humility is one of the most beautiful virtues that a person can possess, though contemporary thought sees humility as a form of cowardice.[3] In living this beautiful virtue of humility, Christians surely should not be cowardly, for Christ himself said: "I am gentle and humble of heart" [Matt. 11:29]. Christ was surely not a coward but the greatest of heroes. So Christians have no reason to be ashamed of themselves when they live this virtue properly.

What does it mean to be humble? It means much more than submitting oneself to a higher authority, more than merely being at someone's service. Humility requires of course that we owe God the Lord, who gives us everything, the greatest obedience. At the same time, we must not forget that we have to obey this world's authorities. But it may sometimes happen that we must not obey this world's leaders and lawmakers because we judge that in obeying them we may in fact act incorrectly, wrongly.[4] In such a situation, we should not speak insults and grumble. Rather, we should pray. Furthermore, a public statement offered at the right time or an authentic request could be more necessary for us than many hours of reviling or lamenting behind the backs of these authorities.

Again, it is Christ himself who taught the greatest obedience, even in relation to this world's authorities. He was obedient until death, even until death on a cross [see Phil. 2:6–8]. Christ could have had the power to distance himself from every injustice. He could have scattered his evildoers as a wind would blow away a house of cards. What would we poor human beings do if Christ had exercised this kind of strength and power against us? Would any of us exist any longer? We must also ask God to give us the understanding so that we know when, to whom, and where we must be obedient.

We must always and in general distinguish between the party and the state. There are currently among us Christians who are obeying when they need not do so and who are resisting when they should obey. If we excuse such people for their deeds and actions, then we can almost always find permissible any action on the basis of the words: "We no longer know what to do today." The people who are saying these words today are not dumb in entirely other matters. Yet we cannot and may not pass judgment about such people, for we do know how unclear human understanding can often be at times.

---

3. Drawing on the ideas of Friedrich Nietzsche, N.S. propagandists held that Christian faith values the "weak" or "soft" virtues, for example, in the Beatitudes, Matthew 5:1–12. [RK]

4. This insight shaped FJ's refusal to take the oath of unconditional loyalty to the Führer. [RK]

However, we cannot approach God with these same words of excuse, for God sees into our human understanding and knows what we have actually thought.

"Jesus, meek and humble of heart, form our hearts according to your heart." We could and should pray this short, beautiful prayer often during each day.

On Prayer

We should never say "We must pray," but "We can and may pray." Why? Because God does not compel us to do anything. God allows us free will in faith and also in prayer.

We are responsible to our Lord God if we still can pray, for very few people today can still pray. Their souls are often so worn down and ill that they can no longer bring a proper prayer to their lips. And if they pray, it is very often a prayer for the sake of appearance, in which their hearts are not truly engaged. Further, many people now say: "I am postponing my praying and also my becoming a better person until my old age when I'll have an easier time of things." Think about these words. Do we know whether we'll live to old age? And if we are already old, do we know whether we'll be fully conscious until the end of our days? Also, people who are suffering physically do not have much time to pray, for they are struggling to overcome their pain. In their early years, people should come to see that they can no longer pray well when they are physically or mentally weary and spent. We should ask older people whether prayer has become easier in their later years and whether they can now turn to it more easily than they did in their earlier years. They may respond with a well-known adage: "What Hans did not learn as a little boy, Hans will never learn." These words apply to our discussion of prayer: what we would like to do in our later years, we must learn and consistently practice in our earlier years.

Many people ask, "Why do we get so little response to our prayers?" First, there are very few people who are able to pray to God with full faith and trust. Second, we frequently pray only for earthly goods. Yet Christ said: "But strive first for the kingdom of God and his righteousness, and all these things will be given to you as well" [Matt. 6:33]. We usually have things upside down, for we would like to make this world into a paradise. We do not consider perhaps that we have merited punishment for our sins and that we may thank our Lord God when he is so good by allowing us perhaps to make reparation for a great part of our guilt for our sins here in this world.[5] It is preferable, I believe, if we do not need to wait for the fire of purgatory. Many saints have said that there is no pain in this life that is greater than the pain that the poor souls must suffer in the fire of purgatory. Most of us Christians have little respect for the fire of purgatory and do not see that we could make reparation for the guilt of our sins in this world. We should think a bit about this and act accordingly: before we are allowed to enter into eternal glory, we must pay for our guilt to the last penny.

On the Our Father

Let us return to the topic of prayer, and in particular to the most beautiful of our prayers, which God himself has taught us, the Our Father [see Matt. 6:9–13]. If we take a close look at it, we can see how beautiful this prayer actually is.

"Our Father in heaven, hallowed be your name." In this first petition, we praise God's name, for the greatest honor and reverence is to be given to God, the Creator of heaven and earth. For this reason, we should never take God's name lightly or speak it in anger.

"Your kingdom come." In this second petition, we implore that the kingdom of God come to us, that it grows in the church, and also that it is always growing and thriving in us.

"Your will be done, on earth as it is in heaven." This third petition gives the way to the goal. God's kingdom enters into the world and into my soul only when the will of God is realized. Briefly stated, this is the essence of all prayers. What does God intend for us? That we do his will. His will is known not only in his Commandments but also in our lives, in our vocations and our roles. If we would always realize the obligations of our vocations and roles, we would be heroes!

"Give us this day our daily bread." We may and must petition our Lord God for our bread, for God is the One who gives us the bread for our bodies and souls. All of our troubles and efforts would be in vain if God would not give his blessing to them.

"And forgive us our debts, as we also have forgiven our debtors." We are sinful human beings and need God's forgiveness every day. This petition applies even to the smallest venial sins of the day because the Our Father is the

---

5. See "merit" and "reparation" in *The HarperCollins Encyclopedia of Catholicism*, ed. Richard P. McBrien (San Francisco: HarperCollins, 1996), 855–56, 1103–4. [RK]

prayer of the children of God. Nevertheless, one may implore God with full trust also concerning the gravest sins. Hence, a perfect repentance is situated in this petition when a genuine intention of penance is present. Nevertheless, the Lord includes an unchangeable condition: our heavenly Father will forgive us our sins only when we pardon other human beings for their failures. Therefore, it would be an impudent, outrageous act if we prayed the Our Father with hatred in our hearts. Indeed, we would call down on our heads God's punishment and lack of forgiveness. God pardons me as I pardon others—or do not [pardon them]!

"And do not bring us to the time of trial." We petition not only for a pardon of past sins but also for a guard against future ones. And also for a victory over temptation when it is inevitable, thus for a protection from sin.

"But rescue us from the evil one." Deliver us from sin, from the greatest evil that can exist in the world.

When we look over the entire Our Father, we see that it actually contains only two major petitions and a minor one. That we enter into God's kingdom. That we remain out of the kingdom of sin. And between these two main parts there lies the small request, namely, that we receive daily bread.

Therefore, when we devoutly pray the Our Father, we pray the paradigm prayer to which there is no equal. This prayer contains everything which human beings need in order to live happily in this world and also to become eternally blessed!

On Sin

We commit a mortal sin when we consciously and freely initiate and bring about a serious offense against God's Commandments. Why is it called a "mortal sin"? Because in this condition we are dead in relation to heaven. When we live with even one mortal sin, we cannot gain any more merit for heaven by means of all of our prayers, fasts, and charitable acts.

Some of the saints have received from God the grace to glimpse for a few moments the hideousness of mortal sin. Afterward, they said that it would be preferable to run with bare feet on burning coals to the end of the earth rather than again to glimpse this hideousness. We usually have little regard for this. Indeed, it is with laughter and delight that many people commit mortal sins. Many cannot hurry fast enough to tumble into hell. Moreover, all of the evils in the world are the consequences of sin.

People often become ill after they somehow lose something good, such as their home and farm. Many of these people would make significant sacrifices in order to regain what they lost. Yet how do some people — indeed, many people — conduct themselves after they lose the highest good, God the Lord, and eternal blessedness because of their sins? They feel no urgency to become reconciled with God through a good confession and thereby to attain for themselves eternal blessedness. For some people, it is even too much to make the smallest sacrifice in order to make up for their misconduct. They refuse to repent even though the evil of their serious sin is so great that when they commit it, they cannot pay for their offense by means of an eternity in hell, and they contest even the interest on this payment.

We human beings are often very foolish in our thinking and acting!

Woe are we when we no longer have a change of heart and do not resolve to improve ourselves after an occasion of sin!

Consider now venial sins. Should we avoid these? Yes, if something is a sin, then it is nevertheless a serious offense. Many people do not notice how expensive a bottle of wine is and drink it down. Surely, we can blot out this offense without going to confession; we can simply make a perfect act of contrition. Yet whoever does not have a regard for the minor sins has also little fear before the major sins. Many rain drops can sink a large ship if they are not pumped out of the ship in a timely manner. Things can go similarly for us poor human beings if we have little or no regard for our venial sins. In this case, the grace that God has given to us to blot out these offenses will have little or no effect on us. I remain convinced that when people have an earnest desire to avoid every venial sin, even when the sins seem small, then the Lord God rewards them in this life with such riches of grace that they can no longer be unhappy, even amid the greatest afflictions that can come upon us on earth. And how much more will the Lord God reward such people in eternity!

On the Four Last Things

The "four last things" are death, judgment, hell, and heaven.

We know that we must eventually die, but we do not know when, where, and how we shall die. Also, we know that if we die in the state of mortal sin, then we are eternally lost! We can ask ourselves, "Am I ready to die at any time?" If we answer yes, then all is going well. A person who is ready to die at any time can find that life is beautiful. But someone who is not ready to die cannot be happy in this life. If we did not have to die, then we could possess the whole world and not think about death. Yet sooner or later we must think about death. We are not yet so far along in life that we would like to reach out to the Reaper. Nevertheless, my loved ones, let us be ready to die, and then we can be among the most fortunate people in time and eternity. After death, repentance no longer helps us. There is the slogan: "As one lives, so one dies." And there is another: "Where the tree falls, there it remains."

Let us be concerned that we never need to fear the eternal Judge. When we frequently think about the day of our deaths and about eternal life, then we place eternal life more clearly in our sight.

Imagine that the world were a beach of fine sand and that a bird would come every hundred thousand years and carry away one grain of sand. How long would it take before there would be no more sand? After all of this time the world would eventually come to an end, while eternity would still just be starting.

What a terror it would be for us if we were sentenced by an earthly judge to life in prison. Yet it would be an even greater terror if we were sentenced by the eternal Judge to eternal damnation. And the damned in hell have to suffer such great pain that the least pain that they must suffer is so great that we in our earthly bodies could not endure it for one second. Imagine that an earthly judge could condemn us to have a toothache for one thousand years. I believe that there would be no one on earth who could endure this pain without going crazy.

How terrible the penance must be for the damned when they think: "With a little bit more sacrifice and suffering during my earthly life I could have merited heaven!" And if they could return to their earthly existence for one hour, they could do the penance that would earn them heaven.

Now let us raise our thoughts a little from hell to heaven. After he was given a short glimpse of heaven and was permitted a moment before the face of God, St. Paul said: "What no eye has seen, nor ear heard, nor the human heart conceived, what God has prepared for those who love him" (1 Cor. 2:9). Indeed, heaven must be something entirely grand: peace and joy without end.

One time, St. Augustine wanted to write a small book on the many, profound joys of heaven and desired the advice of St. Jerome. But Augustine himself was residing in Hippo, North Africa, and Jerome lived in Bethlehem. As Augustine was writing to the holy man in Bethlehem, incense was burning in his room, and a candle filled the room with a spectacular light. Then, in the midst of this light there appeared St. Jerome himself who — as Augustine afterward learned — had just died in Bethlehem. As Augustine was marveling at what he saw, he heard a crystal clear voice come from the middle of the light: "Augustine!

What do you want? Do you think that you'll be able to contain in a small vessel heaven's great sea of joy? It is as though you were trying to grasp the entire earth in one hand. Will your eyes see what no deceased person has yet seen? Will your ears hear what has not yet been heard by human ears? Do you believe that you will be able to understand what has not yet entered into a human heart and be able to comprehend what has not yet reached human understanding? How will you be able to perceive what is infinite and inconceivable?"

The voice proceeded to describe the blessed state of complete joy for those who dwell in heaven, and it concluded with these words: "Augustine, do not try to inquire into an impossible subject matter. Do not trouble yourself by trying to comprehend what no one can understand unless one is already in the blessed realm, toward which you are hopefully striving. In this life, be content to exercise works that lead you to those delights which you desire to comprehend here."

After these words, the image of St. Jerome disappeared. Augustine became so much at peace from the incense as well as from the light that he subsequently attested to the following: "The eternal light is so transforming that if someone were to remain in it for even less than a day, he would experience innumerable years of life in total enjoyment of all of this world's wonders and delights." (This story is taken from Martin Prugger's *Lehr- und Exempelbuch.*[6])

I believe that if we were to reflect more on eternal life, we would not find it difficult to make sacrifices for the sake of heaven. All people who have been baptized and raised in the Catholic faith likely say to themselves from time to time, "I am concerned about the next life." But when they can do so, they probably push aside the thought that they in fact think only a little bit about God and the next life.

"A Person's Character Shows Itself in Suffering"

This is an adage, and it proves true.

We show ourselves to be weak Christians when, because of a little suffering, we complain to God about the horror of it all. But should the Lord God reward

---

6. FJ is referring to Martin Prugger's *Lehr- und Exempelbuch,* 20th rev. ed., ed. Simon Buchfelner (Augsburg, 1724). FJ's copy of this book is wrapped in a book jacket, on the back of which is written: "Read by Franz Jägerstätter in the winter of 1937–1938. I recommend that others read it." The full title of this book is "Martin Prugger's Book of Doctrines and Role Models, in which the Complete Catechism or the Catholic Christian Doctrines are Presented in an Easily Accessible Form, as well as Clarified and Enriched by Various Wonderful Anecdotes, Parables, and Sayings from the Sacred Scriptures and the Church Fathers." FJ refers again to this anecdote about St. Augustine and St. Jerome in text no. 88 (page 243 below). [RK]

us for the offenses against God that we make by our complaining? Shouldn't God punish us for our complaining?

It would be better to thank God when he sends us some kind of suffering so that we can make reparation in this life for our sins. Or do we believe that we should save all of our penance for purgatory since it will be similar to an enjoyable social gathering? Sometimes we ask: "Isn't it enough that we have had to work throughout the whole day? Where do those people go who have never worked hard during their lives?" We should let God judge other people. We must be happy if we ourselves are not condemned. When we are diligent and hardworking, we are so for the loving God. But we must also ask: "How many of us do all that we do out of love for God? Rather, don't we always want to receive a great reward for what we do?"

[We want] to become richer and more esteemed! To be sure, the Lord God sometimes gives us an entirely wonderful reward in this life. But if we had never committed a sin, we would still have to work and take care for our daily bread. This burden has come upon us because of original sin. In the future, let's not be so shortsighted that we are always looking for rewards in this life. When things become difficult sometimes because of work and suffering, we should think about what Christ has promised for those who love him and do the will of his Father [see Matt. 7:21]. Let us be mindful of the fact that we too are cross-bearers. That Christ, though blameless, suffered for us in order to redeem us. And that we, though guilty, do not want to suffer. Therefore, let us take the cross upon ourselves and not complain about it. If it sometimes becomes difficult, then our reward will be greater. Through the cross to the crown! Through suffering to victory!

On Our Fear of Other People

Nevertheless, we Catholics are often cowards. We are often not worthy to bear the wonderful name "Roman Catholic."

We often live and act as though human beings were our ultimate judge. Many people would live far more Christian lives if they did not have this miserable fear of other human beings. What would happen if we really could live so that many worldly people would always praise us, with the result that God would disdain us for this? How many people are there in general who recount only the good aspects of their neighbors? Most often one speaks about and recounts only the bad things. Therefore, we should never allow ourselves to be confused in our religious lives by the evil tongues of other people. No one will step before the eternal Judge for us. Only our guardian angel will be our advocate and defender. St. Stephen once said, "I am and intend to be Catholic. I am living Catholic, and I am dying Catholic."[7] If we want to be assured a gracious Judge, we must also become Stephens.

How can I do all of my daily activities and all of my work for eternal merit?

To accomplish this goal is not as easy as many people perhaps think. First, it requires a secure, unshakeable faith and a deep trust in God. "This is entirely simple," many people would say, "for I make a good intention at the start of each day, as I say the words: 'Everything for the honor of God!' Or 'My Jesus, everything for your sake!' Or 'In God's name!'" It is wonderful when someone expresses this intention. But now comes the greater question, "Did I truly mean what I said?" If we answer yes all the time, we would often be mistaken. When we are put to an actual test, we go back and forth. We can distinguish true Catholics from the nominal Catholics and non-Catholics in situations of misfortune and hardship.

Consider this little example. A husband and wife begin the day with a good intention as they say: "Everything to the honor of my God!" Then they enter into the day's work, which involves much walking around and continually lifting things — all of the activities of hardworking people on a long summer's day. In the evening, when they are completely tired out, God puts them to the test. How genuine was their intention in the morning? God sends a severe thunderstorm that does great damage in the fields and meadows. If they have truly worked for the honor of God, this destruction will mean nothing to them. On the contrary, they will thank God for this misfortune. However, if they have accomplished their work for earthly profit, then this destruction will upset them. I do not need to say anything more. Everyone knows well enough what can spew out of someone's mouth. Indeed, if someone thinks only in worldly terms, then a misfortune is so terrible that it can determine many days, indeed years, until it is remedied. So we have actual proof that it is not so easy to do everything for the honor of God. If we want to walk a higher path in our lives, we must encounter little and even big tests from time to time. And if we are energetic and dedicated students, we'll not have great anxiety amid these tests. We know, too, that if we do well on them, then we'll face even harder tests.

---

7. The Christian tradition does not attribute these words to the deacon and martyr St. Stephen of Acts 6:8–8:3. FJ may be referring to the St. Stephen who lived in Constantinople during the eighth century and endured persecution and imprisonment.

To be a Christian is actually the highest vocation in the world. Consider that people who make mistakes in their work usually want to improve their skills. They have the intention of becoming very competent, even experts, in their line of work. Shouldn't we who are Christians think in a similar way about our vocation? If we educate ourselves in this calling about which we should be proud, we would not want to make mistakes in living the Christian life. Would we blame our outstanding teacher Jesus Christ when we take the challenging tests that he puts before us, but fail to pass them and hence do not enter into heaven? To be sure, the living God does not intend that we be lost for all eternity or that after our deaths we languish for hundreds of years in purgatory.

Sometimes we say to ourselves: "I am too weak and, even with the best will, cannot make any progress." Good teachers know their students and note who is diligent and who isn't. Would they neglect students who are trying hard but are still not able to do well? No, they would give them special help so that they could attain their desired goals. Similarly, may we Christians imagine anything less from our Teacher just because he was perhaps burdened with fewer weaknesses than ordinary teachers? The loving God will assist weak and struggling Christians with much wondrous grace. Therefore, we must see every test — whether small or great — that God gives us as grace. We can learn something from every test. Each day God sends us numerous small tests such as in patience, in humility, in love of neighbor, and so forth. For this reason, at the end of each day our conscience must investigate and decide which of the tests we answered incorrectly or poorly. When we have failed, we must repent of our sins and failings and resolve to do better the next day on the new tests.

When Catholics are so engaged in their faith that they take note of every small thing that they have done poorly, then God will surely give them more time in this life until they can say: "Teacher, you can now come with your tests, even with the greatest of them, namely, death. Now, dear God, I shall be completely earnest when I pray these words to you: 'Dear Jesus, I am living in you. Dear Jesus, I am dying in you. Dear Jesus, I am yours in life and in death! Amen.'"

On the Blessed Sacrament

Do we truly believe in the true divinity of Jesus Christ in the Blessed Sacrament if we come to the table of the Lord only two or three times during a year?

Sometimes we may envy the Three Kings because they were able to take Jesus into their arms [see Matt. 2:11–12]. Yet they must have made a long, dangerous journey until they were able to experience their good fortune. Nevertheless, hasn't Christ placed us in a far better situation than the Three Kings? We do not need to make a long, dangerous journey. Moreover, we can receive a much greater grace, for we are able to take the same Jesus not only into our arms, but also into our hearts. Sometimes we may think that if we could see Jesus in the consecrated host — as the Three Kings once saw Jesus in Bethlehem — then everything would be entirely different for us. But hasn't Christ said: "Blessed are those who have not seen and yet have come to believe" [John 20:29]. Consequently, there is no doubt that we receive far greater graces in the reception of Holy Communion by not seeing Christ in the sacred host than if we were able to see him there.

Don't we face a very great danger when we are lukewarm and indifferent in relation to the Blessed Sacrament? The Blessed Sacrament is the greatest and most wondrous legacy that Christ has left us in the Last Supper. And the Catholic Church permits us daily to draw from this rich wellspring of grace if we are free of sin. Can't it easily be possible that Christ will exclude us from the inheritance of heaven when we are indifferent about the inheritance that he has left us in the Last Supper?

Consider this comparison. A rich uncle has somehow left us a great amount of money in an account at a distant bank. He has included the stipulation that we must personally withdraw a hundred marks or even a thousand marks every week or perhaps even every day. If we remain away from this account for no good reason, then the money must remain in the bank. Would there be many of us who would continue in our previous work in which we have earned 1 mark or even less? I believe not. And if this account truly gave us this money every week, would we neglect withdrawing it? Would we risk losing the money to the bank? If this generous uncle were alive and were to learn that we had not been withdrawing the money and were in fact indifferent about it, he would be aware of our ingratitude. Likely moved by anger, he would disinherit us and give the inheritance to other people who were more worthy of it.

Although we could make ourselves quite comfortable in this life by means of an actual inheritance from a rich uncle, how much more delighted we should be to receive the great inheritance that our best friend Jesus Christ has bequeathed to us in the Blessed Sacrament. Would it surprise us if God were to remove this rich treasury of grace from us and give it to other people?

Sometimes we hear people say that those who receive Holy Communion frequently are no better than anyone else. This may happen sometimes. Nevertheless, when a field is overgrown with weeds and the farmers pull out only the larger ones among them so that they can then plant good seeds in the field, can the farmers expect a full, rich harvest? I believe not.

If people want to produce high quality fruit, they will find a plot of land from which the weeds are already pulled, and then they will go around pulling out the smallest weeds by their roots. So it is with us sinful human beings if we are not always striving to become better and holier by avoiding even the smallest sin. Even then, it can happen that despite our frequent reception of the Blessed Sacrament we are not truly making progress [toward holiness].

Is it necessary that we strive for holiness, and is it possible that even after doing so we may not enter into heaven?

Everyone who dies with a grave sin and is baptized can enter into heaven even if beforehand he or she must first endure purgatory for hundreds, even thousands of years. Sometimes we hear someone ask: "Do you believe that I'll become a holy person?" It is doubtful, however, that these words will bring someone to holiness. Words such as these sometimes come from someone who would like to ridicule the saints in heaven because of their wondrous virtues.

Aren't the saints in heaven, especially the most Blessed Virgin Mary, our intercessors with God in heaven? Sometimes when people find themselves in an unfortunate situation, they call out to the saints who are expected immediately to send them help, even though these people have previously ridiculed the saints for their virtuous and penitential lives. If we could ask the saints what we should to in order to become eternally blessed, they would tell us nothing different from what the Catholic Church teaches.

On the Feast of the Holy Family

On this day we reflect, in particular, on the Holy Family in Nazareth.[8] We should strive not only to think about this family, but also to imitate it.

Even Joseph and Mary lived among sinful people. Even they had to struggle with the burdens of earthly life and had to acquire their means of existence by working with their hands. They attained the wondrous virtues not as immediate gifts from heaven. The familiar adage applied even to them: "Without suffering, no joy. Without struggle, no victory." So we want to reflect on our own families today and to consider how little we resemble the Holy Family.

First, it is our primary task that we care not merely for the physical well-being of our children and family members, but much more for their souls.

---

8. Since the church celebrates the feast of the Holy Family on the Sunday after Christmas, FJ likely wrote this essay in late December 1941. [RK]

Since our conduct with our children and our relatives is entrusted to us, we must render an account before our eternal Judge. God has given everyone invisible and visible guardian angels. The visible ones are the parents and others who are responsible for the education of the children. It can occur that something bad can come about, even when the parents and the pastors motivate and educate children for what is good by means of their own words and deeds. Unfortunate things can happen through the influence of the evil one who wants to win all people for himself. It can also occur because of interaction with bad children or adults. When children and young people go astray, they can return to the right path because this path was already shown to them at an early age. But how difficult it must be for children who hear and see a lack of true faith in their parents who are supposed to be their visible guardian angels leading them to heaven! Sometimes a pastor can show great care for the children entrusted to him for religious education when these children experience something quite different from their parents who are nominal Catholics.

Nevertheless, small things can bring children and young people to doubt their faith, especially when parents condemn many truths of the faith that the children learn in religious education. Parents should not speak about matters of faith with their children when they themselves no longer know, nor want to know, what is and is not sinful. What a big impact they can have in important matters! In these situations, children and young people must ultimately see for themselves that they should listen to what they learn in their religious education and not to the stupid things that they hear some people say.

Children watch and listen to their father, for he is usually the head of the family and the disciplinarian for serious matters. How can the parents teach their children the high value of the Blessed Sacrament or the Mass when they themselves do not receive communion or even attend Mass? Parents sometimes say that they do not have time for church on some days. However, on such days, they can make time for church when there still exists the personal habit and the social custom.

Children who are poorly educated in the faith often continue to practice their faith as long as they fear the punishment of their parents. Years later, as adults, they may live as lukewarm Christians and interiorly may be more similar to nonbelievers or free thinkers than to Christians.

How can nominal Catholics demand obedience and respect from their children when they extract from their children's hearts, especially by means of their bad example, what the catechists have worked to plant in the young hearts? These Catholics are the same ones who complain about the youth of today and blame other people for this state of affairs. Could not the children of these Catholics say—though with a different meaning—to their parents the words that the child Jesus said to his mother in the Temple: "Did you not know that I must be in my Father's house?" (Luke 2:49).

We Must Always Be Children before God

God is our Father, and we are his children. Whether young or old, we must always feel like children before God. Our whole lives should be ones of making requests to and thanking [God] because we can do nothing on our own. We are mistaken if we sometimes believe that we have produced this or that on our own power and that we do not need to thank God for sending us the power and health to do what we did or the talent to do it. We must also be children when we seek pardon. When some people are offended by someone else, they hold that they do not need to pardon the individual who hurt them until the offender comes to them and repents of his or her wrongdoing. In such cases, one person will not easily pardon another. The one who has offended the other will hold that he or she was in the right. As a result, it often happens that people carry around animosities for many years. How good it would be in instances of offending someone, or of being offended, if people would consider that the other person is a brother or sister — since before God we are all siblings — and truly pardon the offense as soon as possible. If we have lost the sense of being children, then we must regain it, for Christ himself said that those who do not become like little children cannot enter into the kingdom of heaven [see Matt. 18:3].

Are we justified in sometimes being slow to pardon someone? I believe not. There is only One who has the right not to pardon us in eternal life, and this is God. Humiliation and pain were never inflicted on a blameless person as they were on our divine Savior. Yet on the cross our Savior prayed for his enemies and even promised the good thief entrance into heaven [see Luke 23:43]. He also cast a pardoning glance to his betrayer Judas as he betrayed him with a kiss [see Matt. 26:50]. If we do not want to live in arrogant blindness, we sinful human beings must readily pardon one another.

Every hour in which we live in hatred is lost for eternal blessedness, for whoever lives in hatred of another human being cannot enter into friendship with God. Christ himself said: "First be reconciled to your brother or sister, and then come and offer your gift" [Matt. 5:24]. I believe that few Catholics would be able to pray the Our Father every day if they were to realize that [in saying this prayer] they are passing judgment on themselves because they can await no pardon from God until they have pardoned those who have offended them. We sometimes speak with our foes as though nothing had happened while we secretly harbor grudges against them and wait until we can get revenge or can say bad things about them behind their backs. But this is not true pardoning. God will not accept a superficial pardoning, for God knows us better than we know ourselves.

On Love

In conclusion, I want to write a few words about love, for without love everything is dead. If someone accomplishes many good works but without love, all of them are dead. Faith and hope and love surely belong together, and yet the highest among them is love. Faith and hope will someday cease, but love is eternal [see 1 Cor. 13].

Of course, we must differentiate between genuine love and sensual love. Sensual love does not of course endure forever, for it vanishes as quickly as it has arrived. Sometimes when it continues for a short time, it can severely wound genuine love. Also, a marriage that is based only on sensual love seldom lasts very long. And if it does not lead to a separation, it pushes most people into misfortune in this life and perhaps also in eternal life.

Let's return to the idea of true love. Authentic love brings about well-being. It comes from heaven and leads to heaven. It is not jealous. It is not inflated. It endures everything. It pardons everything. It also believes everything. It overcomes everything.

How can we grow in true love? Only through God's grace, which we receive primarily through prayer and a deep faith. Authentic love increases in us so that we can love even our enemies. Then we can and should call ourselves Christians. To love only one's friends is something that the anti-Christ and the heathen can do.

On Reading

Is the reading of good books and journals unconditionally necessary for attaining eternal blessedness? The answer to this question is yes and also no. If the answer were only yes, then we would be [wrongly] saying that it is pointless for nonreaders to seek eternal life.

However, it is difficult for those who do not use this wonderful, God-given gift of reading to move toward eternal life. I'll explain my point with the following example.

Imagine that two individuals must make international journeys to the same destination, and each must travel alone. The one individual prepares long in advance of his trip. He carefully studies the map so that he can memorize the entire route. He learns by heart the names of the important places along the way. Nevertheless, after he sets out, he finds himself from time to time making mistakes, arriving at some points later than he had expected. But in each case, as soon as he sees that he is on the wrong road, he takes out his map, figures out where he has gone wrong, and corrects his mistake. It even happens that he has to travel through a region belonging to an enemy. Suspected of being a spy, he is seized and locked up for a period of time during which he is robbed of his most important papers. He is eventually released. Because he is able to recall from memory the map that he has studied and what he has read about his route, he continues toward his destination. At one point, he finds himself in a land torn apart by a war that has resulted in the road signs being destroyed or falsified. Nevertheless, he overcomes these obstacles and eventually arrives at his ultimate destination, crediting his success to his initial studying and memorizing of the map.

Now consider the journey of the second individual who did almost nothing to prepare for his travels. Although he takes a map with him, he has almost no interest in it for he believes that he can always ask someone along the way. But he encounters the same difficulties as the first traveler. He loses his map. He reads falsified signs. He asks directions from people who either do not know the way or deliberately choose to point him in the wrong direction. We must not forget, too, that this second traveler — like the first — finds himself in an enemy land. Even though he meets people who do not treat him as a foe, he does not ask them for directions because he fears that they will give him incorrect information.

Will this second traveler be as fortunate in reaching his destination as the first was? The answer is obvious, I believe.

This imaginary account of two travelers helps make my point. Does not each of us have to make a far journey, a journey to eternal life? Shouldn't our destination be heaven? And don't each of us ultimately make this journey alone? Moreover, how well will people move toward the desired goal if they make little or no preparation for this long and dangerous journey by reading spiritual books and journals? They must rely entirely on others, yet they do not know whether these other people know the right way. They must also not forget that this journey is one of the farthest and most difficult because it is swarming with enemies who want to control everyone so that no one can attain their high, elevated destination.

There may have been a time when this goal was easier to attain without having to read. Then there were trustworthy guides in many places, guides who themselves were on the right path. A traveler could calmly walk in their footsteps. Further, these guides were not shy about making clear to others when they were going in the wrong direction. But not today! We now find ourselves in an enemy land in which either the guides give us maps that are at best falsified, or they give us nothing. They fail to give us the journals and books that are truly Christian. We do not know whether the guides themselves even have this literature in their own possession. For others have either misdirected our guides — the bishops and the priests — or they have silenced them by means of intimidation. If a guide with the courage has warned his trusting sheep about the dangerous wrong paths, or has led them back to the right path after they had gone astray, then he himself has been removed from his position.[9] What has happened to such guides is not unknown.

Was the church in an earlier era sufficiently concerned to furnish the laity with Sacred Scripture or with many good journals so that people could find their own way when their spiritual leaders were taken away from them or were silenced?[10] How many [leaders] were themselves interested in these books and journals? Many clearly recognize today that it is hard to find the right way. But instead of making the effort to find the right way as quickly as possible, many people say, "Everything will work out all right," or something similar. Praying and trusting in God are appropriate if we are to find the right path. We need the Seven Gifts, for which we should pray to the Holy Spirit.[11] But will merely trusting in God lead us to the right goal?

Who can guarantee those of us who err that we will once again experience an era in which the way to heaven is fenced in with roses so that we can see this path from afar and reach it? Or who can guarantee us an era when those of us who have found the right path will not deviate from it? Are not thousands of people departing from us every day without experiencing such a wonderful

---

9. One of the priests to whom FJ is likely referring was Pastor Karobath.

10. FJ is likely referring here to the biblical renewal movement that the Bible associations of Kloster-neuberg and Stuttgart nurtured during the 1920s and into the 1930s.

11. The Seven Gifts of the Holy Spirit are wisdom, understanding, counsel, fortitude, knowledge, fear of the Lord, and piety. See Isaiah 11:1–3. [RK]

era? Had not people found the right way, and were they not remaining on it during that time when Austria upheld full religious freedom? Was it not a wonderful time?

Come the Last Judgment those people who could not teach young people to read will be held less accountable than those people who possessed this great, God-given gift — which is invaluable — and did not use it for its proper goal.

A Brief Reflection on the Current Era

It is undeniable that times change, and therefore the way to heaven does not remain the same. This way has never been easy to find or to follow. Yet it is even more difficult to find and to follow now than a few years ago when we lived in a land that still upheld religious freedom.

A great stream has engulfed us. Now all of us German-speaking Catholics have to swim and struggle in this stream regardless of whether we jumped into it on our own or whether others pulled us into it. It is the same for all of us so long as we find ourselves in it. There remains for us no other way than to swim against the stream in order to come again to a river bank.

Getting out of the stream will be more difficult for those who jumped into it and also pulled others into it. Their bad consciences have weakened their spiritual strength, and without such strength they will soon give up their struggle against the waves. These people may stay longer in the water, too, because they possess not much strength to pull themselves from the waves, and they will not be quickly thrown a life-saver from the shore. They may eventually be pulled under the waves and washed up dead on the shore.

Is it possible for us while we are still swimming in the current and struggling against it to pull from it others whose powers have already completely dwindled? An adage applies here: "Only with great difficulty will a person who is stuck in a swamp be able to pull out someone else." To be sure, some things are easier in water [than in a swamp]. In order to bring about such a rescue someone must be a very strong swimmer, and the current must not be too wide and forceful. Otherwise, it can easily happen that the rescue attempt can bring about the rescuer's misfortune.

Are there still many people who want to save themselves from this current and who are sturdy enough to swim against it? The church has taken note of this difficult situation for a long time. In an earlier era, it made great efforts to give its members the means to survive or advised them through the disseminating of many Catholic journals and books. One of the greatest and best steps to help people was the [papal] exhortation for the frequent reception of Holy Communion.[12] This means of strength assisted Christians in the first century who had to endure hardships that were not much easier than ours. Even today, Christ has not retracted his words that the kingdom of God is suffering violence, and only those who use force will seize it [see Matt. 11:12].

It is of course very sad today that so many people do not recognize, or do not want to recognize, the dangerous situation in which we find ourselves. Many people claim to be blameless. God will eventually judge to what extent they truly are. Of course, the perpetrators will be held more responsible before God's eternal judgment seat than those whom they have seduced. However, the seduced usually have to bear the consequences in this world of the seduction more than the seducers.

The church's means of strengthening and empowering us are simply pointless for those who do not want to recognize the dangerous situation in which we find ourselves today or who do not want to swim against the stream because to do so is more difficult than to allow oneself to be washed along by the waves. If the current becomes too wide and too forceful, then these strengths will fail even the best swimmers. Nevertheless, we must not give up for there awaits on the river bank the One who hears our calls for help. She is the help of Christians. The Blessed Virgin and Mother of God, Mary.

These reflections were written by Franz Jägerstätter during the war years, 1941–42.

Have forbearance with my many mistakes and my poor handwriting. During my school years, I was a lazy student.

---

12. Pope Pius X stressed the value of daily reception of Holy Communion in *Sacra Tridentina Synodus* (December 22, 1905). [RK]

Chapter 8

Notebook II
1942

Franz Jägerstätter likely wrote in his second notebook during 1942. At the outset, he recalls his dream of January 1938, in which he sees people rushing to the "train" of National Socialism, and hears a voice declare, "This train is going to hell." Using this dream as a lens, he gives his analysis of the political, social, and ecclesiastical dynamics in Austria after four years of N.S. rule. This analysis unfolds in nine essays:

- *"On Today's Issue: Catholic or National Socialist?"*

- *"Brief Thoughts on Our Past, Present, and Future"*

- *"Bolshevism or National Socialism"*

- *"A Game of Deceit"*

- *"On the Loss of Responsibility"*

- *"Is It Still Possible to Do Something?"*

- *"Is There Still a God?"*

- *"War or Revolution?"*

- *"On Dangerous Weapons"*

During 1942 Franz heard what the soldiers on leave were saying about the war in Russia and learned of the combat deaths of young men from his region. Along with most Europeans, he likely knew that Napoleon I (1769–1821) and his Grande Armée were defeated in Russia in the autumn of 1812. Aware of the Wehrmacht's plight on the eastern front, he poses the question: "Has the Lord God perhaps brought a stop to the [N.S.] stream because of the good that still exists there?" [RK]

172

On Today's Issue: Catholic or National Socialist?

A very important question today is this: can someone be both a Catholic and a National Socialist? When the Social Democrats stood at Austria's helm, the church told us that a Social Democrat could not also be a Catholic.[1] And now?

I want to begin by describing a short experience that I underwent on a January night in 1938. I initially lay awake in bed until midnight, even though I was not sick. Then I must have fallen asleep for at least a little while, for I saw [in a dream] a wonderful train as it came around a mountain. With little regard for the adults, children flowed to this train and were not held back. There were present a few adults who did not go into the area. I do not want to give their names nor to describe them. Then a voice said to me, "This train is going to hell." Immediately it happened that someone took me by the hand, and the same voice said to me: "Now we are going to purgatory." What I glimpsed and perceived was fearful. If this voice had not told me that we were going to purgatory, I would have judged that I had found myself in hell. Apparently, only a few seconds passed during which I glimpsed all of this. Then I heard a rushing sound and saw a light, and everything went away. I immediately awoke my wife and recounted to her everything that had transpired.

Before that night I could never of course truly believe that the suffering in purgatory could be so great. The train's significance was initially an enigma to me. However, the longer I have thought about the dream, the more clearly this moving train's meaning has dawned on me. It is now clear that this image represents nothing other than National Socialism with all of its distinct organizations — the N.S. German Workers' Party, the N.S. Public Assistance program, the N.S. Women's Association, the Hitler Youth, and so forth — that were breaking in or sneaking in at that time. In other words, the train represents the N.S. *Volk* community and everything for which it sacrifices and struggles.

Just prior to the dream, newspapers reported that 150,000 young Austrians had recently entered the Hitler Youth and hence had joined the N.S. Party.[2]

Let us consider adults who have property, are civil servants, or manage businesses as well as domestic workers and laborers — people who do not belong

---

1. During the 1920s and into the 1930s, Austria's Social Democratic Party pursued a moderate socialist agenda. For this reason, church officials accused this party of being "Bolshevist" or "Communist." [RK] In this vein, Bishop Gföllner of Linz published a pastoral letter on March 1, 1930, concerning the opposition between the church and Communism. This letter was read aloud at Mass in all Catholic churches in the Diocese of Linz. See *Linzer Diözesanblatt* (1930), 41ff.

2. After Austria's plebiscite on April 10, 1938, the Reich required all youth between the ages of ten and eighteen to belong to the Hitler Youth.

to one of the N.S. organizations and do not put money into the red containers.[3] These people must face a choice: either membership in the N.S. *Volk*
community along with donations to the red containers is necessary for our
sanctification as Catholics, or it is an obstacle to it. If membership is necessary
if we want to attain blessedness, then this is a sign that National Socialism has
expanded its network of organizations [to include the Catholic Church].

I believe that the German-speaking people never participated as strongly in
Christian charitable activities as they are now engaging in the N.S. organizations. Nor were they as ready to contribute their money to church programs.

Nevertheless, it will soon be clear to everyone that a person's donations are
not what's most important in the Reich. People can contribute as much as they
are supposed to, but their donations will count for nothing if they have not
committed themselves to the N.S. Party. For example, the National Socialists
have conveyed the true aim of their Winter Help Work (W.H.W.).[4] In the
village of Mautern I saw a poster that read: "Your contribution to the W.H.W.
is your acknowledgment of the Führer."[5] In other words, by means of the
W.H.W., the Führer is testing people to determine who is for him and who is
against him.[6]

Prior to Hitler's seizure of power [on January 30, 1933], many bishops in
Germany banned National Socialists from receiving communion. But how is
it now in the Reich? Many people who are members of the N.S. Party go to
the communion rail with peace of mind. Also, their children participate in the
Hitler Youth, or they receive instructions from N.S. teachers.

Have the National Socialists now — after more than two years of bringing
about the horrible murders of people — adopted a new orientation that would
allow and even promote the silence of church officials? Have church officials
reached the decision that it is now permissible for Catholics to belong to a party
that opposes the church? Have they given a positive evaluation of National
Socialism?

An ordinary person would surely like to cry out at times. When one reflects
even a little on these matters, one wonders whether those who are the most
upright in our land are making a mistake. After all of the [church's] warnings,

---

3. The red containers were bright red tin boxes, approximately seven inches high, that N.S. members
used to collect money for the N.S. Party and its organizations.

4. The Winter Help Work, Winterhilfswerk, was a N.S. program that gathered money, clothing, and
food for the assistance of people in need. It had great propaganda value.

5. During his military training, FJ passed through Mautern an der Donau on March 2, 1941.

6. Reich leader Martin Bormann wrote on June 6, 1941, that National Socialism and the Christian faith
"are irreconcilable."

a bloody Christian persecution will not occur in our land because the church does almost everything that the N.S. party wants or commands.

Austria would no longer have many good priests in freedom or in their ministry if its Catholic clergy had stalwartly voted no in the plebiscite of April 10, 1938. Instead, church officials praised the N.S. Party for its many good acts and so helped generate 100 percent support for the N.S. state.[7] Things would be no worse today for genuine Christian faith in our land if the churches were no longer open and if thousands of Christians had poured out their blood and their lives for Christ and their faith. This would have been better than now watching silently as there is more and more acceptance of falsehood. Yet many people are impatiently waiting for a liberation from this sad situation.

It would be worthwhile if we were to think about the Führer's words: "If you take care of yourself, then you are taking care of God." I would like to cry out to the people aboard the N.S. train: "Jump off this train before it arrives at your last stop, where you will pay with your life!" I believe that God has clearly spoken to me through this dream or appearance and placed it in my heart so that I could decide whether to be a National Socialist or a Catholic!

I am not throwing stones at our bishops and priests. They are human beings of flesh and blood as we are, and they can be weak. Perhaps they are even more tempted by the evil foe than we are. Perhaps, too, they were too little prepared to take on this struggle and to decide for themselves whether to live or to die. Would not our hearts shake [as theirs must have] if it were to come about that we would have to appear before God's judgment seat and be accountable for a decision that would affect so many other human beings? These thoughts help us appreciate more fully the difficult decision before which our bishops and priests stood in March 1938.

Perhaps our bishops thought that the new state would continue for only a short time and then fall apart and that by means of their accommodation they could spare many martyrs and much pain among believers. Unfortunately, things have gone otherwise. Many years have passed, and thousands of people die every year amid this falsehood. We can easily imagine what a heroic decision it would have been to have opposed what the N.S. state has demanded of the bishops during these recent years. Let's not reproach the bishops so that we make the situation more difficult for them than it already is. Rather, let us

7. In anticipation of their nation's plebiscite on April 10, 1938, the Catholic bishops of Austria issued a pastoral letter on March 27, 1938, advising people to vote in favor of Austria's "annexation" into the "Greater Germany."

pray for them, asking that God enlighten them for the great challenge before which they still stand.

If we seriously observe the era in which we now live, we must conclude that the situation for us German-speaking Christians is far more hopeless and complex than it was for the Christians in the first centuries amid the bloody persecutions. Many will perhaps ask themselves, "Why has the Lord God allowed us to live in such a time?" We should not blame God, nor should we shift the blame to other people. The adage applies here: "Where we put ourselves to sleep is what we lie in." Still today it is possible with God's help — if we make serious efforts and apply all of our strength — to get ourselves out of this swamp in which we are stuck and to become eternally blessed.

We must keep in mind, of course, that suffering during our earthly lives is not the worst thing. Even the saints had to suffer frightfully until God took them into eternal life. The Lord did not spare even his apostles from suffering, and most of them lost their lives through martyrdom. And the prospect of martyrdom did not deter them from working so much for Christ.

Amid our sinful lives, we want to live without suffering and struggles, to have a gentle death, and to attain eternal well-being beyond all of this. Christ himself, the most blameless individual, suffered the most among all human beings and purchased heaven for us by means of his suffering and death. Yet we do not want to suffer for him! If we study history and look into the past centuries, we are not surprised that we are in this situation today. Over the years, a deep and devout faith has increasingly receded, and a new paganism has increasingly pushed ahead. Centuries ago, the good writers of religious history said — indeed, some even predicted — that great misery would come upon human beings if they did not improve themselves.

We need only look at Russia. What great suffering among the people! When will they be liberated from it? Should everything be painless for us now as many people hold?

Brief Thoughts on Our Past, Present, and Future

Despite predictions and wise observations, the future always remains dark for us. The future is usually somewhat different from what mere human wisdom has anticipated. What will the future bring us Austrians, us German-speaking people? Many among us still dream of a wonderful future when the war has ended. We leave everything in God's hands, for God directs and leads our destiny. [We hold that] the wildest currents must stand still before God's word.

However, ever since people have existed, we have learned from experience that God allows human beings free will and that God will intervene only occasionally in the destiny of a human being and of a people. Hence, things can become very different in the future, except at the world's end.

Adam and Eve completely ruined their destiny by their disobedience against God [Genesis 3]. They would not have suffered if they had obeyed God rather than the seducer. Also, God could have directed their thoughts differently. If God had prevented their first sin, he could have spared the suffering of all humanity through the avoidance of this first occasion of sin. Further, God could have even spared his beloved Son from this infinite suffering. And so it will be until the end of the world that every sin has consequences. Woe are we if we want to shift these consequences from ourselves and do not want to do penance for our sins and failures.

Would the majority of people turn themselves around today if God would strike the weapons out of the hands of the earth's peoples? Many people surely hold that Austria and Bavaria would not be affected very much if the war were to take a turn for the worse against Germany. But let's ask ourselves: "Are Austria and Bavaria blameless in that we now have a N.S. state instead of a Christian one? Did National Socialism simply fall on us from the sky?" I believe that in response we need not waste many words. Whoever was not asleep during the last one hundred years knows well enough how and why everything has come about.

I believe that what happened in the spring of 1938 was not much different from what happened on Holy Thursday more than nineteen hundred years ago when [Pilate] gave the Jewish people a free choice between the blameless Savior and the thief Barabbas. At that time, the Pharisees had even handed out money among the people so that they would cry out and also so that they would lead astray and intimidate those who still followed Christ. What did some people allege and fabricate against Christian-orientated Chancellor Schuschnigg and against the clergy, even engaging in support for blood-curdling marches?[8] The few people who did not err and did not give the unfortunate yes [in the plebiscite] were simply called fools or communists.[9] Even today, some people have not relinquished their campaigns against these "fools" in order to win them over to the N.S. *Volk* community or at least to have them give up their

---

8. Kurt von Schuschnigg (1897–1977) was Austria's chancellor from July 25, 1934, until March 12, 1938. Imprisoned by the Reich until 1945, he emigrated to the United States in 1947 and taught at St. Louis University. [RK]

9. As already noted, FJ voted no on April 10, 1938.

ideas! Clearly the joy of victory has not lasted long among many people, and many of these people have come to recognize that things are now quite different from what was promised at the outset. Yet the situation today has not disgusted them nor caused them to revolt. They do not have the courage to separate themselves from this anti-Christian *Volk* community.

They seem to me to be not much different from a young woman of rather good character who has been taken in by a malicious young man, intent on seducing her and satisfying his lust. She may initially find things going well. As long as she has no pangs of conscience, she may feel that everything's fine. Then she may finally come to a true estimation of this fellow or may experience the effects of his sinful ways. She may protest and complain about the seducer because of the effects that she must bear. If she cannot summon the courage to end this sinful relationship, she will not become fortunate. Now she will not love but hate the man.

The young woman will eventually try to end this relationship. But this arrogant fellow will not easily let go of his victim. He'll intimidate her with threats, or he'll demand that she return his gifts to her — gifts from which she does not want to be separated. The woman may pray day and night and not sense a divine response. Not truly wanting to give up the relationship, she will endure every hardship, even when the fellow threatens to kill her or slanders her.

Now reflect for a moment on the situation in Russia. Has the Lord God perhaps brought a stop to the stream there because of the good that still exists there?[10] Will God bring about a liberation from that sad situation during this year? Will the Russian people readily assent as willingly and numerously to becoming a Bolshevik community as the Austrian people did to becoming a N.S. *Volk* community, which is ultimately no better than a hodge-podge? Will we Austrians perhaps emerge from our situation exempt from punishment because most of us are Catholics?

However, woe be us if the words that Christ once spoke about Capernaum are also valid for us: "And you, Capernaum, will you be exalted to heaven? No, you will be brought down to Hades" (Matt. 11:23). If it is to happen in our wonderful Austria that Christ is again to reign, then a Good Friday must come after our Holy Thursday. Christ must first die before he can rise again from the dead. There will be no resurrection for us if we are not ready to suffer and, if need be, even to die for Christ and our faith.

---

10. In his writings, FJ refers to the N.S. movement as "the stream," *der Strom*. Hence, he means here that Russia's weather and terrain as well as the Soviet army are now (1942) halting the Wehrmacht, e.g., at Leningrad, Moscow, and Stalingrad. [RK]

For us Austrians, our Holy Thursday was the sad day of April 10, 1938. On that day, the church in Austria allowed itself to be imprisoned.[11] Since then it has remained in chains. Because of this yes we have not yet undergone our Good Friday. (Many Catholics gave their yes hesitantly and with some anxiety when they in fact wanted to vote a powerful no.) Many among us have already died, though not for Christ but for a N.S. victory. Was a no such an impossibility and more beyond the capability of many people in 1938 than a yes? I believe not.

But what can a no still bring about? Will it require the participation of many people? Without a doubt, one person need not ask others what it would mean and accomplish. For each individual, a no would have value in itself because it would free that individual's soul. In order to come to this personal decision, someone must be ready to stand up for Christ and the Christian faith, even if it means giving up one's life. Those people who have come to this decision can immediately withdraw from the N.S. *Volk* community and make no donations to it. Further, if they want to exercise Christian love of neighbor, they can contribute their wages to the poor without the help of the W.H.W. or of the Public Assistance program. Then they will be free to do with themselves as they want. By their decision, they will not immediately strike a blow, but they will place everything at a distance.

The underworld knows well that it can harm people more when it can keep them as members of the *Volk* community or pull them into it than when it tortures them to death because of their faith. So it happens that evil sees that it is no longer easy to win over a person and that this [dissenter] can become dangerous among other people.

I believe that the Lord God does not make it difficult for us to give over our lives for our faith. We need only think that already thousands of young men have been summoned [by the state] to make their lives available in this difficult time of war, and many have already sacrificed their youthful lives [in combat]. So outsiders, who have occupied our homeland and stolen our goods, are able to demand the lives of our young men and to extinguish the souls of thousands of our children.[12] Our awareness of our guilt as German-speaking people gets increasingly greater with every new victory that we attain for Germany. Why should it be so hard to give up our lives for a king [i.e., Christ] who imposes important obligations on us but also gives us rights, whose ultimate victory is

---

11. FJ is again referring to the Austrian bishops' pastoral letter of March 27, 1938.
12. Beginning in the summer of 1941, the Reich prohibited the religious instruction of children under the age of ten in parts of Bavaria and Austria, except in preparation for First Communion.

certain, and whose kingdom exists forever? By his harsh suffering and earthly death, Christ has redeemed us from eternal death but not from earthly suffering and death. Christ demands from us also a public acknowledgment of our faith, exactly as the Führer Adolf Hitler demands from his *Volk*.

God's Commandments teach us that we have to be obedient to our worldly authorities, even if they are not Christian, but only insofar as they command us to do something that is not morally wrong. We must still obey God more than we obey human beings. And who can serve two masters at once? [see Matt. 6:24]. Many people say to themselves, "We can temporarily remain in the mystery of Christ, until the situation appears different." We need not discuss whether National Socialism will continue forever. But it has already existed for a long time. Also, God's kingdom could soon break in when God would assume all of our rights once and for all so that we would have only our obligations to God.

Could it also not happen that the German Reich would be conquered, with the result that a different anti-Christian government would take over? This victor would seemingly liberate us but could also deny us our rights. We know how it would be for Christian belief under a different government, for example, under Russia or under England and the United States. Things might not be much better under [England and the United States] but perhaps they would be more civilized and, at least for a while, not as brutal as under the Russians.

From where can we expect something better? The Christians in the first centuries were able to think: "If we make sacrifices to the gods as the rulers require of us, we can secretly remain Christian." And some Christians actually did this. At the same time, some rulers did not remain on the throne for very long. But unfortunately their successors were usually not much better, and sometimes they were even much worse. The first Christians had to wait about three hundred years until they could experience the free exercise of their faith for a long period of time. And a somewhat good end emerged out of this difficult swirl of being and nonbeing.

Do we believe then that the Christian renewal of our people, who have already sunk far from Christian faith, could progress so quickly that our children could still experience a Christian society? A society's decline usually goes more easily and quickly than its movement upward. We cannot say that things have fallen apart simply because of our state or our upper classes. Is it not terrible and frightening when one thinks about our society's murdering of children, which

King Herod also undertook? [see Matt. 2:16]. (According to the blessed Catherine Emmerich, Herod likely killed seven hundred children.[13]) Why didn't
the Lord God punish this inhuman king during his earthly life? But what have
we heard from the German and Austrian people during these past years? We
did not need a Herod to command the death of children. Parents themselves
have brought this about with their poor care [of their children].

The learned Professor Hermann Mukermann has given data that the total
number of deaths of German soldiers during the four years of this world war
is less than the total number of deaths of children in Germany each year as
a result of murders and abortions. According to this data, there are two mil-
lion children in Germany every year who lose their lives because of acts similar
to Herod's. Are things much better in our still so-called Christian Austria?
These murders occur not only in our large cities but also in our smallest villages.[14] Can we still speak about a German culture? We sometimes shudder
when we hear about the inhuman acts that the Russians are committing in
this war. Is it any less inhuman when people murder their own children —
children who did nothing for which they should suffer and are entirely blameless? Should the Lord God still work miracles for such a people, as he did
for the Israelites who were able to walk across the Red Sea with dry feet? [see
Exod. 14:22].

We surely know that the church of Christ, the rock of Peter, can never be
conquered because Christ himself has said this [see Matt. 16:18]. We know
that this rock is now being besieged from all sides in order to destroy it. But
these efforts will not succeed! It is almost a miracle itself that two nations [i.e.,
the Third Reich and the Soviet Union] — each with the goal of destroying the
church — are now tearing each other apart.[15]

Bolshevism or National Socialism

It is very sad when we hear again and again from Catholics that this war, which
Germany is leading, is perhaps not unjust because it will eradicate Bolshevism.

---

13. Anne Catherine Emmerich (1774–1824) was a stigmatic and mystic in north Germany. Her visions,
as written down by the Romantic poet Clemens Brentano, are reported in *The Dolorous Passion of Our Lord
and Saviour Jesus Christ and Life of the Blessed Virgin Mary.* [RK]

14. FJ may be referring to the village of Ybbs, in which he heard about "sad scenes" at the mental hospital.
See his letter of February 27, 1941 (page 66 above). [RK]

15. In his notes for this essay, FJ wrote that God might be allowing the Reich and the Soviet Union to
destroy each other. He also noted that, according to the blessed Catherine Emmerich, Satan would afflict
the earth in the 1940s.

It is true that most of our soldiers are located in evil Bolshevist lands and that they must defend themselves, even though they want to do nothing harmful. But we must ask ourselves a short question: Against what are these soldiers fighting, Bolshevism or the Russian people?

When our Catholic missionaries went into pagan lands in order to make people Christian, did they go in with fighter planes and bombs? Did they seek to convert people and improve their lives through such means? Most of the noble fighters for the Christian faith wrote home that if they could only distribute enough material goods, they would be able to accomplish their goal more quickly. Of course, they also prayed often, for they owed their greatest progress and conversions to the prayer that accompanied their work.

When we inquire a little into history, we come again and again to the same conclusion: when one nation takes over another by means of war, it usually does not enter into this nation in order to improve the life of the people there or to bestow gifts on this people but in order to obtain something there. If we are fighting against the Russian people in order to take something from their land, what good can we do? But if we are fighting simply against Bolshevism, why are we so concerned about such things as ore, oil, and farmland? Further, have our enemies actually come against Christian belief with weapons in order to eradicate it? Yet whose blood is now nourishing the new seeds that are sprouting up more abundantly than they were previously? Is not this happening as we make the blood of Bolshevists flow out? Are not new [Bolshevist] seeds springing up as a result of our war?

Are we Christians today smarter than Christ himself? Do some of us truly believe that we can rescue Christian belief in Europe from a decline — and perhaps even rejuvenate the Christian faith — by means of this massive shedding of blood? Did our good Savior, whom we should always follow, go against paganism with his apostles as we German-speaking Christians are now going against [Bolshevism]?

Oh, we are a poor people, blinded by our megalomania. Shall we regain our use of reason? We are accustomed to saying: "Nothing comes about by accident. Everything comes from above." But did this war, in which we German-speaking people are fighting against almost all of the earth's peoples, come upon us as a hailstorm, which one must powerlessly watch while also praying that it will soon stop without doing extensive damage? Through the radio, newspapers, public rallies, etc., we knew almost everything that Hitler planned on accomplishing with his N.S. agenda. Further, we knew that [Hitler's] casting aside of war guilt and the extraordinary revaluation of the

German mark could bring no other consequence than what they have brought about.[16]

It was assumed that the Lord God would take away the free will of the world's other peoples and guide their minds so that they would submit themselves without a struggle to National Socialism. But God leaves every human being with a free will. And we Austrians could have exercised our free will on April 10, 1938, after the Germans had taken our land into their possession. Neither God nor the Germans had taken away our free will. And we still have this free will today. I believe that God will not accuse us of sinning if we finally replace our yes — which many people now perhaps regret — with a no. In any case, other peoples have a right to ask God for peace, also asking that God strike weapons out of our hands.

Isn't it an act of disdain if we ask God for peace when we do not truly want it? We must lay down our weapons. Is the guilt with which we have burdened ourselves still too small? At best we may still ask God that he allow us to regain our use of reason in order finally to recognize that other individuals and peoples still possess the right to live in this world. Otherwise, God must upset our calculations through his power, for [left to ourselves] we German-speaking Catholics would compel the earth's peoples to submit to the yoke of National Socialism.

We want to take delight in our thieves' booty, and yet we want to shift to other people responsibility for all that has occurred!

A Game of Deceit

Aren't we more or less playing a game of deceit? Do we not know that we must produce good and noble fruit in order to be admitted into the kingdom of heaven? But isn't it impossible for deception to lead to perfection?

When and how is someone deceitful? Deception occurs when we express ourselves to other people differently from how we are in reality. It happens when we act in public differently from what we are thinking, saying, and writing in private.

Is it in general possible today to speak and enact in public what we are actually thinking? Because of our civil obedience we must sometimes behave differently from what we have in mind. This civil obedience should not go so far, however, that we allow ourselves to perform bad actions.

---

16. On June 9, 1933, the Reich partially suspended its interest payments to other nations because of its alleged lack of funds.

We know that God would not command us to do something impossible. In our current situation, we must not always act upon what we are thinking. And we must not always say what we are thinking. One can and should be silent to a certain degree. We would surely bring difficulties on ourselves if we always told our neighbors what we think of them. We must at times remain silent and swallow our words, which do not always need to be spoken. Further, people do not always want to listen when someone has a lot to say because they themselves must remain silent at this time. To be sure, it is doubly hard not to be deceptive when one is living in a nation that limits religious freedom.

If deception meant nothing disadvantageous for eternal blessedness, then it would make no difference whether we had religious freedom or not. Is being false bad if no one suffers because of it? Yes, because through our deception we always harm ourselves the most, [and] because through it we also offend God and harm his church. An adage applies here: "As we live, so we die." It very often happens that someone cannot stop playing his or her game of deception even in dying. God will severely judge those Christians who no longer go to church or to the sacraments or who have withdrawn from the church and have even punished other Christians [for going to church]. Unless they undergo a conversion, such people will surely not enter the kingdom of heaven.

When people have at least partially given up their false game, others can know to some extent whom they have before them. And I bet that these people have to suffer less pain in hell than those people who have swindled others throughout their entire lives, who have always deceived their pastors and neighbors. Did not Christ himself say: "So, because you are lukewarm, and neither cold nor hot, I am about to spit you out of my mouth" (Rev. 3:16)?

Many people ask themselves, "Why should I show respect to this person who is a bad individual and who is not respectful of me?" First, we should never return evil for evil [see Matt. 5:39]. Second, we have no right to be disrespectful to someone who is perhaps bad because in God's presence this bad individual is still my brother or sister. Further, we may actually help improve this bad individual. Also, we ourselves want to become good Christians and hence be better than those whom we regard as bad people. We must act respectfully and uprightly in relation to others unless we want to reap only scorn and disdain. Is it any wonder that we Christians often hear others say, "They are this way." By playing a game of deceit, we actually bring disgrace upon the whole Catholic Church, for others link together all of us Christians.

Where do things stand today regarding honesty? Are people being honest when they as members of the N.S. Social Service organization or of some other

N.S. organization make sacrifices and ask for donations so that their activities stand out? In all of this, they believe that they are deceiving and misleading the other N.S. members. However, our opponents are not dumb. They recognize that such people still attend church on Sundays and still show that they are apparently religious and that these people are therefore misleading either one side or the other. "No one can serve two masters" [Matt. 6:24]. N.S. officials allow such people to have things both ways at least for a while because they know that these people are ultimately fooling only themselves and inflicting the greatest harm on themselves and the church. Further, they seldom give an influential position to someone who tries to play two games at once.

Are we perhaps able to bring about a conversion in others when we — in order to attain some kind of favorable appraisal — apparently do everything that the N.S. Party wants from us or orders us to do? What must people of other beliefs think about us and about our Christian belief when we value it so little? We must bring shame on ourselves among true N.S. Party members who made personal sacrifices for their N.S. ideals [prior to 1938], who suffered for the N.S. worldview despite the laws against National Socialism at that time.[17] They were not intimidated by imprisonment and death, though their faith concerned only earthly goals. Would they have attained their victories if they had been as cowardly and fearful as we German-speaking Catholics are today? We German-speaking Catholics hope to bring about a glorious victory for our Christian faith without a struggle and want to accomplish this victory after we first struggle on behalf of our N.S. opponents and help them become victorious.

May we reflect on this strategy? I believe that the world has never experienced something similar to this. Humankind is surely very smart and inventive today. But has it ever found that one group of people can be victorious over another without a struggle? I have never heard of such a thing!

On the Loss of Responsibility

At this time, we frequently hear it said that we can and should do with peace of mind [what the state wants] because other people bear responsibility for our actions. Hence, responsibility is shifted from one person to another. No one wants to be responsible for something or to be humanly accountable for all

---

17. After the Austrian government prohibited the N.S. Party on June 19, 1933, numerous party members deliberately defied the ban, knowing that they would be arrested and imprisoned. [RK]

of the criminal acts and horrors that people are committing today. Once in a while, one or at most two people atone for these things.

Am I showing Christian love of neighbor when I commit an act that I regard as bad or at best unjust simply because if I did not do it, I would suffer harm to my body or my business [from the N.S. Party]?

Some people say that others bear the responsibility for our wrongful acts, that our civil and ecclesiastical officials bear great responsibility [for what is happening]. However, instead of making the burden of responsibility lighter for these officials, some people want to place the guilt on them — the guilt that these people themselves could easily bear and that would implicate them deeply in things! Do our officials actually bear great responsibility before God as we sometimes believe, or have we lost our sense of responsibility as others sometimes tell us and as we may often tell ourselves?

Will not God judge every human being in relation to his or her own self-understanding rather than in relation to the position or office that the person has held? Do we know whether the person to whom we want to shift responsibility for our actions sees the matter differently than we do? That he or she holds to be good what we judge to be bad? We know nothing of how differently we human beings perceive things. We can only speak out of our own experiences. It often happens that someone regards something to be entirely good that someone else sees from an entirely different point of view. It may be that in God's judgment someone who held an important position or office bears less responsibility before God than ordinary individuals.

Let's consider an imaginary case. There are two individuals with roles in the N.S. movement who act in the same manner. The first man regards what he does to be good and right, while the second considers the ideas, sacrifices, and struggles for National Socialism to be unjust. This second individual believes, however, that he is far better than the first because he is not so convinced of things, even though he makes the same sacrifices and undergoes the same struggles as his colleague. Further, it does not matter to this second man whether the party for which he makes sacrifices and struggles has benefited from his actions or was harmed by them. The most important thing is what happens to him so that he does not suffer any physical harm.

In my judgment, people bear more guilt for their actions when they fully recognize that these actions are more bad than good and when they nevertheless do them so that no danger and no deprivations will afflict their pampered bodies. (Of course, these people find sweet the words that their actions are the responsibility of other people.) These people bear more guilt than those people who simply do what they do because they see their actions as their duty and, according to their thinking, entirely good.

Is It Still Possible to Do Something?

We frequently hear it said today that we can do nothing more, that it would bring us only imprisonment and death because we can change nothing much in world events. On the one hand, I believe that we would have had to begin more than one hundred years ago [to change things today]. On the other hand, I also believe that, as long as we live in his world, it is never too late to save oneself and perhaps still to win some souls for Christ. There are today people who are no longer able to find the right way amid this great chaos.

The people upon whom we should be able to rely for their good example simply go to Mass. No one clarifies things, either by means of spoken or written words. To be more precise, no one is allowed to clarify things. And so our mindless rat race goes on. As long as something that is partially good happens, we do not notice that we could have acted differently or should have acted differently. Yet woe be us. When need and misery break in some day, then it will come to light whether the things that most people are now doing are truly good and right. At that future time, people will question the goal of today's actions. I am aware, of course, that speaking publicly today about all of this would accomplish very little other than imprisonment.

It is not good that our spiritual leaders have remained totally silent for many years. Words teach, and they gain weight by personal example. Isn't it the case that people today are looking for Christians who will bring clarity, comprehension, and certainty into the darkness, for Christians who stand with the purest freedom and courage amid the absence of peace and joy, amid the self-seeking and the hatred, for Christians who are not similar to wavering reeds pushed here and there by every light breeze, for Christians who do not merely watch to see what their associates and friends will do but who ask themselves: "What does our faith say to all of this, and can conscience bear everything so peacefully that someone will never regret anything?"

Is someone who does not know the right path able to find it when the signposts are stuck so loosely in the ground that they get turned and blow around by the wind? Finding the right path is especially difficult when those who know about this path refuse to answer questions or give false information in order to avoid further inquiries.

Is There Still a God?

How often do we hear it asked: "Is there still a God who sees everything that is happening in the world?" The Gospels report that Christ said to the reapers: "Let both of them [the weeds and the wheat] grow together until the harvest" (Matt. 13:30). Christ did not add that the reapers should then pull out the weeds as though the weeds are more important than the wheat. The Gospels actually teach us very clearly that [God's judgment] will not be as many people expect. It will not be that God will arrive in order to extirpate evil and the evildoers and then that everything will continue to run its course.

To be sure, God will come among us but with great power and glory. What happens then, we also know. If God were to take away the persecutors, there would no longer be martyrs. If God were to remove all struggles from our lives, we would no longer receive the crown of glory. Hasn't God already had compassion on us? Hasn't God already struck the power of hell a powerful blow? Christ has done penance for the guilt of our sins and expiated us. As a result, all of us who accept Christ's teaching and who live according to it can become eternally blessed.

What more do we want? Should Christ allow himself to be crucified again for us? Or was the miracle of Christ's resurrection or the other miracles that he performed so minor that we should still wait for new miracles so that we can then believe in his teachings? Hasn't Christ shown us clearly enough the path to heaven through his words and example? Christ performed the miracles that he accomplished after his ascension into heaven through his apostles, not primarily for the already existing Christian communities, but primarily for the people who did not know about his power so that they could more easily believe in his teachings [see Acts 2:43–47].

Why are we hearing lamentations among us today? Aren't we for the most part still Christians? Doesn't it say in a hymn: "How fortunate is the Christian!"[18] Where is something amiss then today? Are the hymn's lyrics not correct, or do Christians no longer agree with them? The most "fortunate" people are, I believe, not easy to count today. Many people will say, "Oh, this war!" or, "These bad times!" Do we assume that the first Christians lived in rosy times because many were fortunate? We Christians today see ourselves as unfortunate. But is heaven closed for us, or has God's compassion gotten so small that we are not able to hope for the pardoning of our sins?

---

18. These words come from the third strophe of the hymn "Hier liegt vor deiner Majestät," composed by Michael Hayden in 1795 with lyrics by Franz Kohlbrenner in 1777. See the hymn book *Gotteslob*, no. 801.

Christ's teachings and example are not a basis for the distress among us. In light of Christ, we should view these hardships as very insignificant. However, we have great concern about our physical well-being. But should we have this concern if we are Christians? Christ himself said: "But strive first for the kingdom of God and his righteousness, and all these things will be given to you as well" (Matt. 6:33). The first Christians encountered much suffering. Yet do we contemporary Christians no longer know that every hardship that God sends us can be very necessary for our eternal blessedness if we bear it with patience and out of love for God?

It will surely be that hell will exercise an even greater power in this world, but we Christians need not fear it. As great as the power of hell is, the power of God is even greater. Christians who do not securely equip themselves against hell's power with the spiritual means for struggling and defending themselves that Christ left behind for us — e.g., the most holy sacrament of the altar is the highest power — will hardly withstand for very long hell's great power.

War or Revolution?

Many people are of the opinion that this war, which Germany began, is a war just like the other ones that previously occurred. However, it is not a war similar to others in which greed for more land played the key role. Rather, this war is more of a revolution that has enveloped the whole world. The Führer himself has said: "The National Socialist movement is the greatest revolution of all time."

If it were only a war about land as so many others have been and if Germany were actually to end up as the victor, then Catholics at the end of this war would possess the same rights as every other citizen in the German Reich. But if this war is in fact a revolution or a conflict about religious belief, then I could fight for the N.S. Reich as much as I want and yet I — despite all of the exertions and sacrifice that I as a poor soldier had offered — would be seen at the war's end to be an enemy of the Reich because I as a Catholic would still not commit myself to National Socialism. In other words, I would be seen at the war's end as Austrian Christians are seen today, even though they submitted themselves — not freely — four years ago to the National Socialists.

These thoughts alone suffice for someone not to fight for this state or for the N.S. *Volk* community. Further, I believe that many people have forgotten what the Holy Father said about National Socialism in his encyclical many years ago, namely, that National Socialism is even more dangerous than Communism.[19] Since Rome has not withdrawn this judgment, I believe that it is not likely a crime or a sin if someone as a Catholic were to refuse the current obligation for military service — even though a person who refuses military service is surely looking at death. Is it not more Christian for someone to give himself as a sacrifice than to have to murder others who possess a right to life on earth and who want to live in order to save their lives for a short while?

People come up with all sorts of phrases today in order to put the whole situation and the whole struggle into a wonderful light. For example, they say that we "are struggling only for the German state because Christ has commanded us that we have to obey a secular government, even if it is not Christian." These words are entirely correct [see Mark 12:17]. But I do not believe that Christ said that we must obey a state when it commands us to do bad things.

Many say that we should "struggle only for the German state without also struggling for the N.S. Party." But I believe that this is impossible. It is as though I were to trying to fight for God the Father but not for the Son or the Holy Spirit. The German state and the N.S. Party are now two inseparable realities.

Some people speak today of the defense of the homeland. But have we Austrians forgotten 1938 in such a short time? Can I still say that I have a homeland when I live in a state in which I have only obligations and no longer possess any rights? Can there be appropriate talk about a defense of the homeland when we simply invade other lands, are not guilty for doing so, and rob and murder in these lands? What would we Austrian Catholics lose if we were no longer to fight for the German state? Would we lose religious freedom or economic freedom? Have we still not heard clearly enough? What should people do who will not commit themselves to National Socialism? Of course, it would please the party's leaders if we would help them win further victories.

I can never and shall never believe that we Catholics must make ourselves available to do the work of the most evil and dangerous anti-Christian power that has ever existed.

---

19. In 1937, Pope Pius XI issued *Mit brennender Sorge* (March 14) against Germany's National Socialism and *Divini Redemptoris* (March 28) against the Soviet Union's Communism. Bishop Gföllner required that *Mit brennender Sorge* be read at every Mass in the Diocese of Linz. But he did not require the public reading of *Divini Redemptoris*. He also publicly reiterated what he had written on January 21, 1933: "It is impossible to be a good Catholic and a true National Socialist at the same time."

On Dangerous Weapons[20]

People speak today about the very dangerous weapons that human minds have invented and are still inventing. If someone would be able to invent a weapon whereby one could put the whole world into ruins with one blow, wouldn't it still be less dangerous than that before which people [wrongly] show little concern today. This is the spiritual "weapon" that some people are using either to uproot our children's true Catholic faith or to prevent this faith from taking root in them. For almost every weapon there is also a means of defense, and there are also [spiritual] means of defense against these [anti-Christian] weapons. Unfortunately, these means are used very little.

We know that if these defensive means were truly and courageously used, they would result in dead and wounded [Catholics]. Many people would be placed in prison. To be sure, we should struggle for every possibility and offer our lives in this conflict. Shouldn't we risk everything in defense of our children's souls? Should we year after year remain silent and look on defenselessly? I believe that if we continue on this path, we shall one day experience bitter regret and perhaps also eternal sorrow. Are our obligations to lead our children to God somehow today lifted from us just because these obligations are harder to fulfill than they were in earlier decades? I believe not!

The harder the struggle in this life, the more glorious the victory in the next.

---

20. On June 26, 1941, the Reich's Catholic bishops issued a pastoral letter protesting the state's new restrictions on religious instruction and urging parents to assume responsibility for educating their children in the Christian faith. This letter was read at all Masses in the Diocese of Linz on July 6, 1941.

Chapter 9

Separate Essays

December 1941–January 1943

From late 1941 into early 1943, Franz Jägerstätter wrote twelve essays on separate sheets of paper, not in a notebook. These texts are entitled:

- *"'Heavens Send Down Righteousness, and Clouds Water It'"*
- *"On Belonging to the National Socialist Party and Making Sacrifices for It"*
- *"A Just or Unjust War?"*
- *"We Should Be Lay Apostles"*
- *"We Pray for Peace, and Yet We Fight, Sacrifice, and Work for a National Socialist Victory"*
- *"On Not Condemning Others"*
- *"After This War"*
- *"Some Words, Which Apply to All of Us, concerning the Reading of Christian Journals and Edifying Books"*
- *"On Death!"*
- *"Toward a Spiritual Reflection"*
- *"A Reflection on God's Love for Us Human Beings"*
- *"Ten [Eleven] Questions"* [RK]

"Heavens Send Down Righteousness, and Clouds Water It"[1]
(December 1941)

We'll sing these words only for a short time, and then we'll once again celebrate Christmas. Christ surely wanted to bring peace and freedom to all people. Yet

---

1. These are the opening words of an Advent hymn.

there are many people who do not celebrate Christmas every year because peace is lacking in their hearts.

Christ said to his disciples: "Peace be with you" [John 20:19]. Do these words no longer have value for us contemporary Christians because almost the whole world lives without peace? It appears that we are again living in a pagan world and that Christ must be born again and come to redeem us. However, this situation need not discourage us nor weaken our faith, for even nineteen hundred years ago — while Christ himself taught and preached — not everyone found peace.

"Glory to God in the highest heaven, and on earth peace among those whom he favors" (Luke 2:14). Christ surely wanted to bring peace to all people. Yet peace will come only to people of good will. So it always was, and so it will also remain as long as there are people on this earth. For as much as Christ did for us, he could do no more, I believe. He gave his last drop of blood for us. He even left behind his own flesh and blood for us as our food and drink. If we no longer have peace, the cause is now entirely within us. St. Anthony taught that no one is more fortunate and no one is more blessed than those who bear Christ in their hearts.

No wellspring puts forth both sweet water and sour water at the same time. And so it is also with the human heart. For people who have Christ dwelling in their hearts will have no room for discord and envy, hatred and jealousy, vindictiveness, pride and arrogance, deceit and immorality, all of which are the work of Satan. Christ and Satan cannot rule at the same time in someone's heart. If we want to make the world better, we must begin with ourselves. Who would go to their neighbor to extinguish a fire if their own house were burning down?

Is it right for us to pray that others know peace if we ourselves do not have it? An old adage applies here: "Those who are stuck in a swamp are not able to help others out of it."

Would everyone have peace if God were to stop the ravages of the war, which God could easily do? Definitely not! God will not place peace and eternal well-being in us without our cooperation, for God will allow the whole world to fall to ruin rather than to take away our free will. Christ said that the kingdom of heaven suffers violence and is being torn apart, but God will not change his words now or in eternity (see Matt. 11:12).

An alarming instance of this truth occurred for us in 1918. In that year, the ravages of the war came to an end. But did this end bring peace to people's hearts? The war's destruction and killing stopped, but the fires of hate and discord burned within people. The human family had not improved itself. Instead of thanking God, people ravenously plunged into a quest for pleasure and experienced innumerable troubles and emotions. A child had almost no place remaining in the world. Political parties sprang up, and hate and discord burned even more intensely in people's hearts for the next twenty-one years until they ignited in the Second World War.

Many people still hold the view that only a few people bear the responsibility for all of the ravages of the war that has engulfed the whole world. But at the same time they are anxious about this war. This anxiety has sprung up in part because of the war's possible damage to temporal goods. But it has also come about because people hold that they are blameless for everything that happens in world events. But they are seemingly too little concerned about seeking peace for themselves in order thereby to help others attain peace.

If we want to attain peace for ourselves and also for others, we must strive to imitate those who have brought peace to us. God will not remove from his compassion anyone who truly has the will for self-improvement. We may quickly have answers when we receive admonishments concerning peace, especially if we are going to lose. What is the source of these admonishments that arise in our consciences? It must be remembered that things will go better in eternity for the greatest sinners who have acknowledged their guilt, repented, and have a sincere intention to improve, than for those people who in their entire lives have committed perhaps only a few mortal sins, have no concern about their venial sins and have no desire for self-improvement.

No century has unfolded without a war and its ravages. War has affected people who had obtained peace for themselves and had shied away from no sacrifice for the sake of peace — which they themselves experienced and tried to bring to others. Among these peace-seekers were our saints, who saw themselves as fortunate if God sometimes sent them great suffering. Many even prayed for suffering, for they did not desire earthly fortune and material success. Patiently they bore their crosses following their Savior. God did not impose peace on these holy men and women, but they themselves often made great efforts for it as they overcame the world. Indeed, even the most Blessed Virgin Mary had to exert herself in order to obtain great grace from God. She herself spoke of this to St. Elizabeth, the abbess of the Monastery of Schönau at Bingen.[2] The Blessed Mother [reportedly] said: "My daughter, know that I

---

2. The writings of St. Elizabeth (1129–64) of the Monastery of Schönau at Bingen on the Rhine were widely circulated but never officially recognized in the Catholic Church.

saw myself as nothing and as less worthy of God's grace than others and hence persistently asked God for grace and virtue. And I obtained them but not without my effort. God gave me no grace without my having prepared myself for it by means of fervent requests, continuous prayer, works of penance, and great exertions."

If God sent great grace to the spotless recipient not without great efforts on her part, how much less shall we sinful people attain perfection without our great efforts? Therefore, may no sacrifice be too great for us so that we obtain true peace and so that those who already have peace may preserve it. Whoever does not find peace in this world will not find it in eternity. These short lines of the Christian blessing for houses actually say it all: "Where [there is] faith, there is love. Where love, there is peace. Where peace, there is blessing. Where blessing, there is God. Where God, [there is] no need."

On Belonging to the National Socialist Party and Making Sacrifices for It

Many people continue to ask themselves whether it is sinful for people to be members of the N.S. Welfare organization or of the N.S. Party, or for parents to allow their children to participate in the Hitler Youth. To make a judgment we must proceed without finally relying on what other people tell us.

I myself have often inquired into this matter. On one occasion, someone told me that we can belong to the N.S. Party or contribute to the Winter Help Work without giving the matter any further thought. This person said that it makes entirely no difference if we engage in these activities because Rome has canceled its ban [against membership in the N.S. Party]. However, I did not believe this answer, and so I inquired further into this matter with a higher religious authority. He told me that the first answer was not true because Rome has still not made a decision about [National Socialism] in general.

I now believe that it is pointless to ask priests about this matter. First, they have no more specific instructions from higher church officials. Second, if a priest were to say something different from what the N.S. Party holds and if he himself were betrayed, we know what would happen to him. Third, it can also be that priests themselves are not clear about the entire matter.

During a retreat a priest who is member of a religious order said that many parents come to him with questions about their children. He said further that these parents themselves should already know what they have to do. He

acknowledged the difficult situation in which many parents today find themselves when their consciences tell them something different from what the
party says. Everyone knows that to decide against the party's wishes is likely to
jeopardize one's livelihood.

It would perhaps be better if the church were not to make a decision in this
matter, for many people would not be able to go against the party despite an
ecclesiastical judgment. These people know that with one blow their entire
life would be ruined. Moreover, as long as the church has not made a definite
decision in this matter, accountability before God for many people will not be
so difficult.

All of us who were educated in the Catholic religion know that we are not
allowed to participate in political parties that are enemies of the church or to
contribute to such parties so that they can have a wider influence. My conscience has much to say about all of this. I believe that if people have a full
recognition that this political party that they are joining or have joined or to
which they have contributed is an opponent of the church and if these people
continue to contribute to it so that they obtain earthly advantages, then they
may find themselves facing eternal disadvantages.

We should not, of course, pass judgment on others when they participate
in this or that, make contributions, or engage in N.S. fund-raising. We do not
know whether they have a full recognition that the party to which they belong
is an opponent of the church. Or if they know this, they may not know that
belonging to such a party is not allowed by the Catholic Church. There are
also many people who even believe that to contribute to the N.S. Party is a
Christian act.

Further, we must also make an important differentiation. There are those
people who belong to the party, voice the party's convictions, and have a full
recognition [of the party's opposition to the church] but act out of weakness
and fear. These people have no intention of harming the church even if their
actions have this consequence. Further, there are those people who participate in the party with the full intention of harming the church of Christ. The
accountability before God is unequal between these two types of people.

So we see that we ourselves must not judge this person or that person, and
we must set aside a judgment about others. No one can cheat God, regardless
of what excuses one may bring before him. God alone knows and recognizes our weaknesses and how far our recognition [of the party's character]
extends.

A Just or Unjust War?

What can it benefit me if I obey and execute the evil orders of the Führer and, in doing so, commit no sin but also am not able to attain perfection?

Moreover, if someone who chooses not to follow the Führer's evil orders is alleged to be doing something seriously sinful, then it is impossible for someone today — amid the greatest persecution of Christians that has ever happened — to sacrifice his or her life for Christ and the Christian faith.

Does it make then no difference today whether we are carrying out a just or an unjust war? Perhaps I would have come to a different answer to this question if I had not read so many Catholic books and journals.

How can people today declare many men and women of earlier times to be holy — men and women who put their lives at risk — when most of these men and women would have refused to carry out the evil orders that are now required of us? Is there anything more evil than when I am required to murder and rob people who are defending their homeland only so that I might help an anti-religious power attain victory and then be able to establish a world empire with belief in God or, to be more accurate, with no belief in God?

Today there is talk only about the evil Russians. There is apparently no longer an issue concerning the people in the other countries against whom we have done much and continue to do much [harm]. Yet Christians who are soldiers must shoot people or beat up people, and they are told to think that when they shoot these people, they are sending their souls to travel for eternity in hell. Isn't this crushing for Christians who are soldiers, especially when they realize that these people are engaged in a more just struggle [i.e., defending their homelands] than the soldiers themselves? Shooting good people would also be easier if the shooters were halfway good marksmen so that the dying would take only a moment. But most importantly, the shooters themselves would be eternally fortunate if they were fighting for a just cause.

Must it be sinful when a citizen of the Reich chooses not to follow the orders of the Führer? One knows very clearly that if people are not members of the N.S. *Volk* community or do not contribute money to it or collect money for it, they can put their lives at risk, lose their livelihoods, or plunge their families into great need.

In this situation, we should rely equally on the gifts of wisdom and understanding by saying the seven petitions that we pray to the Holy Spirit. But if we must blindly obey the Führer, then what need have we for much wisdom and understanding? Yet aren't we Christians called to become true disciples of Christ?

Let us consider these imaginary cases. If Christ had received the charge from Pilate to kill and rob people for the sake of some evil cause, would Christ have obeyed him? Or would the executioners have sinned if they had contradicted Pilate's order by not scourging Christ and not nailing him to the cross? We should not quickly answer these questions. For now, I believe, it suffices simply to have posed them.

We Should Be Lay Apostles

To lead souls to Christ is one of the most wonderful tasks to which God more or less ultimately calls all of us. It is sad in our current situation that we laity are not able to rescue a few more souls. We look on helplessly as close relatives and many souls, for whom we bear responsibility, are drowning in this stream in which all of us are now swimming. We may not even advise them on how they could be rescued from it. Yet we laity would be able to give some of them necessary advice on how to make it to the other river bank. Our spiritual leaders, on whom we rely the most and should rely, now remain silent. Or they tell some of us even the opposite of what we should do if we are to be rescued from this dangerous stream. As long as they do this, it is of course better that we laity remain entirely silent. If people are already weak and find themselves bewildered, we could lead them into even greater bewilderment through our advice.

As long as our priests and bishops are giving us no advice about the dangerous situation in which almost all of us are finding ourselves or are offering us poor advice, we laity must at best pray to God that he allow us to succeed in reaching the other river bank as soon as possible. So other people can at least see and perhaps follow the example of how this person or that person has been fortunately rescued on the other river bank.

We Pray for Peace, and Yet We Fight, Sacrifice, and Work for a National Socialist Victory

Many German-speaking Catholics, who do not hold N.S. convictions, are praying for peace, hence contrary to the N.S. goal of victory. Yet we should be Catholics not only in prayer but also in action. Just as the N.S. goal of victory cannot be reached only by means of prayer, we who do not hold N.S. convictions cannot attain peace if we only pray for it.

The National Socialists fight, sacrifice, and work for victory and, as a result, they have attained a great deal and accomplished some great victories. Yet how much are we — who are not National Socialists — fighting, sacrificing, and working for peace? Should the Lord God bring us peace only as a result of our prayer? If it is a sin when we Catholics fight, sacrifice, and work for the N.S. victory, then it seems to me to be entirely impossible that we would find God granting our prayers for peace, for in our actions we are doing the exact opposite of what we are praying for.

We know that we are not able to get to heaven without prayer, for without God's grace and help we would soon give up advancing toward what's good. The grace of God, I believe, is effective in us only as long as we cooperate with this grace. I believe that we could pray at great length to become holy, but if we do in our actions what is the opposite of what leads to holiness, then we shall not become saints even in thousands of years. It would surely be more pleasant if we could want something and be able to attain it, and if God would place in our laps what we want simply through our merely asking for it without our efforts and troubles.

Who can simultaneously be a soldier for Christ and a soldier for National Socialism? Who can fight for the victory of Christ and his church and at the same time fight for the N.S. idea and its ultimate victory?

On Not Condemning Others

While I have surely pounded hard against National Socialism, I am not permitted to attack National Socialists. To do so would go against the Commandment concerning love of neighbor. We should condemn the N.S. views or convictions but not the people themselves who hold these convictions. It belongs to God alone to judge people and to condemn them. All of us are brothers and sisters before God.

We know that the greatest Commandment concerns loving God, and after this there is the Commandment about loving one's neighbor [see Mark 12:28–34]. I would like to place these highest Commandments in everyone's heart. Pertinent here is the adage: "What you do not want others to do to you, do not impose on others" [see Matt. 7:12]. We are able to give many more death blows with our tongues than with our hands. With our words, we can quickly destroy a person's honor. What it does to us when we learn that someone has made known our mistakes or has disgraced us, so it also does to others whether these others are poor or rich, of high or low rank. Even if others treat us unfairly many times or offend us, we should not harbor hatred against them or hold a grudge against them.

To what person was more injustice and a greater offense done than to Christ himself? And how did Christ himself respond to this? Doesn't God have the power to immediately destroy us and send us to hell when we offend him? Even after all of the great disgrace and pain that people could inflict on a human being, Christ still prayed on the cross for his enemies [see Luke 23:33–43]. And how often is he still offended by us! And he always gives us a time of grace in which we can improve ourselves. At the same time, God is ready to forgive us when we ask him for this and when we have the sincere intention to improve ourselves.

Of course, we ask God to forgive us even when we are not ready to forgive our enemies from our hearts and to hold no grudge against others, perhaps even when we have a desire for their destruction. Don't we pray in the Our Father with its verse: "And forgive us our debts, as we also have forgiven our debtors" [Matt. 6:12]? If we are not ready to pardon our enemies, it is better that we entirely omit this verse from the Our Father. Otherwise, we will only invoke God's nonpardon on ourselves.

Many people would now ask themselves: "If we were really to act as has been described here and to see this as the best course for all Catholics, what are we saying about our sons, brothers, and spouses who are now fighting on the front or have already fallen in combat?" We must truly turn this judgment over to God. We have neither the right to damn nor even to declare holy. [We cannot judge] whether someone participated freely in this war or was compelled to do so.

I do not agree with the view that an individual soldier bears no responsibility for the whole [war] and that this responsibility belongs to only one individual [i.e., Hitler]. Clearly many who are still in the homeland bear more responsibility because of their N.S. convictions than many of the soldiers who shoot hundreds of people because they are simply doing their duty. Most of these soldiers are participating in this war because they are ordered by the state to do so, and to refuse to obey the state's orders would result in their certain deaths. We hope that there are not many soldiers who are fighting with the aim of destroying other individual human beings and peoples nor of making people into slaves so that they themselves can be their masters.

In any case, we cannot and should not judge other people because it is possible that they will come — perhaps only in the last moments of their lives — to a recognition of their actions and repent of them and so become eternally fortunate. I would like to add that we must remain concerned about our relatives and friends who belong to the N.S. movement. But we must be concerned more about their eternal well-being than about their temporal well-being. The state takes care of the temporal well-being of its soldiers, though often very insufficiently. For this reason, we are also able to undertake activities of corporal mercy by sometimes sending soldiers a care package. However, we should be most concerned about their eternal well-being, for the state has little or no concern for soldiers' eternal well-being. Even when soldiers could hear a sermon, many of them stay far away out of human fear. But in our letters we can impart Christian admonitions and teachings to soldiers who are our relatives and friends.[3] They are not able to evade these letters; they must receive them. Of course, if they toss these letters into the wind, this is their own responsibility. In any case, we are relieved of our obligation.

After This War

I want to write down here some thoughts that are running through my mind. These ideas on paper may differ somewhat from what they are in my mind. But they will at least be similar to what I am thinking.

We hear today many Catholics say that a period of bloodshed for the Catholic Church will break out after the war [if Hitler wins]. If so, one must anticipate that the Reich's persecution of Catholics will be the same among German-speaking Catholics as among other Catholics. Of course, we must wish that this conquering of peoples will soon come to an end and that the heavy, dark clouds — which I see building up over German-speaking people — will disperse. I surely see nothing good for all peoples, for no land or people on this earth is so wealthy that it can engage in the war as it is today without there coming about wide disruption of what existed prior to the war, even among the victorious nations.

As I see it, the worst things will come upon the German-speaking people because they bear the major guilt among all of the peoples for what has occurred. May the Lord God not regard my thoughts as sins! Even if all peoples share some guilt, not everyone will have it to the same degree. Perhaps I would not

---

3. FJ sent a letter of this sort to Hans Rambichler on November 11, 1941, and a similar one to Franz Huber on August 8, 1942.

have such a dark view of the future of the German-speaking people if I relied only on what was told to us before 1938 concerning the goals of the people with N.S. convictions. Unfortunately, [since 1938] we have felt the impact of these goals on our own bodies.

We would very much like to wish that at least a great amount of good will come about for the German-speaking people and that the majority of people will be prepared to become disciples of Jesus Christ. For Christ suffered for all of us, and God desires that all people become blessed. It does not even belong to us to condemn either the National Socialists as a group or as individuals. But as Catholics we must condemn and reject the N.S. convictions and the ideas of those people who believe that we are not able to become fortunate on this earth through the teachings of Christ. It is a certain sign that such people know too little about the Christian faith. Because our faith offers so much, we shall become fortunate through it not only in eternal life but also already here in this world. So we Catholics have not the least reason to allow our faith to get somehow combined with other teachings.[4]

The Catholic Church has not yet declared that the N.S. Party is an opponent of the church and hence has not said that it forbids Catholics, under the pain of sin, from belonging to the party. The church has remained silent on this matter. Nevertheless, we surely know what this party is and how it stands in relation to the church. Many Austrians will be able to remember the words of the Holy Father in the encyclical that came to our ears as drastic changes were occurring in Austria: that the National Socialist danger is as dangerous for us as the Communist danger.[5] (I cannot now remember the exact words and did not write them down at that time.) Someone could immediately ask, "Would the Communists be better to you?" But am I compelled to choose one of these two parties? It is almost certain that if people are not now connected with the N.S. *Volk* community, then their livelihoods and their very lives are in danger.

There are today many people who belong to this *Volk* community without holding its convictions simply in order to receive its earthly benefits. But I believe that there is a great danger in being involved in this way. Whoever wants to receive the advantages of this *Volk* community must also put up with the disadvantages that can arise in it. When people enter into a marriage, they

---

4. The "German Christians" sought to unite the teachings of Jesus Christ and the teachings of Adolf Hitler. They even placed photographs of the Führer on their churches' altars. [RK]

5. Pope Pius XI's encyclical *Mit brennender Sorge* (March 14, 1937) appeared in the Diocese of Linz's newspaper, along with the comment that "the dangers which the church has faced in Germany are also our own dangers" (*Linzer Diözesanblatt* [1937], 49–50).

must bear the sufferings that can arise in it. While someone's bond with the *Volk* community is not eternally binding as it is in marriage, it is such that to withdraw from this community is life-threatening.

Is death itself so horrible for us Catholics that we must gladly do everything so that we can lengthen our lives? Must we experience all of life's enjoyments? Would we find much in this world to be difficult if we were to keep in mind the eternal joy of heaven?

Is this war, which Germany began, a just one? Further, are there no disadvantages for people's souls when they are members of the N.S. movement and make continual contributions to the N.S. Party? For us Catholics, the Christian faith itself has actually not changed much since we came under N.S. rule.

Some Words, Which Apply to All of Us, concerning the Reading of Christian Journals and Edifying Books

What books and journals should we Catholics read? Nothing other than the letters from God that God wrote through human hands. They should show us the way to heaven and unite us ever more closely with God and with our eternal home.

How many people are there who, having originated in heaven, want now to know nothing more about heaven and the loved ones who dwell there? Aren't all of us wanderers far from home who desire to return sooner or later to heaven?

Consider this short comparison. A husband is called to military duty and has left behind at home a wife of personal integrity who cares deeply for her husband and sends him one letter after another. But this husband himself is not concerned about these letters and has apparently no interest in what his caring wife writes to him. He simply lays these letters aside unread and involves himself in various activities or dissipations. His wife learns from an anonymous writer about her husband's behavior. After many months, the husband receives a military leave. He naturally wants to spend these wonderful days at home and manages to get there. Will everything at home reach the fulfillment that the husband desired? I believe not. Will his wife — knowing how he regarded her letters with indifference — still be able to believe in her husband's love, even if shortly before returning home he declares to her his love for her, even speaking of God?

Will it go any better for us when our time is up and our days in this world come to an end? How should we undertake the journey to our eternal home? Do we believe perhaps that God does not know how we were indifferent to his letters? Will God prepare a lovely dwelling place for us in heaven, to which we want to go after our deaths? Does it make a difference to act on behalf of anti-Christian powers when there exists the power to evade them? Does it make a difference to withhold from people Christian journals and books because this literature establishes the best ties with God and our eternal home? Shall we be found by God to be better than those people who did not want to allow this Christian literature to reach other readers if we ourselves did not read it and were completely indifferent about obtaining it for ourselves? Did not Christ once say: "I wish that you were either cold or hot. So, because you are lukewarm, and neither cold nor hot, I am about to spit you out of my mouth" (Rev. 3:15b–16). So to whom do we belong?

On Death!

Many people would give a great deal if they could lengthen their lives, though not in order to become more perfect but simply in order to live longer. For many people death is something fearsome. Although for us Catholics death no longer has its sting, there are still many of us who readily put up with everything only because we do not want to die.

Death was something fearsome until Christ opened heaven's door for us and left for us many means of grace so that we can more easily attain eternal happiness. Shall we make ready God's joy if we have little longing for heaven? If we always want to postpone our deaths in order to stagger around in this dangerous world?

We know that most times death is connected to great pain and that Satan will risk everything with many people in order to rob us at the last moment of eternal happiness. Shall we spare ourselves all of this if we are able to keep death far away from us for a long time? In any case, won't we remain very anxious that the evil foe will still conquer us at the last moment? Our strength will clearly not extend into this fight. However, we can pray fifty times or more each day: "Holy Mary, Mother of God, pray for us poor sinners now and at the hour of our deaths. Amen." Is it likely that the Blessed Mother will abandon us in our final hour if we say this prayer each day?

We know to be sure that all of eternity depends upon our death, either eternal happiness or eternal damnation. If we already have such a great anxiety about death because eternity depends upon it, shouldn't we approach the table of the Lord with this same fear? At this table, the bread of life conduces us either to eternal life or to eternal damnation. We may think to ourselves that we can eventually go to confession if we are receiving communion unworthily. But do we know that God will allow us enough time to confess our unworthiness or that we shall still receive the grace to repent in our final hour? Therefore, we should prepare ourselves when we are approaching the table of the Lord as we would if we were preparing ourselves for death.

How little we cherish the immense merit that will come to us through the reception of the eternal bread. Consider how fortunate many people would feel if someone were to give them an entire kingdom. Couldn't we compare such a gift with a single worthy reception of communion? Yet not for long, for if someone could give us the entire world with all of its wealth and kingdoms, this would still be nothing in relation to a single, worthy reception of communion.

Think now about how infinitely fortunate we are to be able to go often to the table of the Lord. We should consider that there are still Catholics who need the time of grace and almost daily approach the table of the Lord, and yet they unfortunately behave so that we cannot differentiate them in their daily lives and activities from others who renounce receiving communion even once each month. We know that among millions of recipients of communion hardly two are exactly the same. Surely in every host there is the same Christ who contains the same high value. It can dawn on us how the reception of communion will enrich us. It depends many times on our faith and on our preparation.

We should approach the table of the Lord as though it were our last reception. We must be ready therefore to give God everything: property and goods, body and soul. We must even be entirely prepared to die. The more we give to God, the more God will give to us. God knows us. He knows all of our thoughts. He knows our wills. He knows how we would actually prepare ourselves if he would demand everything from us. If we are able to approach the table of the Lord with such a willingness and surrender to God, then God will allow his wealth of grace to be imparted to us in the richest measure. So true peace and happiness will enter into our hearts.

After every reception of communion, we should say the following prayer: "My Lord and my God, I accept death whenever, wherever, and however it may encounter me according to your most holy decree. I accept it willingly with all of its anxieties, pains, and sufferings, and I receive it out of your fatherly hands."

If we are however not ready to die, then it is better that we omit this prayer. Otherwise, we'll make ourselves into liars immediately after receiving communion. Catholics who have great well-being are often able to approach the table of the Lord and surrender themselves entirely to the will of God, and they will live in peace even in the worst times and will always have joy. They know that when God sends something hard into their lives and they bear it with patience, then even this hardship will lead them to eternal salvation. "Glory to God in the highest heaven, and on earth peace among those whom he favors!" [Luke 2:14].

The following text is hard to place chronologically. Written on paper of a very poor quality, it reads as though Franz Jägerstätter is paraphrasing it from a published text such as a catechism and adding some of his own thoughts to it.

Toward a Spiritual Reflection

There is one God and three divine Persons. God the Father created us. God the Son has redeemed us. And God the Holy Spirit sanctifies us.

Why has God created us? That we might serve him, love him, and worship him in order to become eternally happy. Is God pleased when we meditate frequently on eternal happiness? It would very much displease God if we were to reflect only a little on heaven. Eternal joy, eternal delight, light without darkness, and everything eternal without end. If we meditate often on all of this, then sacrifice in our lives will become easier.

However, heaven was not always open to us. It was closed to us because of the sin of the first human being. But God has had mercy on us. The Son of God offered himself and became a human being, suffered for us, and died for us. If we do not attain eternal happiness, we have done this to ourselves. God is so compassionate that the greatest sinner need no longer doubt it. Yet we should not take advantage of God's compassion, for death can come to us unexpectedly.

The examination of conscience! How have I sinned today in my thoughts? In my words? In my deeds? Through omission?

A Reflection on God's Love for Us Human Beings

God's love for us human beings is so great that we can never comprehend it with our human understanding. Although we often offend God and even seriously offend him, God still persistently loves us. Otherwise, God would not time and again forgive us. Could we imagine a greater love?

And we have not yet said enough about this love and forgiveness. Christ has even made atonement for our sins. He has freely taken on himself the greatest suffering that a human being could bear. And if that were not enough, Jesus Christ also sacrifices himself countless times every day on our altars in order to reconcile us with God the Father. Jesus even offers himself as food and wants to come to us sinful human beings.

Now we must see our love of our neighbor in relation to God's love of us. Shouldn't we Christians become increasingly like to Christ? Although we shall never be offended so horribly by other human beings as we offend God, we are far — in relation to God — from forgiving our neighbors. We would never speak ill of our neighbors if we would truly care for them. Therefore, love of our neighbors is the greatest act of gratitude that we can show God for his love. Love is the first thing that God requires of us, and whoever walks in love remains in God and God in them! [see 1 John 4:7].

Franz Jägerstätter wrote out the questions below three times, and even added an eleventh question in one of these drafts. This eleventh question is included, even though he entitled this text "Ten Questions."

Ten [Eleven] Questions

Who can and will answer these questions for me?

1. Who will give us the guarantee that it is not sinful to belong to a party that aims to eradicate the Christian faith?

2. When has the church's teaching office given its approval so that someone may do and obey everything that the N.S. Party or its state commands or desires us to do?

3. If everything is found to be right and good that is done by someone who belongs to the N.S. *Volk* community — such as collecting money for it and contributing to it — then must it not be that everything that does not conform to this *Volk* community's wishes must be declared evil and unjust? Both ways cannot be good.

4. What kind of Catholic would venture to declare that these military campaigns of plundering, which Germany has undertaken in many lands and is still leading, constitute a just and holy war?

5. Who would venture to maintain that only one individual [i.e., Hitler] of the German-speaking people bears responsibility in this war? And if only one individual is responsible, why then must so many millions of German-speaking people still give their yes or no to the war?

6. Since when are deceived people who are dying without repentance and without amending their committed sins and failures—which they were deceived into committing—allowed to enter into heaven?

7. Why are people, even in Austria's church, now honoring the fighters for National Socialism as heroes? Haven't we for the past five years completely condemned these fighters among us?[6]

8. If we can declare the German-speaking soldiers, who have relinquished their lives in the fight for the N.S. victory, to be heroes and saints, how much more highly should we regard the soldiers in the other lands who were intent on defending their homelands after they were suddenly attacked by German-speaking soldiers and taken away [to prison camps]? Can we still view this war as God's punishment [of other peoples]? If this war is producing so many heroes and saints, wouldn't it be better to pray that this war continue until the end of the world than to pray that this war end soon?

9. How can we still educate our children to become true Catholics today when we are supposed to teach them that some activities that previously were seriously sinful are now good or at least not sinful?

10. Why should we now regard as just and good those activities that the masses are undertaking? How can people successfully get to the other river bank when they are defenselessly pulled along by the stream?

11. Who can succeed in simultaneously being a soldier of Christ and also a soldier for National Socialism, in simultaneously fighting for the victory of Christ and his church and also fighting for the victory of National Socialism?

---

6. FJ's mention of "five years" of N.S. rule in Austria implies that he wrote this essay in the winter of 1943. [RK]

Chapter 10

Notebook III

Late 1942 or Early 1943

During late 1942 or early 1943, Franz Jägerstätter wrote seven questions on three pages in his third notebook. Then he abruptly ended the list of questions for unknown reasons. He may have drafted these questions in order to prepare himself for explaining to others his refusal of military service. Franz likely mentioned these questions of conscience when he spoke with Bishop Joseph Fliesser of Linz in the winter of 1943.[1] (Bishop Fliesser succeeded Bishop Gföllner, who died in 1941.) Further, he probably also raised these questions during his numerous interrogations by military officials, beginning on March 2, 1943.

1. How can someone combine being a soldier of Christ and also being a soldier of the N.S. revolution, simultaneously fighting for the victory of Christ and his church and also for the victory of National Socialism?

2. Doesn't it seem laughable when people say that no one can truly decide whether this war, which Germany initiated against so many countries, is just or unjust?

3. During this difficult time, I have often heard it said that every father must be his family's priest. As father and priest, he must be accountable for his family and friends before the judgment of God. Since a father has this great responsibility, I would like to ask whether a father should watch in silence if his family and friends actively participate in and promote the N.S. victory. If a father evaluates things and acts according to the fundamental convictions of the Catholic faith, he can think that, as a matter of conscience, he must occasionally give an evaluation and judgment [concerning National Socialism] that differs from what some pastors are currently telling their parishioners. Is a father as priest allowed to do this for his family and friends?

---

1. On FJ's meeting with Bishop Fliesser, see Zahn, *In Solitary Witness,* 58. [RK]

4. Shouldn't we become even greater saints than the first Christians? Yet we are much more obedient to the state than they would be. They offered sacrifices to the [state's] gods only if no one would ultimately undergo much harm, and they saved their lives. What is demanded of us Christians today? We are expected not only to offer sacrifices but also to attack, rob, and even murder people so that a N.S. world empire [*Reich*] will come about. Nevertheless, people who decide not to obey the state's commands are accused of doing something seriously sinful. Wouldn't it be worthwhile to learn from the lives of the saints so that we would know how the first Christians would have responded to today's evil commands?

Can one person accuse another today of no longer having a love of our homeland? Do we Austrians even still have a homeland in this world? If a country is my homeland, then it should give me not only obligations but also rights. Do we still have rights today? Are we incapable of improving our knowledge [of current affairs], and would we become a threat to the state if we did so? And what would happen to us? If a homeland is still worthy of being defended, even by its citizens who cannot voice their views, then no one would want to attack the German Reich today.

I believe that at one time we still had a right of national defense. To be sure, we had this right four years ago.[2] Many people are better off when they are ignorant about things. Because they remain ignorant about today's events, the majority of people would ultimately not act differently if they were truly allowed to make a decision. Shouldn't we then make a reproach against Christ because he has instituted the most holy sacrament of the altar? This sacrament may count against the majority of Catholics in eternity, because we have failed to draw strength from it in today's situation. As a result, heathens may fare better in hell than we Catholics.

5. Why today's lamentation among Christians? Other than withdrawing from the church, we can do nothing more evil than what the N.S. Party wants from us Catholics.[3] Can we fulfill the party's expectations and commands without somehow committing a sin? Suffering and dying are not the worst things for a Christian. We know that we must die someday, and faith teaches us that whoever is intent on not suffering in this life must undergo suffering in the next.

---

2. Since FJ is referring to Austria prior to March 12, 1938, he may have written down these thoughts in late 1942. [RK]

3. In their pastoral letter of June 26, 1941, the German bishops wrote: "There exist the sacred duties of conscience from which no human being can free us, and which we must fulfill even if it costs us life itself."

Today we hear words of consolation, such as: "Be at peace, and wait patiently." People who want to do otherwise are told: "Nothing needs to be done." Today's situation and these words of advice are comparable to this imaginary scene. People find themselves in a house that is engulfed by flames, and they hear someone outside the house call to them: "Be at peace. The fire will not continue much longer. Soon the entire house will fall down." Can someone guarantee the people that they will not suffocate in the smoke before the house collapses and that they will not be struck by the debris as the house falls in?

6. In the past it often happened that a city or an entire nation would allow its moral character to decline quite low. Then some citizens would rise up and try to save what could still be saved. The just people among these citizens would feel compelled to make atonement, and the formerly unjust people among them would seek to do penance. But what do we hear today about atonement and penance? Why did the people of the past feel the need to do penance? Would they accept today's view that they had done nothing wrong by withdrawing from the church or that only a few people had withdrawn? Hasn't much occurred in recent years that people will eventually regard as wrong and unjust?

Today we frequently hear people say that we can do nothing more and that if we were to say something, we would find ourselves in prison or dead. They add that we cannot change much in world events. However, did things go much better for our missionaries who often brought about no results other than the reward of their own imprisonment or death?

I perceive that many words will not accomplish much today. Words teach, but personal example shows their meaning. Even if we are as silent as a wall, we can nevertheless do much good. People want to observe Christians who have taken a stand in the contemporary world, Christians who live amid all of the darkness with clarity, insight, and conviction, Christians who live with the purest peace of mind, courage, and dedication amid the absence of peace and joy, amid the self-seeking and the hatred. People are looking for Christians who are not like a wavering reed that is pushed back and forth by every light breeze, for Christians who ask primarily about the teaching of Christ and our faith, Christians who do not watch to see how their associates will respond to this or that point. If signposts are set in the ground so loosely that they can be turned by every wind and, as result, point in this direction and then in that direction, is someone for whom the way is unfamiliar able to find the right path?

7. We often hear people ask whether there is still a God who sees everything that is taking place. Yet we know, as the Gospels recount, what Christ said to the reapers [about the weeds and the wheat]: "Let both of them grow together until the harvest" (Matt. 13:30). He did not add that they should then pull out the weeds as though the weeds were more important than the wheat. The Gospels clearly teach us that things will not be as many people think: that God will come among us.... [*The text abruptly ends here.*]

Chapter 11

Notebook IV

May–August 1943

This fourth and last notebook has a bright orange cover on which Franz Jägerstätter penned "Written in prison." It contains two sections, the second of which comprises this chapter and follows after this introduction.

The notebook's first section starts with Franz's heading "Calendar for the Year 1943" under which is a list of successive dates, beginning in May and stopping at the end of July. After some of these dates, Franz has written what happened, for example: "May 24, Interrogation" and "July 6, Trial." Further, he has given the church's holy day or feast day after its date, and he has also noted the dates on which he received letters, for example, "July 22, received letter of July 13."

There is another noteworthy aspect to Franz's list of dates. Beginning on May 22, Franz wrote a number after each date, except on Sundays and the days on which he was interrogated or went to trial. At the start there are two-digit numbers such as "60," "65," "76," and "94." But there are eventually three-digit numbers such as "200," "200," "181," and "185." It is likely that each number records how many envelopes Franz made on that particular day. As a prisoner, he was expected to fold and glue envelopes for the Reich's use. It is likely, therefore, he kept a record of his production numbers.

These production numbers stop after July 5. On July 6, he would not have made envelopes because he was on trial before the Reich's Military Tribunal. After being sentenced to death on that day, Franz was forced to wear shackles on his hands and feet around the clock until his death. (He was freed from them during his visit with his wife, Franziska, and Pastor Ferdinand Fürthauer on July 13.) Given the constriction of his hands, Franz was no longer able to work on the envelopes. Moreover, as a result of the shackles, Franz subsequently wrote his reflections in a tiny, almost illegible handwriting.

The fourth notebook's second section begins with Franz's heading "What Every Christian Should Know." Under this heading, Franz wrote down 199 distinct reflections on the Christian life, and numbered each of them. He erred, however,

213

in his numbering. After writing entry "no. 60," he wrote entry "no. 70." In any case,
entries no. 1 through no. 187 are terse statements, while no. 188 through no. 208
are relatively long reflections. Franz even gave headings to his last entries. Further,
the last twenty entries include long biblical quotations that Franz wrote down,
copying them from the Bible that he kept in his cell, the Stuttgarter Kepplerbibel,
edited by Professor Dr. Peter Ketter (Stuttgart, 1939). The text below gives the
biblical citations, but does not include the biblical quotations themselves.

What Every Christian Should Know

1. St. Joseph is a magnificent model of silent and prompt obedience. We recognize true Christians less by their words than by their actions. (See Matt. 1:18ff.)

2. Christ's disciples should keep other people from the erosion of their ethics by means of the salt of supernatural values. They should add salt to ethics, not to life. Their light should enlighten, not blind. (See Matt. 5:13–16)

3. Christ demanded a religion of conviction and action.

4. Whoever wants to avoid bad action must rein in human desires. Un-ordered desires grow into lustful glances. The lustful glances prompt evil actions. (See Matt. 5:27ff.)

5. We should pursue our rights, and yet love of neighbor is a higher value than cold rights. (See Matt. 5:38ff.)

6. Love of enemies is not a weakness of personal character but a heroic power of the soul and the imitation of the divine model. (See Matt. 5:43ff.)

7. Calmly enacting God's love accomplishes the most over a period of time because it flows out of one's inner sources, not out of a perverted self-seeking or compulsion. (Matt. 6:1ff.)

8. Those who are too proud to pray to God with other people will soon no longer pray alone in their rooms. (See Matt. 6:51)

9. Jesus presupposes that we fast. But we should do it in the right sense. (See Matt. 6:16ff.)

10. Each of us stands before the decision whether or not to serve God. Those people who choose earthly existence allow wealth to become their gods. Detachment from earthly things should not, however, spring from convenience. We can remain interiorly free and happy when we are concerned about our livelihoods as though everything comes from us, and we can simultaneously trust like children in God as though everything depends on God's help. (See Matt. 6:25)

11. The Pharisees' spirit, which Jesus castigates, is doubly detestable among Christians. We should not believe that we are devout if we are lovelessly judging others. (See Matt. 7:1ff.)

12. Since our own strength does not suffice, we should implore God in humble prayer. (See Matt. 7:7ff.)

13. Doing for other people what we want them to do for us is better than not doing to them what we do not want them to do to us. (See Matt. 7:12)

14. Those who want to find the right way to eternal well-being should not walk with the majority of people who are usually timid about making sacrifices, and they should not entrust themselves to leaders whose actions differ from their words. (See Matt. 7:15ff.)

15. Authentic spirituality comes about not by talking about God, but by living according to God's command. Without this obedience, even wonderful acts mean nothing. (See Matt. 7:21ff.)

16. Discipleship to Christ requires heroism. A weak and wavering personal character is good for nothing. (See Matt. 8:18ff.)

17. For the Gadarenes, the salvation of their neighbors would have made up for the loss of their herd of swine, and they would have come to faith. But for people who live only for an earthly life, a few swine are of more value than supernatural goods. (See Matt. 8:28ff.)

18. Sacrifices without compassionate love are valueless. The righteous need no special invitation [to show compassion]. (See Matt. 9:10ff.)

19. Belonging to Christ requires the courage to acknowledge him [as the Christ]. (See Matt. 10:17ff.)

20. Jesus demands that his followers place peace with God and the church higher than peace with one's relatives, that they place discipleship to him higher than fear of pain and death, and that they place the life of the soul

higher than the life of the body. He does not want to bring to a family the disruption that springs from a lack of love and from self-seeking. But he wants no idle peace that violates the duty of conscience. (See Matt. 10:34–39)

21. The greater the grace, the greater the responsibility. (See Matt. 11:25)

22. We need to be responsible not only for our actions but also for our words. (See Matt. 12:33ff.)

23. Jesus himself taught that his church on earth will include people who are not good Christians. The great separation will come at the end of time. (See Matt. 13, the parable of the sower.)

24. Whoever sacrifices everything for God's cause has made the best swap. (See Matt. 14:1ff.)

25. The Jews were called marriage-breakers because they broke their trust with God, who entered into a covenant with them.[1] (See Matt. 12:39ff.)

26. Jesus declared the apostle Peter to be the foundation of the church and promised him the primacy, the most authoritative position in the visible church on earth. Therefore, Christ himself established the papacy. (See Matt. 16:13ff.)

27. The divine law protecting children, which Christ himself proclaimed, shows the value of the soul of every human being. No sacrifice is too great in order to save a soul. (See Matt. 18:5ff.)

28. Church authority includes the power to punish serious offenders by excluding them from the community. God himself honors these punishments by the church. (See Matt. 18:15ff.)

29. True love does not ask about the boundaries of the obligation to love, but pardons others as often as it has the opportunity. Such opportunities occur every day in a family. (See Matt. 18:21f.)

30. The apostles were afraid of unbreakable marriage vows. At the same time, Jesus presented the freely willed renunciation of marriage out of love of God as a higher form of life. In doing this, however, he did not present married people as less perfect Christians. The measure of perfection does

---

1. This entry and others in the notebook show that FJ unfortunately held the erroneous views of Judaism that predominated among Catholics in his day. [RK]

not depend alone on being married or being celibate but on the love and faithfulness with which someone fulfills the obligations of his or her way of life. (See Matt. 19:1ff.)

31. A child has a sacred right to be led to Christ through religious instruction. The strict obligation to bear responsibility for this instruction rests on parents and educators. No one should hinder parents and educators from fulfilling this responsibility. (See Matt. 19:13ff.)

32. We may delight ourselves with our good works for eternal life, but God is independent in his assessment. (See Matt. 20:1–6)

33. It is better to atone repentantly for a committed mistake than to connect a spiritual attitude with interior dishonesty. (See Matt. 21:28–32)

34. Both Commandments are equal. They are two sides of the same command because love of neighbor is love of God made visible. (See Matt. 22:34–39)

35. The world's Judge will appear unexpectedly but visible to everyone. All people will quickly and certainly gather at the place of judgment, as birds that detect booty from afar. (See Matt. 24)

36. Time and again, the Lord urges watchfulness. The parables here make this same point. (See Matt. 24:32–25:46)

37. The bridesmaids are friends of the bride. Their carelessness concerning their fate is their foolishness. Each person must secure his or her salvation. (See Matt. 25:1–12)

38. God requires from everyone conscientious work in one's vocation. What is decisive for the reward is not one's greater or lesser talents but one's faithfulness in the use of the talents that one has received. (See Matt. 25:14–30)

39. The guilt of the damned is that they did nothing good. Caring for the needs of others does not alone suffice for salvation. Someone can deserve hell because of sins other than failure to perform works of mercy. (See Matt. 25:31–46)

40. The terrifying self-destruction shows what a people can do to itself when it lends its ear to conscienceless agitation. (See Matt. 27:24ff.)

41. The feeling of God's abandonment was the most terrifying pain for Jesus' human nature. (See Matt. 27:45–46)

42. With an awareness of divine power, Christ entrusts to his apostles and their successors the offices of teacher, priest, and pastor until the end of time. (See Matt. 28:18ff.)

43. Jesus' example shows that even fully engaged daily work still allows time for communication in prayer with God. (See Mark 1:35)

44. The Holy Spirit is the benefactor of every grace and the spirit of truth. Whoever opposes his grace and struggles against the truth with lies is not capable of repentance. (See Mark 3:28–29)

45. Our bond with God's will must be stronger than our love of our family and relatives. (See Mark 3:31–35)

46. Religious belief must manifest itself in the external world and encompass all of life. Faithful collaboration [with God] draws new grace to itself. Negligent individuals soon lose everything. (See Mark 4:1–9)

47. Christ spread the seed of God's word on earth and is allowing it to mature on the basis of its inner strength until the harvest at the judgment of the world. (See Mark 4:26–29)

48. The disciples of Jesus must learn to perceive the suffering of their master as unavoidable and to apprehend the religion of Jesus as the religion of the cross. (See Mark 8:31) The salvation of the soul takes precedence over everything else.

49. Whoever wants to show us a way other than the way of the cross in discipleship to Christ keeps us from eternal salvation with Satan's help. (See Mark 8:32)

50. Neither ambition nor the need for riches but humble service characterize a disciple of Christ. (See Mark 9:33–37)

51. Whoever permits the dissolving of the marital union places the Jewish view over the Christian. (See Mark 10:1–12)

52. God's grace may inspire a person freely to renounce earthly goods. (See Mark 10:17–22)

53. No one other than Jesus has more decisively required nor shown better through personal example that the community's need takes precedence over the individual's need. (See Mark 12:38ff.)

54. Whoever finds delight in a betrayal and pays for this betrayal to occur is worse than the betrayer himself. (See Mark 14:10–11)

55. The God-man seeks solace with his disciples. In difficult times we need someone who understands us. Yet we find the best solace — as the human nature of Jesus did — in trusting prayer and in a courageous yes to God's will. (See Mark 14:32–42)

56. Christ the King, enthroned in heaven, lives and continues to work on earth through his church. Baptism joins us with Christ in the community of life. (See Mark 16:14ff.)

57. The handmaid of the Lord exercises maternal service and familial duty. True love of God is visible in active love of neighbor. (See Luke 1:39–56)

58. As the rising sun brings on the day, so God sends the Redeemer as the light of the world. (See Luke 2:29ff.)

59. Remaining steadfast to the Father's will is the most authoritative norm for Jesus. He approaches everything in relation to this, even if he must prepare his mother and his foster father for pain. (See Luke 2:42–50)

60. To be tempted is no sign of a lack of desire to please God. It is important to ward off the tempter by means of a strong resolution and a calm outlook, as we marvel at them in Jesus. (See Luke 4:1–13)[2]

70. In this life, there is no ongoing security against the devil's temptations. (See Luke 4:13)

71. This woe is addressed only to those rich people who place their satisfaction, their consolation, in their wealth and who yearn for nothing higher. (See Luke 6:24)

72. This woe pertains not to a sense of happiness but to frivolous exuberance. (See Luke 6:25b)

73. In Christ's kingdom there are no rigid rights. Rather, self-giving love is the highest authority. In place of self-seeking, Christ upholds selflessness. Christ never spoke well of injustice and acts of violence. A higher readiness to sacrifice oneself is required of Christians than of nonbelievers. (See Luke 6:27–35)

---

2. FJ inadvertently jumped from no. 60 to no. 70.

74. [There are] people who live in the state of grace and make the love of God the basis of their souls, whose works are supernaturally good fruit. "Love God, then do what you will!" (See Luke 6:43ff.)

75. To belong as a child of God to the kingdom of Christ is a higher grace than to be the greatest prophet of the Old Covenant. (See Luke 7:18–28)

76. No earthly authority has the right to enslave a person's conscience. God's rights surpass the rights of human beings.

77. Just as Paul sees himself as a debtor to everyone, so every Christian is responsible for the salvation of other human beings. No one is independent in religious matters. (See Rom. 1:8ff.)

78. Those people who are ashamed of their belief in Christ show that they do not know him. (See Rom. 1:16)

79. Clear insight into the will of God increases responsibility. Religious belief is disgraced when life stands in contradiction to [God's] teaching. (See Rom. 2:12–24)

80. What makes a human being pleasing to God is not external membership in a religious community but right conviction and right action in accordance with the Old Covenant as well as with the New Covenant. (See Rom. 2)

81. What neither pagan philosophy nor Jewish law are able to concede is what every human being attains through belief in Jesus Christ. His redeeming death gives those who join themselves in faith to Christ the "glory of God," that is, the supernatural life of grace. No nation is any longer favored by this. (See Rom. 3)

82. What happened in Abraham is important in every human being: not the law but faith is for everyone the way to salvation. This must be a strong faith that does not waver when everything seems to be lost. (See Rom. 4)

83. Sin has created the enmity between God and human beings. Christ's redeeming death has brought peace. Out of pure love, Christ did so much for us sinners. What more can we, the redeemed, expect! Steadfast optimism suits Christians. (See Rom. 5)

84. The Spirit of God teaches us not to accept suffering in dumb resignation but to adopt a positive attitude toward it. (See Rom. 8:14–25)

85. Having received great riches in Christ, Christians may not give them-
     selves indolently over to rest or to pleasurable licentiousness. The no-
     bleness of salvation brings with it the obligation for a pure life. To be
     a Christian and simultaneously to be a sinner would be absurd, as it
     would be absurd to be both living and simultaneously dying. With bap-
     tism, which is bestowed by means of submersion, the old human being
     has become dead to sin, and a new human being is raised with Christ
     out of the baptismal water, bound to the risen One in a unity of life. By
     means of his fully realized suffering unto death, Christ has done away
     with every sin, as a criminal atones the entire guilt. A relapse into sin
     means slavery to desires. (See Rom. 6:1–14)

86. All Christians have the lifelong obligation to avoid sin, whose slaves they
     once were. They belong entirely to Christ. Striving for salvation is not
     only the task of each individual but of all of the redeemed together.
     Eternal life is the attractive award. (See Rom. 6:15–23)

87. For those who love God, there is only one particular misfortune: sin.

88. Working together are the call of God and the answer of human beings,
     the gift of grace from heaven and the free collaboration of creatures. We
     must become one with Christ. Otherwise, we are not Christian.

89. Our receiving of God's grace and compassion does not occur first of all
     because of us but because of God himself. Our own will is not the basis
     of our receiving grace. Yet without our wanting and striving for grace,
     God cannot send it to us. When human beings do not want grace, then
     God abandons them to their evil will. Human beings never have the
     right either to compel God, the Creator, to grant them justification or
     to complain about God. (See Rom. 8 and 9)

90. People cannot excuse themselves because of their lack of knowledge con-
     cerning the conditions of salvation. Whoever will not hear when God
     proclaims the truth should not wonder when others become recipients
     of the grace which was offered to them. (See Rom. 10)

91. There exists an irreconcilable opposition between the Christian faith and
     the world's spirit. Whoever does not want to reject the world will surely
     become unfaithful to Christ.

92. In the Bible God himself speaks to us and gives our hope an unshake-
     able foundation. If all of the books written by human authors would

have nothing more to say to us, our souls would still be able to direct themselves to God's word.[3]

93. Communal prayer is the best way for a community to fight for Christ's cause.

94. The validity and effectiveness of baptism depends not on the worth of the one who baptizes us. Rather the effects of baptism come about much more because of the people who instructed us in the faith and how they did it.

95. The success of the proclamation of faith depends not only on the preacher but also on the spiritual disposition of the hearers themselves. If "the sense of Christ" leaves us, we shall never understand the standpoint of a truly religious person.

96. Superficial people find occasions to complain about what church officials do and allow.

97. Christians who allow themselves to be governed by feelings of inferiority [because of their faith] show that they do not know how rich they are because of their relationship with Christ. (See Rom. 15:14ff.)

98. The authentic and simple truths of the Sacred Scriptures offer us more guarantees than [the truths of] this or that well-known contemporary writer or teacher.

99. The physical hardships cause by the devil should lead sinners to repentance and so to the saving of their souls.

100. Nominal Christians do the most harm to the church. (See 1 Cor. 5:12)

101. Nowhere is the love of human beings recognized as such a high value as in the religion of Jesus. However, this love does not fuel a cult of the human body. There is no "right of the human body" that permits us to misuse our bodies for sin. Paul gives an answer to this pertinent issue. He does not intend to identify the single and highest goal of marriage when he speaks of marriage as the God-given means for stilling our strong, natural drives. Both spouses have the same rights and the same obligations in relation to this matter. Neither partner may abridge the rights of the other without good reason or even demand in the least something that

---

3. These reflections show that FJ drew strength and hope from the Bible's words during the final weeks of his life. [RK]

repudiates God's law and the sacred character of marital life. Not only the vocation to celibacy consecrated to God but also the vocation to marriage is a grace. The unbreakable character of marriage is therefore a command of the Lord and is valid for everyone. The church can change nothing in this matter; even less can the state change it. (See 1 Cor. 7)

102. Someone should prefer celibacy to marriage not in order to have a pleasant life but in order to serve God with undivided abandonment and "to be holy in body and soul." (See 1 Cor. 7:32ff.)

103. An action that is permissible in itself can become sinful because of its external circumstances. The Christian faith is the religion of love, not of rigid rights. (See 1 Cor. 8)

104a. As someone who understands human nature, the apostle Paul knows that he is not able to save everyone. Nevertheless, he summons everyone in order to lead at least some people to salvation. (See 1 Cor. 9:19–23)

104b. The vocation to Christian faith is an extremely serious matter. Taking on the name alone does not fulfill this vocation, nor are spiritual words sufficient.

105. Time and again, the apostle Paul stresses that the community's worship is first of all directed for the well-being of the whole, not only for an individual's emotions. Liturgy is communal service before God. (See 1 Cor. 11:17–33)

106. The apostle's report concerning the resurrection of Jesus is not a legend or a private interpretation but a testimony, confirmed by many witnesses, to a historical event of the recent past. This report is a primary piece of the ancient Christian confession of faith. (See 1 Cor. 15)

107. Out of our belief in life beyond death there grows the courage for the right form of life on earth. This courage creates heroes. (See 1 Cor. 15:30–31)

108. Consoling others is understood best by those who themselves have undergone profound suffering and have so moved closer to God on the way of the cross. (See 2 Cor. 1:3ff.)

109. As the same medicine can bring health to one person but death to another, so it is with the effects of the message of faith. (See 2 Cor. 2:15ff.)

Similarly, the liturgy speaks in the *Lauda Sion* of the impact of the sacred Eucharist: "To the malicious it becomes death and hell. To the good, the source of their lives. So different are the effects of this bread." The spiritual disposition of the individual is therefore decisive.

110. As the servant of the New Covenant, the apostle stands high above Moses. The Old Covenant is based on the letter of the law, but the Spirit of God reigns in the New Covenant. There death, here life. (See 2 Cor. 3:4ff.)

111. External hardships and persecutions are not able to break the interior resistance of those people who live and act in Christ. When one's gaze is directed to eternal life, this world's afflictions lose their terror. (See 2 Cor. 4:7–18)

112. The human body is the perishable tent of the soul, its earthly garment. God has prepared for us in heaven an eternal dwelling place and a glorious, festive garment. Our souls yearn for this, but the taking down of the earthly tent and the taking off of the earthly garment, our physical deaths, remain somewhat painful. (See 2 Cor. 5)

113. Paul's opponents mock him when Paul expresses himself with unrestrained spiritual zeal. The saying "Overstate nothing" was always said by those who were directed not by Christ's love but by self-love and hence feared that life could become "unpleasant." (See 2 Cor. 6)

114. True love believes in the good in the other person and wants it to awaken and unfold, even if this love must experience labor pains in the process. (See 2 Cor. 7)

115. Ethical heroism grows out of Christian repentance. It is the sign of inner strength. Out of weariness with the world there proceeds contempt for other human beings and cowardly self-loathing. (See 2 Cor. 7:8–11)

116. God is not surpassed by the generosity of human beings. (See 2 Cor. 8:9)

117. When the poor praise God and ask his blessing upon their good actions, they express the most loving gratitude for their well-being. (See 2 Cor. 9)

118. Exaggerated patience leads to weakness. (See 2 Cor. 10–13)

119. To the whole Christ there belongs not only "the broken figure of the slave" on Good Friday, but also the [figure of the] victor over death on Easter morning. (See Eph. 1:19–23)

120. It has always been the case that people who are weak in their faith care-fully scrutinize this faith and church officials' exercise of authority. (See 2 Cor. 10–11)

121. Religious belief is a whole. Someone cannot accept one individual in love but reject another. Belief flows forth not from nationality and race but from a living faith in Christ. To think otherwise is to fall back into Jewish narrowness and spiritual servitude. (See Eph. 2:11–21)

122. The best strategy for dealing with our human desires is to engage in the work of the Spirit, in the positive virtues. (See Eph. 4)

123. The fruits of the spiritual life are love, joy, peace, patience, gentle-ness, goodness, faithfulness, a sweet temper, moderation, abstinence, and chastity. When such fruits of the Spirit ripen through grace, a person no longer needs law, which is only directed against sin. (See Col. 3)

124. The fraternal reprimand is an ethical duty. No one should speak as Cain did: "Am I my brother's keeper?" [Gen. 4:9]. To be a Christian is to be responsible for everything among us. Yet a consciousness of one's own inadequacy calls for modesty. (See 1 Thess. 2)

125. The Christian duty "to do good in all things" is not violated by the ad-monition that we should also exercise loving actions within our specific Christian community. These actions are called for here as the crowning of our actions for the well-being of all people. (See 1 Thess. 5:12)

126. The apostle exhorts [us] not about earthly gifts, but about the highest gifts that God may bestow: the Spirit of wisdom and divine revelation. (See Eph. 3:14–19)

127. Christ, enthroned in heaven, is not far from us nor a stranger to us. He as our head and we as his members form one completely mysterious real-ity, the mystical body of Christ, the church. In the church, Christ is fully acknowledged as the Savior and draws the church's members into the di-vine life which flows from Christ, the head. The statement, "Outside the church there is no salvation" is thus not an arrogant assertion, but an ex-pression of a necessity of nature, an expression of the law of supernatural life.[4] (See Eph. 4:1–16)

---

4. Concerning this statement by Cyprian of Carthage, see Francis A. Sullivan, S.J., *Salvation outside the Church?* (New York: Paulist Press, 1992). [RK]

128. Just as deceased persons never return to life on their own strength, so sinners cannot obtain the lost life of grace on their own strength. The folly of the idea of a human being's self-redemption is evident here in relation to the greatness of the compassionate love of God for us sinners. (See Eph. 4:7)

129. The resurrection of Christ is the basis, model, and guarantee of our spiritual reinvigoration. Eternal life starts with our justification and is fully realized in our being raised from the dead and our becoming holy in heaven.

130. The church is a living organism. The whole body draws its life from its head whose love is moving among its members. (See Eph. 4:15–16)

131. Vice deprives a person of the desire for the spiritual. A life of vice is brutish. (See Eph. 4:17–31)

132. When someone sees Christ in others, being subject to them is not difficult, at least in marriage and the family. (See Eph. 5:25–33)

133. On marriage. A husband is a reflection of Christ, the Savior, whose body is the church. A wife is a reflection of the church, the bride of Christ, whom Christ has loved to full self-giving. She brings [everyone] together not out of self-seeking but out of the desire for mutual sanctification. Each spouse becomes the other's second "I." This unity in duality is joined with Christ in the supernatural community. A marriage is thus infinitely more than a "worldly thing." (See Eph. 5:21ff.)

134. Religious individuals express gratitude as they pray for others. (See Eph. 6:18ff)

135. Joy in Christ is the blossom sprouting up from the roots of grace. For the apostle Paul, to be permitted to suffer for Christ is simultaneously grace and joy. (See Phil. 1:19ff.)

136. Restlessness for Christ never allows genuine Christians to become fully satisfied. Holding fast to the proven One, Christians are always struggling on. (See Phil. 3:7–16)

137. Christ suffered on the cross in order to redeem the entire human family. And because every Christian is a member of the mystical body of Christ, God also intends a certain degree of suffering for every Christian. Since there is suffering in the living unity of the mystical Christ, we can even

speak of today's "suffering Christ" or "persecuted Christ." This [suffering of Christians] is for the benefit of the church, the mystical body of Christ, which will be fully realized when the suffering and struggling church is entirely transformed into the triumphing church. Out of this profound mystical suffering arises the joy of suffering for others. (See Col. 1:15ff.)

138. Just as the world knows nothing about the glorified Christ, so it will know nothing about the supernatural life of Christians until there comes about the great turning point with the universal judgment. When an internal religious life is lacking, all external [religious] activity is only an appearance. (See Col. 3:1–4)

139. Love as the outer-wear is the "uniform" of Jesus' disciples. His disciples are known by their love. (See Col. 3:9–15)

140. Parental authority should not be misused, especially as a result of moods. Children who are misunderstood and treated unfairly are intimidated and embittered. (See Col. 3:21)

141. We should avoid imprudent and untimely zeal when we're with people who do not belong to the church. (See Col. 4:5)

142. Christians' conversations should bring together wisdom and strength, engaging grace and healthy, penetrating acuity ("salt"). Saccharine good deeds are repugnant. The salt of wisdom is given to everyone in baptism so that "it remains in them always." (See Col. 4:6)

143. St. Augustine says, "Pray without ceasing." This means: "Unceasingly yearn for eternal life from the One who alone is able to give it." We should offer up to God all of our work, joy, and suffering. The spirit of prayer must live in us, even when we are not able to undertake special prayers because of our work. Then work as worship becomes our prayer. (See 1 Thess. 1:2–3)

144. God never does his work halfway, except when the evil will of human beings hinders him. (See 1 Thess. 3:6–13)

145. Our joining with Christ does not protect us from earthly suffering but puts suffering in the perspective of eternal value. (See 2 Thess. 1:3ff.)

146. Whoever acts out of love, as a just person does, experiences the law of God more as a support than as a burden. (See 1 Tim. 1:3–9)

147. No one is excluded from God's saving will. The human nature of the Redeemer is uniquely raised up because only Christ as the God-man could suffer and die. (See 1 Tim. 2:4ff.)

148. Slaves can find no basis in the Christian faith for their deficient respect for the pagan master. Further, they take away nothing from their Christian master when they are equally recognized as brothers in God's presence. (See 1 Tim. 6:1–2)

149. For all of eternity God has decided to bestow grace on us through Christ. Through Christ's incarnation, this grace has been revealed and has become part of us. (See Heb. 1)

150. The great significance of the Bible for the configuration of the Christian life — for the formation of our conscience, will, and whole person — comes to light in these words. It should not happen, therefore, that someone possesses an entire series of spiritual books, but does not possess the "book of books" [i.e., the Bible] in which God speaks to human beings. (See Heb. 2:1–4)

151. Christians should not live as the unfruitful fig tree with ornamental leaves of faith. Their fruits are the activities of loving their neighbors. (See Matt. 21:19)

152. God has called his Son to engage in Lordship over heaven and earth. The Son, the image of the Father, is thus the same essence with the Father and is almighty as the Father is. This will become evident when the Son of God comes in his glory for the judgment of the world. In other words, Christ goes beyond the angels; he is God. (See Heb. 2:5ff.)

153. It should fill us with the strongest trust that Christ is the Son of God and yet is nevertheless not distant and alien. He entered into all of our inadequacies, except sin [which is our] turning away from God. (See Heb. 4:15)

154. The person of Christ not only stands over the high priests of the Old Covenant, but also his service is far more sublime. He himself is our mediator not in an earthly dwelling but in heaven. The covenant secured by him brings about his inspired acknowledgment of God and the ongoing forgiveness of our sins. (See Heb. 8–10)

155. Corresponding to this glorious morning prayer are Christ's last words, "It is finished" [John 19:30]. A true Christian has the same orientation:

"See, God, I have come to do your will." This [orientation] reveals true love of God. (See Heb. 10:7)

156. The sin against the Holy Spirit is this: to oppose the recognized truth. This sin begins with the conscious decision to remain away from a community's worship because someone is tepid and contrary. (See Heb. 10:23–25)

157. Moses is an illuminating model for those who, out of a true spirit of faith, gladly renounce a prestigious earthly position so that they are not unfaithful to their convictions. The apostle Paul made a similar sacrifice for Christ. (See Heb. 11:24ff.)

158. Christ spoke and still speaks to us from heaven through the Holy Spirit and through his message of faith. (See Heb. 12:25ff.)

159. At the end of time, "the form of this world will pass away," and there will follow a "new heaven and a new earth" with ongoing existence. (See Rev. 21 and Heb. 12)

160. At no time should the image of Christ be formed according to the world's liking; otherwise it will be a false image. (See Heb. 13:8–9)

161. Reining in one's tongue, exercising day-to-day love, and being a person not "of this world" are the three indispensable elements of authentic religiosity. Doing these exhaust all [religious] obligations. For God has expressed how we have to honor him. This is established not to our liking. (See Jas. 1:26–27)

162. The wonderful title "the royal law" expresses the supreme character and universal obligation of this command to love one's neighbors. (See Jas. 2:8)

163. Through the disastrous fire of sin, the tongue can insert corruption into human life. Hence, it can be an instrument of hell. (See Jas. 3)

164. An adulterer in the pervasive, spiritual sense is any sinner, [that is,] anyone who does not remain faithful to God and relies solely on the world. (See Jas. 4:4)

165. This thought in the Old Testament is often expressed literally and also figuratively: God requires wise love of a person and also whole, undivided love. We belong to God alone, not to anyone else. God recognizes our

weakness, and accordingly allots his grace to those who are humble. (See Jas. 4:5ff.)

166. Greed becomes the sin "crying out to heaven" when the greedy withhold from workers their well-deserved payment. (See Jas. 4:13–5:6)

167. For individual Christians as well as for the entire Christian community, the time of conflict and suffering is short in comparison to eternal life. (See Jas. 5:7–8)

168. The thoughtless taking of an oath betrays a lack of truthfulness. Everyone should be able to rely on the yes or the no of a Christian.[5] (See Jas. 5:12)

169. Christians are preordained to faith by God the Father, sanctified in baptism through the Holy Spirit, and called to obey the Son of God and to be sprinkled with his blood, that is, to be purified from sins and sanctified through Christ's blood. (See 1 Pet. 1:1–2)

170. Christian hope is living because of the resurrection of Jesus Christ, which guarantees Christians their own resurrection and transfiguration. (See 1 Pet. 1:3ff.)

171. Despite their suffering Christians may attain a joyful self-awareness. God has richly favored them. Salvation in Christ, for which the prophets yearned, and the truth of the Gospel, in which the angels themselves recognize an elevation of their well-being, are the glorious possession of Christians. (See 1 Pet. 1:6–12)

172. Just as hikers, laborers, and boxers wear loose-fitting clothes so that they can move more easily, so too Christians should prepare themselves to work or to struggle in God's service and to advance toward their goal as they cast aside all that hinders them. (See 1 Pet. 1:13)

173. Christians belong to a royal priesthood. They are kings because they are called to rule in heaven. They are priests because they are consecrated by God to bring forth spiritual offerings of worship, humility, and self-denial, in short, good works. At confirmation, every Christian receives the sacrament of the lay priesthood in order to collaborate in the work with the ordained priesthood in the building up of God's kingdom. (See 1 Pet. 2:9)

---

5. This reflection is pertinent to FJ's refusal to take the military oath of unconditional obedience to the Führer. [RK]

174. The apostle expects that a devout, chaste, and good wife will have a greater influence on her husband than missionaries with their preaching. (See 1 Pet. 3:11)

175. The exemplary life of a Christian is the best advertisement for the faith. However, it does not protect believers from persecution by people of ill will. (See 1 Pet. 2:12)

176. Time and again, the apostle instructs the young Christian community that the call to Christian faith does not mean a guarantee against suffering and persecution on earth. On the contrary, it is more often the case that innocent suffering for Christ is a sign of election, hence, a cause for joy. (See 1 Pet. 3:14–22)

177. God gives to us in grace the most sublime of which we are capable: God invites us to participate in his divine nature through supernatural life. This nobility obliges us to live a pure life. God's gift becomes a challenge to us. (See 2 Pet. 1:1ff.)

178. We should not apply our small human measure to God's promises. God is the Timeless One, the Eternal One, and therefore also the Patient One as well as the Just One and the True One. God's day always comes early enough. No one can withdraw from God's judgment. (See 2 Pet. 3:8–9)

179. Consciousness of sin is not a subservient sense, not a feeling of inferiority, but a noble self-recognition in the light of the utter holiness of God. (See 1 John 1:8–10)

180. Love of the God-rejecting world is unreconcilable with love of God, for no one can serve two masters. (See 2 John 2:15)

181. Sin goes against the law established by God. As a result, sinners cannot come to God. (See 1 John 3:3ff.)

182. The seed of God is the sprout of divine life, implanted through sacred baptism in the soul; it is grace that makes us holy. As long as this grace is in us, we live in communion with God, and all of our actions are holy. However, the life of grace can be lost. It dies through someone's conscious turning from God — a turning that occurs in serious sin, in mortal sin. (See 1 John 3:1ff.)

183. Active love of neighbor out of love of God is the best means of salvation for the anxious soul and the surest sign of being a child of God. (See 1 John 3:11ff.)

184. Christian love of neighbor presents most surely a person's joining with the invisible God. It is a proof of God's existence by means of action. (See 1 John 3:21ff.)

185. The apostle removes the slavish fear that is incompatible with love. By contrast, the childlike fear of offending God is an expression of deferential love. (See 1 John 4:17–18)

186. Along with apostolic urgency to instruct those with doubts, to rescue those in danger, and to win back those who have fallen away, it is also necessary to be watchful for oneself so that aversion to evil is not lost. (See the Letter of Jude)

187. The watchword of Christians amid conflict is not "Resist power with power," but "Resist power with patience and perseverance in faith." (See the Letter of Jude, verse 20)

From this point until the end of the notebook, Franz Jägerstätter simply wrote a phrase for each entry, and then wrote out the verses from the biblical text appropriate to this phrase. (Printed below are the biblical references but not the biblical quotations themselves.) Arising each morning with the awareness that this could be his last day, Franz Jägerstätter nurtured what he called his "inner peace" by penning into his notebook (with his chained hands) those biblical texts that were strengthening him. In other words, he engaged in the writing of biblical verses as a form of meditation. [RK]

188. From the Letter of the Holy Apostle John.[6] Do not sin. 1 John 1:5–2:2

189. Keep the Commandments. 1 John 2:3–11

190. Sin not. Do not love the world. 1 John 2:12–17, except verse 14b

191. A sign of being a child of God. 1 John 2:29–3:9

192. Let us love the brethren. 1 John 3:10–24

193. God's love for us. 1 John 4:7–10

194. Our love for God. 1 John 4:11–21

---

6. FJ inserted his heading concerning the "Holy Apostle John" after "188," whereas he subsequently inserted his headings between his entries, e.g., between "194" and "195." [RK]

From the Letter of the Holy Apostle James

195. Pray for wisdom. James 1:5–11

196. A warning about the sins of the tongue. (Difficulties.) James 3:1–12

197. On true wisdom. James 3:13–18

198. A warning about jealousy and strife. James 4:1–10

199. Concluding admonitions. James 5:12–13

From the Letter of the Holy Apostle Peter

200. On brotherly love and ethical purity. 1 Peter 1:22–25

201. Christian obligations. 1 Peter 2:11–12

202. Admonitions to everyone. 1 Peter 3:8–17

203. An admonition for patience. 1 Peter 4:12–19

204. The assurance of salvation. Rom. 8:31–39.[7]

From the Letters of the Holy Apostle Paul

205a. The great song of love. 1 Corinthians 13:1–13

205b. On comfort amid suffering. 2 Corinthians 4:13–5:10

From Matthew's Gospel

206. On the two ways. Matthew 7:13–14

From Luke's Gospel

207. On persevering in prayer. Luke 11:5–13

From Matthew's Gospel

208. On trusting and persevering. Matthew 10:26–42

---

7. This entry belongs under the heading below since it is from Paul's Letter to the Romans. [RK]

Chapter 12

Last Thoughts

July–August 1943

After being sentenced to death on July 6, 1943, Franz Jägerstätter lived from one day to the next without knowing when he would be executed. He apparently coped with each day by writing his reflections on "What Every Christian Should Know" (pages 214–233 above) and also by occasionally expressing his thoughts in an essay addressed to Franziska and his family. Whereas he manifests a meditative, almost serene spirit in "What Every Christian Should Know," he conveys his passion and pain in the five texts that somehow eventually reached his wife. Since Franz speaks in these letters of his refusal to take the military oath of unconditional obedience to the Führer, he was likely prompted in part to write these essays as a follow-up to his twenty-minute meeting with his wife and pastor on July 13. Since these texts did not receive headings from Franz Jägerstätter, they are listed here according to their archive numbers. [RK]

Text no. 84

Who fares better in this world: the person who places earthly life before eternal life or the person who puts eternal life before earthly life?

What does this life offer to those who prize eternal life more than earthly life? Many people usually regard believers as buffoons. They hold that these believers get in this life nothing other than work and concern and suffering. But this is not completely true. There is much work in this world that cannot be paid for with earthly recompense. Believers are fortunate and at peace because they know that God will reward them with eternal riches. They know that no suffering need occur for itself alone since God will reward everything with abundant recompense.

People are unfortunate if they sin, for sin is the greatest evil and misfortune that exists in general for human beings. As long as people live in serious sin, they gather for themselves not the least merit for eternal life.

How well do things go for unbelievers who place earthly life ahead of eternal life or who no longer believe in eternal life? They do not need to work at anything, and they decrease what they care about. They have nothing to suffer for, or they seek payment for their suffering. But can they avoid difficult times or elude death?

Unbelievers often experience good fortune. But bitter regrets and serious woes unfortunately usually follow such times. Moreover, even in good times something can happen that is not supposed to occur, and then a person can come into conflict with this world's laws.

Do unbelievers still find something enjoyable if they turn to food and drink and simply seek to satisfy themselves for many days or even for many years? I believe that they do not, for the more we live in moderation, the more we find ourselves in good health. So who fares better in this world: believers or unbelievers?

Text no. 85

Franz Jägerstätter wrote this next reflection in red crayon on an unfolded piece of stiff paper of the kind used for "a letter-card":

My dear loved ones, the hour draws ever nearer when I shall give my soul back to God, the Lord. I could say many words of farewell to you, and it is hard to imagine saying no more good-byes to you.

I would have gladly spared you the pain and the suffering that you have borne on account of me. But you surely know that we must love God more than we love our family, and that we must be ready to let go of everything that we love on this earth and that is dear to us rather than to offend God in the least. And I would not dare to offend God on account of you. We know what suffering God could have sent you on account of me!

It was surely hard for our dear Savior to give his dear mother pain because of his death. And what are our sufferings in relation to those which those two innocent hearts suffered for us sinners? Moreover, what must a farewell [at death] be for those people who do not fully believe in eternal life and who, therefore, do not have much hope for a reunion? If I could not have trusted in God's mercy and forgiveness for all of my sins, then I would have hardly had peaceful days during my solitary time in prison.

Although people have accused me of criminal behavior and condemned me to death, be consoled knowing that in God's eyes not everything is criminal that the world perceives to be criminal. I hope that I do not have to be afraid of the eternal Judge because of this [so-called] criminal behavior.

My death sentence should be a warning for you. God, the Lord, will not treat us much differently if we perhaps think that we do not need to obey everything which he commands us to believe and follow through his church. However, [if we do not follow God's Commandments,] the eternal Judge will condemn us not merely to an earthly death but to an eternal death.

Therefore, I have nothing more urgent to set before you than that you resolve to keep all of the Commandments and to avoid every sin. You should love God, our Lord, and also your neighbors as yourself [see Mark 12:28–34]. On these two Commandments rest the entire law. Keep these, and then we have reason to hope for an imminent reunion in heaven.

One must not think poorly of others who act differently than I have. It is much better for everyone to pray than to pass judgment on others. God intends that everyone should become holy.

Many people simply believe that things must be as they are, that they should do what is unjust, and that others have responsibility for this [situation]. They also hold that whoever has the mind and the will should be able and willing to obey all regulations. For them, to take the military oath is not to lie. However, someone else may say beforehand: "If I cannot uphold and obey everything that I promise in this oath, then I commit a lie." I am of the mind that it is best that I tell the truth, even if it costs me my life: I cannot obey [the oath] in all of its aspects.[1]

Neither God nor the church gives a commandment requiring that we must — under the burden of sin — commit ourselves in an oath to obey [human] authorities in all matters. So do not have a heavy heart when others declare that I am sinner. You can have peace of mind if you take [my love of] my family as evidence [concerning me]. For it is because of my family that I am not permitted to lie, not even if I had ten children. My greatest request is the one that I have already conveyed to you: raise the children to be devout Catholics as much as it is possible for you. They do not yet have a great understanding of [Catholicism].

---

1. As already noted, according to defense attorney Feldmann the Reich's Military Tribunal might have reconsidered its death sentence of FJ if he would have taken the military oath. But FJ told Franziska Jägerstätter and Pastor Fürthauer on July 13 that since he would be lying if he were to take the oath, he would not take it. Here FJ reiterates this point. See Zahn, *In Solitary Witness*, 84–96. [RK]

Out of my own experience I can say that life is painful when one lives as a lukewarm Christian. To exist in this way is to have more the existence of a vegetable than truly to live. If a person were to possess all of this world's wisdom and be able to claim half of the earth as his own, he could and would still be less fortunate than a poor person who can claim nothing in this world as his own other than a deep Catholic faith. I would not exchange my small, dirty cell for a king's palace if I was required to give up even a small part of my faith. All that is earthly — no matter how much, nor how beautiful — comes to an end. But God's Word is eternal.

I can assure you that if you — in the state of grace — would merely pray with reverence the Our Father for the children, you would give them a greater gift than if you could give them the greatest wedding gift that a millionaire could give his daughter. Many people would laugh at these words. But they are true.

Now my dear children, when your mother reads you this letter, your father will already be dead. I would have gladly come to you, but the heavenly Father wanted it otherwise. Be well-behaved and obedient children. Pray for your father so that we shall see each other soon in heaven!

My dear wife and my mother, forgive me for all the ways in which I have offended you and have made you suffer. I surely forgive you. And I ask that everyone in Radegund, whom I have made suffer and have offended, forgive me.

Also, give my greetings to Hilda.[2]

Text no. 86

Franz Jägerstätter wrote the text below — similar to text no. 85 above — in tiny print on a piece of stiff paper that was used for "a letter-card":

Who can fully appreciate the value of a Catholic's deep and devout faith? No one except God. It is not a free choice but a duty for a Catholic to believe everything that God has presented for us to believe in Catholic doctrine. It is also a duty to uphold all of the laws of God and the church.

To be devout Christians and to strive after sanctity is nothing more than to seek to fulfill God's will in everything. Such Christians may still of course sin, even though they believe everything that God has taught us to believe and to

---

2. FJ is referring to his daughter Hildegard Auer.

have the certain will to die rather than to offend God by freely choosing to sin. It would indeed be a sin to tell a lie in a situation of need, though many people judge that this would not be a sin. People can think of themselves possessing a faith that believes everything and also having the will to uphold everything that God and the church require. God does not deny his help and grace to such people, and they will never easily sin.

There are still many Catholics — though how many would one still find in the German Reich? — who would renounce a wonderful job or a wonderful career or would even renounce a house and a farm rather than to offend God by means of a venial sin. They would even have their heads cut off rather than to offend God by means of a venial sin![3]

Indeed, a venial sin is something so significant that we should renounce our lives rather than to commit one. A sin — even a venial sin — is an offense against God. And an offense against God is something so significant that we can never fully comprehend it with our human understanding. If a mortal sin is so significant that someone would be in hell for all eternity if he or she did not atone for it, then a venial sin must also be significant. If someone were given the choice, which would be more preferable: on the one hand, to claim the whole world as one's own (or at least as much of the world as one desired) and in doing so to offend God by committing a venial sin or, on the other hand, not to offend God and to remain a poor wretch for one's whole life? Many believers would choose the latter!

There is nothing overstated in these words. To believe and to uphold all of this is the duty of every Christian. One can think of the sacrifices that the saints took on themselves. It is easily understandable that the saints would never be understood by worldly people. Such people characterize the saints as fools while they live in this world.

To strive for holiness is the duty not only of some individuals but of everyone. Many people would think of themselves as fortunate in this life if they could truly live their faith and avoid sin. There are no more fortunate people in this world than these. And if they were the greatest sinners, they would still fear God and trust in God's mercy, [believing] that God has removed all of their sin and has done so for all of eternity. Even if they have experienced suffering, affliction, defamation, and persecution, they have endured all of this with patience and out of love of God. The mere thought of eternal joy, which

---

3. FJ was aware that the Reich might seize his family's home and farm after his execution. He also knew that he would be executed by the guillotine. [RK]

they await, prevails against all suffering and sorrow. They do not have bitter hearts. Anger, hate, and the desire for revenge are alien to them. A constant peace governs their hearts.

St. Anthony said, "No one is more blessed and no one is more fortunate, than those people who possess God in their hearts." Such people are not anxiously concerned about their earthly future, even when their prospects are bleak, for they know that the more suffering that God sends to them [on earth], the greater will be their joy in heaven.

So there can be no higher and greater good for a person in this world than a deep and devout faith! If people could teach their children all of the world's knowledge, it would be nothing if they could place a deep faith in their hearts. Even with all of this world's wisdom and knowledge, someone can be one of the most unfortunate people in the world.

But is it even possible to place such a faith in the hearts of children? With God's help nothing is impossible. Of course, this is the primary task of parents. If parents do not live what they teach, catechists — even when they show great concern for the children — will have difficulty being successful in teaching the children to be good Catholics.

Parents themselves usually plant the primary and greatest poison of unbelief in their children's hearts, first through their bad example and then through their thoughtless words. As a result, weeds take root in the souls of their children and grow up with the children. They get bigger and increasingly displace the noble fruits of faith until the weeds of unbelief are victorious. At this point, children become adults who are unfortunate in this world and in eternity unless God comes to help them with special graces so that they themselves go on to seek the good way and to eliminate the weeds of unbelief from their souls. Despite their great caution, parents can often plant poisonous weeds in the hearts of their children through their association with other children and adults.

What is therefore the challenge that parents face? They must diligently look into the souls of their children. From time to time, they must test — with goodness and gentleness — their children in the faith so that they can detect where poisonous plants have established themselves. Gardeners must be very diligent if they want to keep their gardens free of weeds, and must often inspect things. Otherwise, the best dung and the most diligent watering doesn't much help their best plants. Of course gardeners must also be careful when eliminating the weeds; otherwise they will damage the best plants.

The education of children in the faith is therefore the most difficult challenge facing parents. People who have been raised in the faith have to struggle in their youth in order not to succumb to the great dangers that threaten them. If they err, they can pull themselves together with God's help because they can repent of their sins since they still believe in what is right and what is sinful. However, how can those who experience the struggles of youth be victorious if the poison of unbelief has already taken root in them?

There exists no greater crime than intentionally ruining or bringing to ruin the faith of children and adults. If someone were capable of destroying all of the world's churches — which could of course be rebuilt — he would have undertaken a crime less serious than if he were capable of turning people from their faith so that they were lost for all eternity. In fact, someone is now accomplishing effective blows against us, as a result of which many believers are falling aside.[4]

To be sure, someone could ask me, "Do you cherish more those people who are destroying the churches?" I believe that every Christian knows clearly enough that nothing better can be expected from the kind of man who would destroy churches. But in my judgment, there is someone who is allowing the churches to stand and yet is having success in destroying souls. He even contributes to the building of churches, but works with trickery and cunning. This man is more destructive than the one who sets out to tear down churches and imprisons all of the priests.[5] Will the existence of church buildings be helpful if people no longer believe very much or believe nothing at all? Are the priests still much help to us if they must remain silent when they should be speaking out? Do doctors help much when they have someone lying there covered with blood and yet are forbidden from bandaging the patient?

Text no. 87

Franz Jägerstätter wrote the text below on the back of a letter to him from Pastor Karobath. Then, after writing on the back of Karobath's letter, Franz continued his own letter on the front, putting his words in the original letter's margins. Pastor Karobath sent his letter to Franz on July 20, 1943, and subsequently estimated that Franz Jägerstätter used it for his own letter on July 29.

---

4. In this comment and his subsequent ones, FJ is referring to Hitler. [RK]

5. FJ judged that Hitler was more destructive of the Christian faith than Josef Stalin. Hence he disagreed with the German-speaking bishops and Vatican officials who held that Bolshevism, not National Socialism, was the greatest threat to the church. [RK]

My loved ones, I want to express a small reproach to you amid the great suffering which you already have to endure. I wish to rebuke you if you are experiencing anxiety and worry concerning the future of your material needs as you live with the threat that someone will dispossess you of our family's home and farm because of me.[6]

I believe, as you know, that when people have great suffering in this life and bear it with patience, then they will have still greater joy in heaven. Or do you perhaps believe that if someone dispossesses you of our home and farm that you will immediately die of hunger? Think about the fact that there is One who rules over us. Further, you would not be the first people who have been dispossessed of their property.

Now my dear wife, I want to present you with a small case that is similar to mine. You have said that I do not need to lie if I were to take the oath. Let us assume that you were faced with a choice, either to lose our farm [by refusing the oath], or to promise in the oath that you would obey everything that some people told you to do concerning our farm and your deeding of it to someone else. You yourself know how these people demand everything. What would you then do?

If you would refuse to take the oath, then these people would threaten you concerning the children, as they did to me. You would know beforehand that you would be lying if you were to take the oath because you would eventually not obey everything that these people would require of you — unless, of course, you would no longer care for your children because you had hardened your heart. Does there exist a great difference between what would be demanded of you as a farmer and what can be demanded of a soldier?

If I believed that the Führer alone must bear responsibility for everything that he orders people to do, then I would not do what I am doing.

I know that it was definitely not easy for you when you visited me here and were not allowed to give me even a mouthful of your food. The soldier in the room with us did his duty and wanted to harm no one in doing it. Nevertheless, you perhaps wondered how he could be so hardhearted. It could easily be that he has enforced the same regulation with children as well as with adults, and that he is obligated to do so or to be punished because of his acceptance of the N.S. Party.

---

6. As already mentioned, FJ was likely told that if he did not submit to the Reich's orders, he would bring about the state's seizure of his family's home and farm. [RK]

Couldn't we also say that the church has not forbidden us [from obeying the Führer], and hence that it is simply our duty to obey civil authority? This is the kind of reasoning that has prevailed since the plebiscite.

I can also tell you that I am not the first Catholic to oppose what's going on, and I'll surely not be the last.[7]

I believe that if someone had said to us six years ago that in a few years almost all of us Catholics in Austria would be undertaking terrible acts for National Socialism — acts which at that time were illegal for us in Austria — this someone would have been regarded as the greatest fool in the world. Yet today the fools are those who do not do these things. So do the times change.

It is good that in God's eyes not everything is criminal that the world perceives to be criminal. I am accused of criminal conduct and have been sentenced to death for criminal conduct. [In this view] God must change his Commandments and his moral convictions from time to time. I believe that you still remember what was said during the turmoil [in 1938] about National Socialism: "One should not always ask and be asking himself whether or not he is responsible for something. What someone does, does not matter to God."

Pray continually for a strong faith, for all of us still need our faith as a rock. Without faith, we'll lose our hope in eternal life.

A test of the strength of your faith can and will come upon you. This storm, in which all of us are now swimming, has not yet fully burst upon us, though it is already worse than if we were caught up in a literal rainstorm. At present, even the still waters are very dangerous. . . . [8]

A house that is situated for a long time in water and is not built on rock will slowly collapse, especially if a storm breaks upon it or if the water continually swirls around it. And today's storm or its swirling waves of water will be unavoidable for us. Would I have a strong enough faith, necessary [for what I face], if my family and the priests were not encouraging me in my situation? Also, think a little about whether these priests, who have assisted me and encouraged me, would still be free today under this regime [if their words to me were publicly known]. Would we have much merit for eternal life if we had acted with no sense of responsibility, if we had wanted to work as some people have for their own prosperity or for the destruction [of others]?

The education of children will increasingly be a great responsibility and also a great merit for eternal life. If a time of bloodshed for the church soon breaks

---

7. Among those whom FJ had in mind was the priest Franz Reinisch who was executed on August 21, 1942, because of his refusal to take the oath of allegiance. See Zahn, *In Solitary Witness*, 96. [RK]

8. The text has a gap here.

upon us, as some people anticipate, then [it will fall] to you, dear wife, and to a good catechist to educate our children without my help. And if this regime — which opposes faith — is victorious, then one will face a choice as soon as the war ends: either to be imprisoned and possibly be put to death, or to allow the children to be educated as this regime wants.

Text no. 88

Now I'll write down a few words as they come to me from my heart. Although I am writing them with my hands in chains, this is still much better than if my will were in chains.

God sometimes shows his power, which he wishes to give to human beings, to those who love him and do not place earthly matters ahead of eternal ones. Not prison, not chains, and not even death are capable of separating people from the love of God, of robbing them of their faith and free will [see Rom. 8:31–39]. God's power is invincible.

"Be obedient, and submit to authority." These words are flying today at a person from all sides, especially from people who no longer believe anything that exists in Sacred Scripture and that God has commanded us to believe. If someone were to concern himself with what these people are saying, then he would assume that heaven is in fact in this world. For instead of being concerned about saving me from serious sins and directing me toward eternal life, these people are concerned about rescuing me from an earthly death.

They always want to prick my conscience concerning my responsibilities for my wife and children. Is the action that someone does somehow morally better because this person is married and has children? Or is the action better or worse because thousands of other Catholics are doing it? Has smoking a cigarette also become a virtue because thousands of Catholics are doing it? Is someone permitted to lie in taking an oath just because he has a wife and children? Did not Christ himself say that whoever loves wife, mother and children more than me is not worthy of me? [see Luke 14:26]. On what basis do we ask God for the Seven Gifts of the Holy Spirit if we should adhere to blind obedience in any case?

For what purpose did God create all human beings with intelligence and free will if it is not our place — as many are now saying — to decide whether this war, which Germany is conducting, is just or unjust? For what purpose does someone need to recognize the difference between good and evil?

I believe that someone can calmly adhere to blind obedience only when one will surely not harm anyone else. If people were totally honest today — as some Catholics are, I believe — they would have to say, "Yes, I see that the acts that I am required to do are not morally good, but I am simply not ready to die [for refusing to do them]."

If God had not bestowed on me the grace and power to die for my faith — if this is demanded of me — then I would be doing the same as the majority of people are doing. God can give someone as much grace as God wants. If other men and women had received as much grace as I have obtained, they would have perhaps done much more good than I have done.

Many people are perhaps of the opinion that they are suffering for the faith and giving their lives for the faith when [the N.S. Party] requires that they withdraw from the Catholic Church. But I venture to say openly that people die for their faith only when they are ready to suffer and die rather than to offend God through the smallest, thoughtless sin. Those people who are ready to die rather than to offend God through a little, freely chosen sin gain greater merit for themselves than those people who withdraw from the Catholic Church when it is demanded of them. We are required under the pain of serious sin to lose our lives rather than to leave the Catholic Church. A saint once said that if someone were capable of putting an end to hell by means of telling one small lie, this person should still not tell the lie because he or she would offend God by doing so.

Something that was seen to be clearly ridiculous in the nineteenth century is now something that some people frequently think and say. Indeed, we have changed in many things, but God has not removed even one dash or comma from his Commandments. Why does someone always want to postpone death, even if only a little, as though one did not know that it must eventually occur? Did our saints try to do this? I believe not.

Or do we doubt God's compassion and see hell awaiting us after our deaths? I would surely deserve hell because of my many serious sins. But Christ came into the world not for the righteous but in order to seek out all who are lost [see Matt. 9:13]. Therefore, sinners do not need to doubt God's compassion. During his passion, Christ showed us God's love in his outreach to the good thief [see Luke 23:39–43]. Could people have a calm fifteen minutes in this life if they had to think that God the Lord will not forgive them, and that therefore there remains nothing else for them than to wander for eternity in hell? Wouldn't such ideas bring people to doubt any longer in life after death or to imagine hell as a place of enjoyment where there is always merriment?

If a good friend were to promise us a beautiful and lengthy holiday trip — of course, without cost and with first-class accommodations — would we be always postponing this journey or saving it for our old age? I believe not. And what then about death? Do we not have a lengthy journey to make from which we cannot return? Can it been seen in a more joyful perspective than an earthly one when we see that we can fortunately land on heaven's shore?

Of course, we should not forget that before arriving in heaven we must undergo purification in the fire of purgatory. But this process does not continue forever. And those people who were concerned in this earthly life to help the poor souls in purgatory and to give appropriate veneration to the Mother of God can be sure that they will not need to stay long in purgatory.

It would likely become a moment of dizziness if one were to think about the eternal joy of heaven. We are fortunate when we experience a little joy in this world. But what are the short moments of joy in this world in relation to that which Jesus has promised us in his kingdom? No eye has seen nor ear heard and no human heart has grasped what God has prepared for those who love him [see 1 Cor. 2:9]. One time, when St. Augustine wanted to write a book about the joy of heaven, St. Jerome — who had just died — appeared to him and said: "Just as there is little in this world that you can grasp with your hands, so there is little about the joy of heaven that you can express in a book. You are not yet at that place to which you are diligently trying to go." If the joy of heaven is so great, shouldn't we dismiss all of this world's delights?

Franz Jägerstätter's martyrdom came to international attention in 1964 when Gordon C. Zahn published his study In Solitary Witness: The Life and Death of Franz Jägerstätter. *Soon afterward, Bishop Thomas D. Roberts wrote about Franz's life and death in the course of the Second Vatican Council's discussion of conscience amid the drafting of* Gaudium et Spes, *the Pastoral Constitution on the Church in the Modern World. The Archdiocese of Linz initiated the process for the beatification of Franz Jägerstätter in 1997, and — as already noted — declared him "blessed" on October 26, 2007.* [RK]

Appendix

People and Events
in Franz Jägerstätter's Life

The two sections below, arranged by Robert A. Krieg, provide information pertinent to FJ's letters and essays. The first provides biographical information concerning the Jägerstätter family and their neighbors and friends. The second lays out a chronology of FJ's life and writings in relation to the history of the Third Reich.

Biographical Information

Family Members Frequently Mentioned in the Letters

The various nicknames for the same individual are placed in parentheses after the person's name.

Franz Jägerstätter (Franzl). May 20, 1907–August 9, 1943. The son of Rosalia Huber and Franz Bachmeier, who died in 1915 in the First World War. Franz was eventually adopted by his mother's husband, Heinrich Jägerstätter. In 1936, he was given ownership of the Jägerstätter home and farm in St. Radegund. FJ married Franziska Schwaninger on April 9, 1936.

Franziska Jägerstätter, née Schwaninger. Born in 1913. A daughter of Lorenz and Maria Schwaninger, she grew up in Hochburg, a village near St. Radegund. After marrying FJ on April 9, 1936, she moved into his family's home, joining Franz and his mother.

Rosalia Jägerstätter (Rosl, Rosal, Rosi). Born on September 1, 1937. Married name: Sigl. The first daughter of Franz and Franziska.

Maria Jägerstätter (Maridl, Maridi). Born on September 4, 1938. Married name: Dammer. The second daughter of Franz and Franziska.

Aloisia Jägerstätter (Loisi). Born on May 5, 1940. Married name: Maier. The third daughter of Franz and Franziska.

246

Hildegard Auer (Hilda). Born August 1, 1933. The daughter of Franz and Theresia Auer Kirsch.

Rosalia Jägerstätter, née Huber. September 4, 1885–October 30, 1949. The mother of Franz. On February 19, 1917, she married Heinrich Jägerstätter (d. May 8, 1933).

Lorenz Schwaninger Sr. (Schwanninger). July 19, 1876–November 24, 1953. The father of Franziska Jägerstätter, he often assisted Franziska in Franz's absence.

Maria Schwaninger, née Zeitmayer. May 22, 1877–May 26, 1977. The mother of Franziska Jägerstätter.

Rosa Schwaninger (Resi, Resie, Rosi). One of Franziska's sisters, she assisted Franziska in Franz's absence.

Neighbors and Friends Frequently Mentioned in the Letters

Leopold Arthofer. 1899–1977. A pastor in Kronstorf and a friend of Pastor Karobath. Arthofer was imprisoned on February 11, 1941, because of his statements against the N.S. Party. Incarcerated at the Dachau concentration camp from April 4, 1941, to April 4, 1945. After the war, Arthofer published an article about FJ and also his autobiography *Als Priester im Konzentrationslager* (1947).

Anton Eckinger (Toni Strohhofer). A son of Johann Eckinger.

Johann Eckinger (Hans Lang, Strohhofer). A neighbor who assisted Franziska in Franz's absence.

Maria Eckinger (Mari, Thomas-Mari). A neighbor. The wife of Thomas Eckinger.

Thomas Eckinger (Lang). A neighbor. A son of Johann Eckinger, and the husband of Maria Eckinger.

Ferdinand Fürthauer. 1911–2000. A priest. The pastor in St. Radegund from August 1940 to July 1945. He accompanied Franziska to Berlin in July 1943.

Johann Hofbauer Sr. A neighbor who operated a Gasthof (pension) until he and his wife were forced by the Third Reich to close it, perhaps because of his son's opposition to National Socialism.

Johann Hofbauer Jr. (Johann Pleikner). 1903–61. The son of Johann Hofbauer. He was a pastor in Burgkirchen. Because he criticized the N.S. Party, he was imprisoned from October 30, 1941, to April 4, 1945.

Lidwina Hofbauer (Lid). A neighbor and the mother of Johann Hofbauer Jr. Wife of Johann Hofbauer Sr.

Franz Huber. 1923–2005. FJ's cousin and godson.

Josef Karobath. September 1, 1898–January 4, 1983. A priest. Pastor in St. Radegund from 1934 to 1940 and from 1945 to 1970. Arrested on July 7, 1940, for his criticism of National Socialism. Released on August 23, 1940, because of lack of evidence. Assigned to marginal pastoral duties in Wolfern as well as in Enns and Laakirchen from September 1940 to 1945.

Franz Krenn. 1899–1958. A priest, musician, and composer. The parish administrator in Ostmiething from 1933 to 1935, and then the pastor in Geinberg until he was forced to resign because of his criticism of the N.S. Party. Prohibited from pastoral ministry, he served as an organist in Enns until after the war.

Heinrich Kreutzberg. A priest in Berlin. A chaplain to Catholics at the Berlin-Tegel prison, he met with FJ during the final weeks of his life. Franziska Jägerstätter sent him a letter of gratitude on September 5, 1943.

Rudolf Mayer. 1906–43. From Raab in Upper Austria, he and FJ met during their military training in Enns. They entered the Third Order of St. Francis together on December 8, 1940. After being separated by their military duties, they remained in correspondence. As Franz awaited his execution, he wrote to Franziska (August 8, 1943) that Rudolf Mayer may have recently died in combat in Russia. He was correct.

A Chronology of Franz Jägerstätter's Life
and the History of the Third Reich

May 20, 1921. FJ turns fourteen, and ends his formal education.

1927–30. FJ works in the iron mines in the Steiermark region.

January 30, 1933. Adolf Hitler (b. 1889) is named Germany's chancellor. In 1934, he becomes the nation's president and "Führer."

March 28, 1933. The German bishops agree to drop their prohibitions against membership in the N.S. Party.

July 20, 1933. Cardinal Eugenio Pacelli (Pope Pius XII) and Vice Chancellor Franz von Papen formally sign the Concordat between the Vatican and the Third Reich.

August 1, 1933. The birth of FJ's daughter Hildegard Auer.

April 9, 1936. The marriage of FJ and Franziska Schwaninger. They honeymoon in Rome.

March 14, 1937. Pope Pius XI issues *Mit brennender Sorge*, condemning National Socialism. This encyclical is read at all Sunday Masses throughout Germany and Austria.

September 1, 1937. The birth of Rosalia Jägerstätter.

January 1938. In a dream, FJ sees a train being boarded by youth, and hears a voice declare, "This train is going to hell." Upon awaking, he judges that the train represents the N.S. Party, and that the voice is his conscience, hence, the word of God.

March 11, 1938. Hitler "annexes" Austria, making it part of the Third Reich.

April 10, 1938. FJ votes no in Austria's plebiscite.

September 4, 1938. The birth of Maria Jägerstätter.

February 10, 1939. Pope Pius XI dies. On March 2, Cardinal Pacelli is elected Pope Pius XII.

September 1, 1939. The Wehrmacht invades Poland, thereby igniting the Second World War.

April 9, 1940. The Wehrmacht invades Denmark and Norway.

May 5, 1940. The birth of Aloisia Jägerstätter.

May 10, 1940. The Wehrmacht invades Luxembourg, the Netherlands, and Belgium.

May 13, 1940. The Wehrmacht invades France. Italy enters the war.

June 17, 1940. As required, FJ reports for military training at Braunau am Inn, Hitler's birthplace.

June 22, 1940. France signs an armistice with the Third Reich.

April 21, 1941. FJ receives a military deferment in order to manage his family's farm. He becomes the sacristan at St. Radegund's church.

June 22, 1941. The Wehrmacht invades the Soviet Union.

December 7, 1941. Japan attacks Pearl Harbor, and the United States declares war on Japan. On December 11, Hitler declares war on the United States.

January 20, 1942. Hitler's Wannsee conference decides to implement the Reich's "final solution" against the Jews.

August 21, 1942. Franz Reinisch, a priest from the Tyrol, is executed at the Brandenburg-Görden prison for refusing to take the oath of allegiance to the Führer.

September 1942. The Wehrmacht's Sixth Army attacks Stalingrad (Volgograd).

September 1942–February 1943. Five soldiers from St. Radegund die at Stalingrad.

October 1942. The British Army routs the Wehrmacht at Alamein, North Africa.

February 2, 1943. The Wehrmacht's
Sixth Army surrenders at Stalingrad,
and the Soviet Union's forces begin their
unrelenting drive to the west.

February 1943. FJ meets with Bishop
Fliesser at Linz.

February 22, 1943. Sophie and Hans
Scholl, the student leaders of the anti-Nazi
group "White Rose," are executed in
Munich for treason.

February 22, 1943. FJ receives his military
induction notice.

March 2, 1943. At Enns, FJ refuses military
duty, and is incarcerated at Linz.

April 5, 1943. Dietrich Bonhoeffer,
Protestant pastor and theologian, is arrested
along with others who were plotting to
assassinate Hitler. He is incarcerated at the
Berlin-Tegel prison.

May 4, 1943. FJ is transferred to the
Berlin-Tegel prison.
May 24, 1943. FJ has a hearing with the
Reich's Military Tribunal.

June 29, 1943. Max Metzger, a Catholic
priest and pacifist, is arrested for treason,
and eventually imprisoned at the Berlin-
Brandenburg prison.

July 6, 1943. The Reich's Military Tribunal
condemns FJ to death.

July 11, 1943. Pastor Fürthauer and
Franziska Jägerstätter receive defense
attorney Feldmann's letter, urging them to
come to Berlin. They depart by train on
Sunday, July 12, and arrive in Berlin on
July 13.

July 13, 1943. Franz and Franziska are
allowed to meet for twenty minutes at
the Berlin-Charlottenburg prison. At
10:00 p.m., she boards the train back to
St. Radegund.

July 14, 1943. The Tribunal confirms FJ's
death sentence.

August 9, 1943. The Tribunal reconfirms
its death sentence of FJ, who is executed at
the Berlin-Brandenburg prison at 4:00 p.m.

August 13, 1943. In Berlin, the Reich executes the Austrian priest Jacob Gapp, S.M., a critic of National Socialism.

August 19, 1943. The German bishops issue their Decalogue Letter, condemning the Reich's murder of innocent victims.

September 8, 1943. Italy surrenders to the Allied forces.

April 17, 1944. Max Metzger is executed at the Berlin-Brandenburg prison.

June 6, 1944. D-Day, the Allied forces land in northern France.

July 20, 1944. The attempt by Claus von Stauffenberg to assassinate Hitler fails.

February 2, 1945. Alfred Delp, S.J., executed for treason.

April 9, 1945. Dietrich Bonhoeffer is executed at Flossenbürg.

April 30, 1945. Adolf Hitler commits suicide in Berlin.

May 7, 1945. Germany agrees to an unconditional surrender.

August 17, 1943. FJ's ashes are buried in a Berlin cemetery.

August 9, 1946. FJ's ashes are buried at St. Radegund.

1997. The Archdiocese of Linz initiates the process of the Catholic Church declaring Franz Jägerstätter a saint.

October 26, 2007. FJ is declared "blessed" at the Linz Cathedral.